Digestive Health.

The Physician Billing Process

Avoiding Potholes in the Road to Getting Paid

Deborah L. Walker, MBA, FACMPE
Sara M. Larch, MSHA, FACMPE
Elizabeth W. Woodcock, MBA, FACMPE, CPC

Medical Group
Management
Association

MGMA®

Medical Group Management Association
104 Inverness Terrace East
Englewood, CO 80112-5306
877.275.6462
Web site: www.mgma.com

ii

Medical Group Management Association (MGMA) publications are intended to provide current and accurate information and are designed to assist readers in becoming more familiar with the subject matter covered. Such publications are distributed with the understanding that MGMA does not render any legal, accounting or other professional advice that may be construed as specifically applicable to individual situations. No representations or warranties are made concerning the application of legal or other principles discussed by the authors to any specific factual situation, nor is any prediction made concerning how any particular judge, government official or other person will interpret or apply such principles. Specific factual situations should be discussed with professional advisors.

Item 6116

Copyright © 2004 Medical Group Management Association

ISBN: 1-56829-230-9

Printed in the United States of America
10 9 8 7 6 5 4 3 2 1

About the Authors

Deborah Walker, MBA, FACMPE, is the president of Medical Practice Dimensions, Inc., a health care consulting firm based in Southern California. Walker is known for achieving sustainable changes in medical practices that give them a competitive position in the health care market. She assists medical practices and health care organizations in improving their business operations by reducing administrative costs, rightsizing staff, improving billing and collection performance, enhancing productivity and efficiency and developing physician incentive compensation plans. With more than 22 years of expertise in health care, Walker is a sought-after consultant and speaker in the field. She holds an MBA from UCLA's Anderson Graduate School of Management; she is a PhD candidate at the Peter F. Drucker and Masatoshi Ito Graduate School of Management, Claremont Graduate University; and she has achieved Fellow status in the American College of Medical Practice Executives. Walker has authored numerous articles on medical practice operations issues, she is a frequent keynote speaker at national health care forums and she is the co-author of the book *Rightsizing: Appropriate Staffing for Your Medical Practice*.

Sara M. Larch, MSHA, FACMPE, is chief operating officer at University Physicians, Inc., the faculty practice plan at the University of Maryland School of Medicine. She is involved in designing and implementing processes that support billing and collection, in monitoring process performance and in leading and implementing change. Larch has more than 20 years of medical group experience in single and multispecialty practices both small and large. In addition to a public administration degree from Miami University, Ohio, she has a master's degree in health sciences administration from Virginia Commonwealth University and is a Fellow in the American College of Medical Practice Executives. She is past board chair of the Medical Group Management Association and is past president of both the Academic Practice Assembly (APA) and the Association of Managers of Obstetrics and Gynecology (AMGO). Larch is a professional speaker on topics such as billing and reimbursement, practice operations and women in leadership.

Elizabeth W. Woodcock, MBA, FACMPE, CPC, is a popular author, speaker and consultant. Woodcock has focused on medical practice operations and receivables management throughout her career. Combining innovation and analysis to teach practice operations and management, she has delivered presentations at regional and national conferences to thousands of physicians and managers, authored several practice management manuals and textbooks, and published numerous articles in national health care management journals. She is the author of the books *Mastering Patient Flow to Increase Efficiency and Earnings* and *Mastering Patient Flow: More Ideas to Increase Efficiency and Earnings*. She is co-author of the book *Operating Policies and Procedures for Medical Practices*. Woodcock is a Fellow in the American College of Medical Practice Executives. In addition to a bachelor of arts degree from Duke University, she completed a master's of business administration in health care management from the Wharton School of Business of the University of Pennsylvania.

Contact Information:

Deborah L. Walker, MBA, FACMPE
Medical Practice Dimensions, Inc.
TEL: 562-592-9930
dwalkerbwa@msn.com

Sara M. Larch, MSHA, FACMPE
University Physicians, Inc.
TEL: 410-328-1722
slarch@upi.umaryland.edu

Elizabeth W. Woodcock, MBA, FACMPE, CPC
Woodcock & Associates
TEL: 404-373-6195
ewwoodcock@mindspring.com

Dedication

This book is dedicated to our husbands – Kirk Keegan, Richard Smith and Richard Woodcock – who provide their love and support and encourage us to pursue our dreams. We also dedicate this book to our parents, who instilled a love of learning and achievement and who have continued to offer their unquestioned support.

We are indebted to those individuals who have generously shared their knowledge with us – our clients, colleagues and the physicians, practice administrators and billing staff who have attended our workshops and seminars over the past 10 years. Your innovation and dedication amid constant change in health care never cease to amaze us.

Table of Contents

Chapters 2 through 9 provide a step-by-step review of each of the billing potholes. Each chapter includes a description of the billing function; advanced practices; a practice blunder case study; case exercises; and figures, tools and policies.

List of Figures

List of Tools

List of Policies and Procedures

Foreword

What do we mean by physician billing, and why should an entire book be dedicated to this subject? Physician billing, also known as Part B or professional fee billing, encompasses the many steps needed to translate a health care service into a billing claim and to follow that claim until it is paid. Unlike purchasing a typical commodity, reimbursement for the professional services provided by a physician is not at all straightforward. Rarely is it a simple process of exchanging cash for services rendered. For example, once physicians sign a contract with a payer, they may not even know the exact level of reimbursement the payer intends to pay for the service, as payer fee schedules are not always made available. The billing and collection process involves a number of steps that must be performed in a timely and accurate fashion – with limits to process variability – if a medical practice seeks to optimize its revenue performance.

There are a number of publications that discuss physician billing; however, most of these discuss one aspect or only a few steps in the billing process. We will provide a step-by-step review of the entire billing and collection process, from patient registration to collections. As we proceed on this journey, we will discuss potholes in the road to getting paid and advanced practices adopted by better performing medical practices – potholes and advanced practices we have learned during our careers as consultants and practice administrators responsible for the revenue cycle in the medical practice.

This book will enable medical practices to enhance revenue performance by optimizing key billing and collection processes. There are more than 5 billion claims generated in the United

States each year. It is reported that 30 percent are rejected, with only 50 percent of these ever resubmitted. That means that 15 percent of the total claims are not adjudicated. The Centers for Medicare & Medicaid Services (CMS) indicates that it rejects 26 percent of the services it processes, with 40 percent of these never rebilled; thus, a total of 11 percent of Medicare claims are not adjudicated.[1] A recent report cited that one in five claims is underpaid or under-allowed, representing 5 percent of net revenue.[2] CMS has recently shortened the amount of time practices have to appeal denied claims. As reimbursement continues to decline from both government and third-party payers and as it gets more and more difficult to ensure a "clean" claim is submitted to payers, medical practices need to examine *leading* billing and collection indicators and ensure they are using advanced billing practices to optimize reimbursement and profitability.

Medical practices can use this book to (1) analyze their current performance, and (2) initiate change efforts to enhance performance. We provide specific tools, resources, and policies and procedures at each step in the revenue cycle to promote improvements in your medical practice. We highlight advanced practices in the form of bulleted segments to draw attention to processes adopted by better performing practices. These advanced practices will help you identify ways you can enhance billing and collection performance in your own medical practice. Additionally, we outline the problems of a fictitious medical practice, Practice Blunder, which provides case studies of billing and collection practices that should be avoided. Questions follow each of these case studies to prompt the reader to consider tools and techniques that will improve Practice Blunder's revenue cycle.

We hope you enjoy the journey as we translate a clinical service into an adjudicated claim and as we share tools and best practices to help you avoid the potholes in the road to getting paid. We fully expect that in our lifetimes we will see an innovation that will solve all of our billing potholes – perhaps a smart card that permits instantaneous transmission of services performed and electronic transfer of payment for these services. Until such a time, however, we need to work with due diligence to optimize the billing and collection process and ensure the fiscal viability of medical practices so they can continue to meet the health care needs of their communities.

---

[1] Centers for Medicare & Medicaid Services. Baltimore (MD); [cited 2000 Dec, www.cms.hhs.gov].

[2] Medical Present Value, Inc. San Antonio (TX): © 2004. Available from: www.mpv.com/pr2002.07.01.

Introduction

The accounts receivable (A/R) in a medical practice is the largest single balance sheet item. Consequently, it is important to actively manage this asset. The billing and collection process for physician billing is a labyrinth of process steps, hand-offs, decisions and pathways that take billing staff on a daily rollercoaster ride through health care reimbursement. Many of us remember from civics courses in grade school how a bill becomes a law. The illustration on the next page demonstrates the complexity of how a health care service becomes a paid bill. It is a convoluted web of steps that requires due diligence, attention to detail and persistence.

Reimbursement for physician health care services has steadily declined. Today, it is not unusual for a medical practice to report a gross collection rate of 60 percent or less. That means that for every $1 of health care services billed, the physician receives only 60 cents. Thus, it is important to bill for the service correctly the first time to avoid additional expenditures associated with billing rework.

Many of the medical practices that we visit review data relative to the billing and collection process on a monthly basis. Typically, they review gross charges, net collections and procedure volumes. Unfortunately, these performance indices represent *lagging* indicators rather than *leading* indicators to effect change in the medical practice. By the time these are available at month's end, it is often too late to effect change that is needed to bring about financial success. This book discusses *leading* performance indicators and advanced billing practices that permit medical practices to manage billing and collection as an important asset.

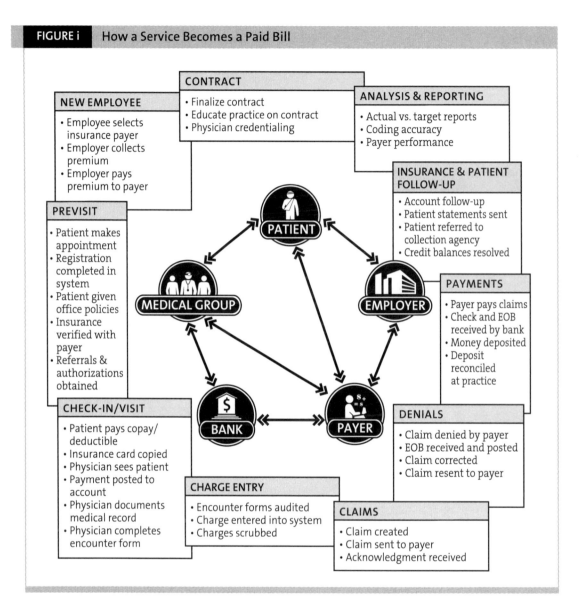

FIGURE i How a Service Becomes a Paid Bill

CONTRACT
- Finalize contract
- Educate practice on contract
- Physician credentialing

NEW EMPLOYEE
- Employee selects insurance payer
- Employer collects premium
- Employer pays premium to payer

ANALYSIS & REPORTING
- Actual vs. target reports
- Coding accuracy
- Payer performance

INSURANCE & PATIENT FOLLOW-UP
- Account follow-up
- Patient statements sent
- Patient referred to collection agency
- Credit balances resolved

PREVISIT
- Patient makes appointment
- Registration completed in system
- Patient given office policies
- Insurance verified with payer
- Referrals & authorizations obtained

PAYMENTS
- Payer pays claims
- Check and EOB received by bank
- Money deposited
- Deposit reconciled at practice

CHECK-IN/VISIT
- Patient pays copay/deductible
- Insurance card copied
- Physician sees patient
- Payment posted to account
- Physician documents medical record
- Physician completes encounter form

CHARGE ENTRY
- Encounter forms audited
- Charge entered into system
- Charges scrubbed

DENIALS
- Claim denied by payer
- EOB received and posted
- Claim corrected
- Claim resent to payer

CLAIMS
- Claim created
- Claim sent to payer
- Acknowledgment received

Diagram nodes: PATIENT, MEDICAL GROUP, EMPLOYER, BANK, PAYER

Before we get started on the *journey on the road to getting paid*, we suggest that you complete the following assessment to evaluate the billing and collection process in your medical practice and to determine how much you may be able to improve your revenue performance.

FIGURE ii	Practice Self-Audit: Is Your Practice Leaving Money Uncollected?

	Yes	No	Unknown
1. Our practice collects cash equal to or greater than 95 percent of the collectible (net) charges.	___	___	___
2. Our practice verifies insurance eligibility prior to every ambulatory care service and all inpatient services.	___	___	___
3. Our practice knows when copayments are due and collects them at the time of service from all patients.	___	___	___
4. Our practice knows when to collect deductibles, co-insurance and other patient responsibility balances.	___	___	___
5. Our practice has management reports which enable us to review the quality of our staff's registration activity.	___	___	___
6. Our practice's registration data is accurate and of high quality.	___	___	___
7. Our claims are rejected by payers less than 5 percent of the time.	___	___	___
8. Our practice offers credit cards as a payment option at all sites and on patient statements.	___	___	___
9. Our practice physicians and staff know what contracts we have and what the critical elements of those contracts are to ensure compliance and appropriate reimbursement.	___	___	___
10. Our patient statements are understandable and informative to our patients.	___	___	___
11. Our billing office tracks rejections and provides feedback to front-office staff.	___	___	___
12. Our practice has cash controls in place to ensure all money is accounted for each day.	___	___	___
13. Our practice captures information needed to ensure prior authorization for services.	___	___	___
14. Our practice reviews each patient's account for previous balances due prior to his/her appointment and informs the patient that this amount is due.	___	___	___

Total your responses: _____ Yes _____ No _____ Unknown

Use the guide below to assess your medical group.
Unknowns:
If you recorded any *unknowns* we encourage you to focus on these particular sections of the book.
Number of No's:
☐ 10 – 14 No's = Dramatic improvement in revenue in your practice is possible.
☐ 4 – 9 No's = Possibility of significant improvement.
☐ 1 – 3 No's = Some improvement is possible.

Note: If you found yourself wanting to answer *maybe* or *sometimes*, count that as a *No*. If your practice's performance is inconsistent, then there is opportunity for improvement in your revenue.

© 2004 Walker, Larch, Woodcock. Reprinted with permission.

We are certain that some of you have performed extremely well on this assessment instrument. We congratulate you on your adoption of advanced practices in the billing and collection process. Others of you have a few unknowns to explore. Regardless of how you performed on the self-audit, we hope this book expands the breadth and scope of your knowledge related to the detailed billing and collection steps required to maximize reimbursement and optimize profitability for your medical practice.

Oversight of the billing and collection process by state and federal agencies and other regulatory bodies has been heightened in recent years. It is important to remember that there is significant variation among states related to specific billing requirements. There is also variation among the hundreds of payers with which you contract.

As a consequence, we need to remind you of the following:

None of the information or material presented is intended to encourage action on the part of the reader that would be in violation of federal or state law or violation of insurance contract terms. When questions of a legal or regulatory nature arise, the reader is strongly encouraged to seek appropriate legal counsel.

CHAPTER 1

The Revenue Cycle: An Overview

T he revenue cycle begins at the time the contract is signed with an insurance company, or payer. This contract determines which patients may seek services from which providers, and it outlines the terms of claims processing and reimbursement. This billing process continues through patient scheduling, obtaining and verifying insurance information, and alerting patients to outstanding balances on their accounts. This requires a well-coordinated effort between the front office and billing office to ensure optimal billing and collection activities. The entire process of billing and collection, what we term "the revenue cycle," must function in a streamlined fashion for it to be as effective as possible.

In this chapter, we cover:

- The revenue cycle
- Front-end and back-end billing
- Billing and collection potholes
- Performance workload ranges
- Cost to rework a claim
- Recurring themes

The Revenue Cycle

The revenue cycle for a medical practice includes multiple functions that must be performed at optimal levels by all involved physicians, nonphysician providers, staff and managers. The revenue cycle is depicted in the figure below. The long horizontal arrow represents the entire revenue cycle, while the shorter arrow shows what has traditionally been considered the "billing office."

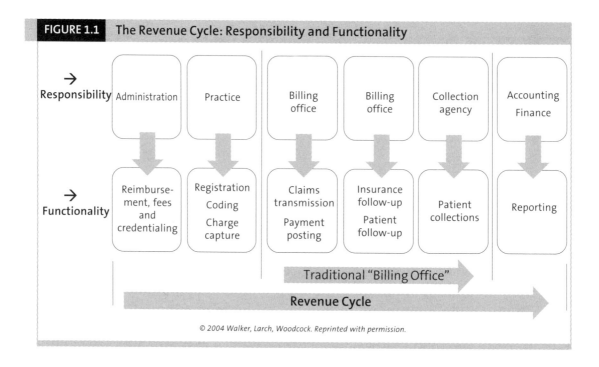

FIGURE 1.1   The Revenue Cycle: Responsibility and Functionality

→ Responsibility

| Administration | Practice | Billing office | Billing office | Collection agency | Accounting Finance |

→ Functionality

| Reimbursement, fees and credentialing | Registration Coding Charge capture | Claims transmission Payment posting | Insurance follow-up Patient follow-up | Patient collections | Reporting |

Traditional "Billing Office"

Revenue Cycle

© 2004 Walker, Larch, Woodcock. Reprinted with permission.

A more detailed depiction of the revenue cycle is shown in Figure 1.2. This figure outlines critical tasks in the billing and collection process that must be performed. Note that what has historically been considered billing and collections is only one box in the entire process. Payer contracts, previsit functions, front-desk/visit functions, charge entry functions, account follow-up functions, and reports and analysis are all steps that could include potholes in the road to getting paid.

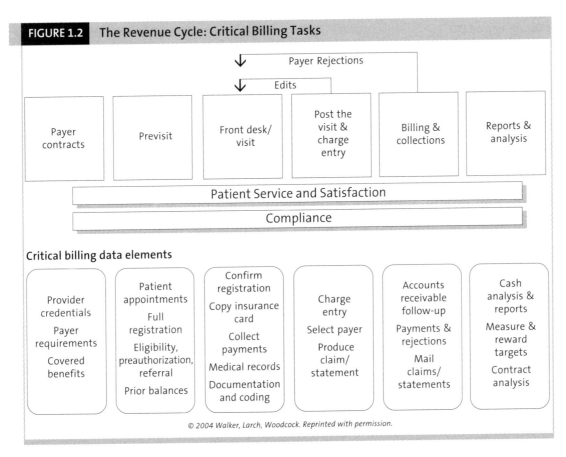

FIGURE 1.2   The Revenue Cycle: Critical Billing Tasks

© 2004 Walker, Larch, Woodcock. Reprinted with permission.

As indicated in the figure above, a medical practice should give patient service and satisfaction intense scrutiny. We have observed numerous instances in which patients have been pleased with the service provided by the physicians and office staff, only to become extremely agitated with the method and manner by which billing has been conducted. Practices also need to attend to compliance issues throughout the revenue cycle. Compliance with relevant laws, regulations and established policies and procedures represents good business practices for a medical practice and reduces variation in the billing and collection process.

Front-end and Back-end Billing

The billing process is often described as having both a front end and a back end. In the past, it was possible to consider billing to be a back-end, localized function performed by staff assigned to the billing office. As more care became "managed," however, the end-to-end process evolved so that billing now starts when the patient calls to make an appointment. Front-end billing functions are typically performed at the practice site(s) where the patient is seen. Back-end billing functions are typically performed in a central billing office, which may or may not be at the practice site. The interface between both of these functions — front-end and back-end — needs to be transparent to ensure accountability and to optimize revenue performance.

The front-end and back-end billing functions are listed in the figure below. As one might expect, all of the functions outlined represent *reimbursement functions* for the medical practice. It is clear that billing and collection is no longer only a back-office responsibility. Billing is now the responsibility of everyone, including physicians; non-physician providers; managers; and front-office, clinical and billing office staff.

FIGURE 1.3   Front-end and Back-end Billing Functions

Front-end Functions	Back-end Functions
• Appointment scheduling	• Billing edits
• Registration (demographic and insurance)	• Claims to payers
• Check-in process	• Accounts receivable follow-up
• Checkout process	(by payer type)
• Referrals and pre-authorizations	• Statements to patients
• Coding	• Payment posting
• Charge capture and entry	• Payment variance analysis
• Financial counseling	• Denial posting and resolution
• Cash at time of service	• Reporting results and analysis

• Training and performance management

• Contracts, credentialing and compliance

• Information systems and technology support

© 2004 Walker, Larch, Woodcock. Reprinted with permission.

Billing and Collection Potholes

The flowchart in Figure 1.4 on page 6 depicts the key billing and collection process steps. In examining the physician billing process, we first outlined the responsibility and purpose of the revenue cycle and then we identified critical billing tasks. Now we view physician billing at the level of process steps. This figure outlines the major potholes in the road to getting paid. The key potholes to navigate in the physician billing process include:

Pothole 1:	The Previsit Process
Pothole 2:	The Patient Check-in Process
Pothole 3:	The Charge Capture and Charge Entry Process
Pothole 4:	The Claims Process
Pothole 5:	The Payment Posting Process
Pothole 6:	The Account Follow-up Process
Pothole 7:	The Denial Management Process
Pothole 8:	The Patient Collections Process

In the next eight chapters, we discuss each pothole and provide a step-by-step examination of the optimal billing and collection processes for a medical practice. In examining each of the potholes, we describe expected performance outcomes and advanced practices that lead to optimal process performance. We include case studies to help readers diagnose problems and develop action plans, and we provide checklists so readers can diagnose their current process performance. In each of the process steps, we provide relevant tools and policies and procedures to help make the changes that enhance revenue performance.

After the chapters devoted to each of the billing potholes, we present Chapter 10, Rightsizing the Billing Office, which includes methods to determine if you have the right number and mix of staff for your billing office. We provide sample organizational charts, competency assessments and incentive compensation plans, and discuss methods to actively involve your staff in the performance of your revenue cycle.

In Chapter 11 we discuss technology to enhance your revenue cycle, including electronic funds transfer, document management, scrubbing software and other technology to leverage the performance of your billing operation.

Chapter 12 presents insights regarding a frequent debate – whether to centralize, decentralize or outsource your billing. We review the advantages and disadvantages of each of these strategies, and discuss how to determine the best fit for your practice.

In Chapter 13 we analyze the revenue cycle by benchmarking billing and collection performance and investigating the reasons for low collections through the use of leading

FIGURE 1.4 The Revenue Cycle: Flowchart and Potholes

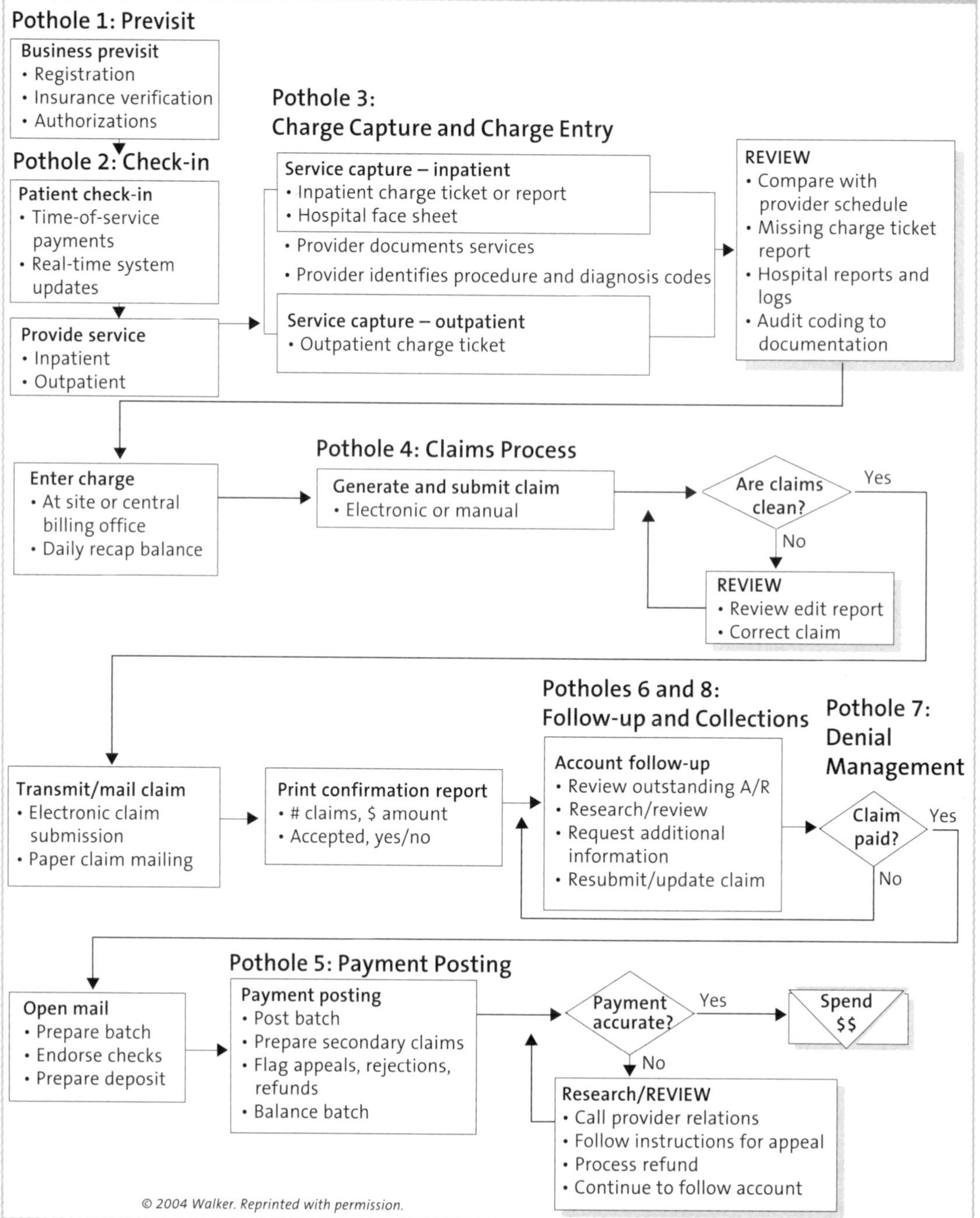

Pothole 1: Previsit

Business previsit
- Registration
- Insurance verification
- Authorizations

Pothole 2: Check-in

Patient check-in
- Time-of-service payments
- Real-time system updates

Provide service
- Inpatient
- Outpatient

Pothole 3: Charge Capture and Charge Entry

Service capture – inpatient
- Inpatient charge ticket or report
- Hospital face sheet
- Provider documents services
- Provider identifies procedure and diagnosis codes

Service capture – outpatient
- Outpatient charge ticket

REVIEW
- Compare with provider schedule
- Missing charge ticket report
- Hospital reports and logs
- Audit coding to documentation

Enter charge
- At site or central billing office
- Daily recap balance

Pothole 4: Claims Process

Generate and submit claim
- Electronic or manual

Are claims clean? — Yes / No

REVIEW
- Review edit report
- Correct claim

Transmit/mail claim
- Electronic claim submission
- Paper claim mailing

Print confirmation report
- # claims, $ amount
- Accepted, yes/no

Potholes 6 and 8: Follow-up and Collections

Account follow-up
- Review outstanding A/R
- Research/review
- Request additional information
- Resubmit/update claim

Pothole 7: Denial Management

Claim paid? — Yes / No

Pothole 5: Payment Posting

Open mail
- Prepare batch
- Endorse checks
- Prepare deposit

Payment posting
- Post batch
- Prepare secondary claims
- Flag appeals, rejections, refunds
- Balance batch

Payment accurate? — Yes — Spend $$

No

Research/REVIEW
- Call provider relations
- Follow instructions for appeal
- Process refund
- Continue to follow account

financial indicators. In this chapter we also demonstrate how to evaluate the cost of your billing operation and present keys to management reporting.

We present approaches to resourcing your compliance efforts in Chapter 14, where we also discuss the Health Insurance Portability and Accountability Act (HIPAA) and its impact, both current and anticipated, on physician billing. This book concludes with additional resources regarding billing and collection that you may want to investigate as you continue to refine your journey on the road to getting paid.

In this book we describe the experiences of a fictitious medical practice, Practice Blunder. Many of these case studies, while based on actual events and findings, have been altered to protect the innocent. The case studies are meant to provide interesting examples of how things can go wrong in the billing and collection process. Case exercises follow each of the case studies to assist the reader in applying the billing and collection tools and techniques. These case studies and exercises are often used in educational curricula, conferences and seminars as physicians, administrators, staff and students work to understand the complexities associated with physician billing. We hope that the reader will learn from the missteps conducted by Practice Blunder and/or recognize with relief that the reader's own medical practice is doing many things well.

Performance Workload Ranges

Throughout this text, we provide typical performance workload ranges for various billing and collection functions. It should be noted that a number of practice-specific factors impact the ability of an employee to function at these levels. The practice's billing process, the technology, the facility, the patient population, the number of tasks assigned to staff and many other factors impact the workload for a particular staff member. Thus, the workload ranges are offered as tools for determining whether there is opportunity to enhance efficiency. The workload ranges are not offered as arbitrary, numerical goals or targets absent actual verification of the workload range expected at a specific medical practice. We suggest that you measure the productivity of your staff, compare it with benchmarks or goals you establish and then move their performance and/or your practice's performance toward the benchmark. Don't use a benchmark to set unachievable or unrealistic goals, as staff and physicians tend to ignore unrealistic benchmarks. Set interim goals and measure performance against those; continue to increase the expectations after improvement is made. You should be making progress toward the benchmark and reward staff at the appropriate intervals. As improvements in technology enhance your processes, improve staff productivity and reduce your costs, your goal should be to outperform these benchmarks.

Cost to Rework a Claim

It is important for physicians and practice administrators to recognize that there is a significant cost to the medical practice if the billing and collection process is not performed correctly the first time. A simple calculation of this cost is provided in the figure below.

FIGURE 1.5 **What Does a Denied Claim Cost Your Practice?**

Scenario 1:
Medical service provided:

Initial charge	$130
Allowed amount	$55
Contractual adjustment	$75
Payment received	$55

Scenario 2:
Medical service provided:

Initial charge	$130
Allowed amount	$55
Denied part of claim	$(30)
Contractual adjustment	$75
Payment received	$25

Cost of service/billing:

Cost to provide service	$29
Cost to prepare and mail claim	$6
Total cost	$35
Practice income after expenses	$20

Cost of service/billing:

Cost to provide service	$29
Cost to prepare and mail claim	$6
Cost to rework claim	$25
Total cost	$60
Practice income after expenses	$(35)

Assumptions:
- Cost to prepare and mail claim = $6 per claim.
- Rework cost based on industry standard of $25 (to rework and resend claim).
- If rework denial is successful, the practice has ability to collect the $30 denied, but cost of billing increases by $25 of rework costs.

In this example, the practice has a charge of $130, of which $55 was received in reimbursement ($75 represents a contractual adjustment). The practice calculated its cost to perform this service at $29 and it calculated its cost per claim at $6. It also calculated the expense associated with rework of the claim to be $25. This included resubmitting a claim to the payer – researching, corresponding with the front-desk staff, requesting the medical record, researching the payer question, reviewing the notes from the date of service, preparing a claim and mailing the claim. The income after expenses – in this example, $20 – would be dramatically reduced if the claim needed to be reworked. This demonstrates why we emphasize doing the work correctly the first time if a medical practice seeks to optimize its revenue cycle.

Recurring Themes

You will recognize a number of recurring themes as you explore each of the billing potholes:

- Putting patients first and developing a patient-oriented billing and collection process;
- Doing it right the first time, minimizing rework and lost revenue opportunities;
- Performing work in real time, rather than batching work to be performed at a later date, thus enhancing efficiency;
- Measuring performance outcomes – both quantity and quality – to recognize early warning signs through leading performance indicators;
- Taking action to lead change in the medical practice involving billing and collection so advanced billing practices can be adopted and implemented; and
- Using data to communicate the need for change and to measure and analyze change efforts.

These principles are important to ensure a successful billing operation. If you adhere to them, your journey on the road to getting paid should be smoother, resulting in improved revenue for your medical practice.

CHAPTER 2

POTHOLE 1:

The Previsit Process

T he previsit process is vital to ensuring accurate and timely receipt of information regarding the patient's ability to pay, yet many medical practices ignore this process. Those practices that disregard the previsit process simply wait for the patient to present for a visit to begin capturing the important information needed to ensure they are paid. And that is where they are getting into financial trouble!

By starting the billing process *before* the patient sees the physician, you can avoid problems related to uncovered services, out-of-network providers, inaccurate insurance information, ineligibility and patient flow delays. In addition, the previsit process is an opportune time to establish expectations regarding your patients' financial responsibility. The implementation of a previsit process is beneficial to your practice, as well as your patients, who appreciate – and increasingly demand – a greater understanding of their responsibility for the care delivered.

In this chapter, we cover:

- Previsit registration
- Previsit insurance verification
- Setting patients' expectations
- Patient financial policy
- Referrals and authorizations

The previsit process ensures that billing is performed *right the first time* and that physicians receive revenue for the services performed. How many times have you heard the front-office staff say "I have too much to do"? And how many times have you cringed when you thought about the level of chaos that is almost constant at the front office? The previsit process is where your revenue cycle begins. Chaos at your front desk is a clear indication that many of the front-office steps should be moved upstream.

The previsit process has typically included many clinical functions, such as preview of the patient's chart, exam room preparation, visit preparation and procedure preparation. Now, the business functions are also being conducted *prior* to the patient visit because there is a greater need not only to enhance revenue performance for the medical practice, but also to ensure that patient-friendly billing occurs during the process. Any paperwork, data capture, data updates, insurance verification and other business functions that you can handle prior to the visit will enhance the patient's experience on the date of visit. Waiting until the patient arrives amid chaos at the front desk before collecting the information necessary to ensure a clean claim is not a good way to start the revenue cycle for your medical practice.

The previsit process involves capturing data prior to the patient visit. This information is required to conduct front-end billing such as registration, demographic and insurance updates, review of patient responsibility balances, verification of insurance and prior authorization for services to be rendered. The front-office staff typically perform these services; however, billing staff can, too. For example, a biller might review the patient visit schedule two days prior to appointment and note the copayment or patient responsibility balance to be collected by front-office staff. Alternatively, this task may rest with the front-office staff as they prepare for the visit from a business perspective. Regardless of who performs these tasks, it is essential to complete them in advance of the patient visit.

The figure below outlines the business functions that need to be performed as part of the previsit process.

FIGURE 2.1 Business Previsit Functions

✓ Determine prior account balance
✓ Verify insurance
✓ Determine copayment level
✓ Determine co-insurance and deductible levels
✓ Learn pre-authorization requirements
✓ Make demographic/insurance updates
✓ Learn patient's no-show history

© 2004 Walker, Larch, Woodcock. Reprinted with permission.

To ensure an efficient and effective previsit process, we present proven strategies to enhance your revenue cycle. The advanced practices that we provide throughout this book are steps you can take to optimize your revenue cycle. They represent billing and collection practices typically found in better performing medical practices.

Advanced Practices | THE PREVISIT PROCESS

■ **Capture Patient Demographic and Insurance Information in Advance of the Patient Visit**
One of the key steps you can take to improve your front-end billing is to obtain patient demographic and insurance information prior to the patient's date of service. There are several alternative means for capturing this registration information for new and established patients.

For new patients, consider the following alternatives:

- Ask new patients to download registration forms from the practice's Web site or send a registration packet to the patient via e-mail; ask the patient to mail or fax the forms to the practice before his/her visit.

- Complete a full registration over the telephone when the patient calls to make an appointment.

- Once the patient is given an appointment, transfer him/her to a registration unit that obtains the full demographic and insurance information over the telephone.

- Schedule a telephone meeting with the patient and then call the patient back to obtain the required information.

We have seen each of the above alternatives work well; the method you select will depend upon the staffing model you have adopted for your practice.

If you don't have enough staff resources to conduct a complete registration of the patient over the telephone, obtain enough information about the patient's insurance to make a verification with the payer (further discussed below). A better performing practice uses the following script: "Ms. Jones, while I'm looking for an appointment time for you, could you be kind enough to get your insurance card out of your wallet?" This leaves ample time for the patient to locate the card, while not extending the call beyond a reasonable time.

For return patients, previsit communication typically takes place during the appointment reminder process that is conducted 24 to 48 hours in advance of the scheduled appointment. At that time, staff remind patients of any outstanding balances and updates to their insurance information. They can also obtain credit card payment for outstanding balances over the telephone.

■ **Verify Insurance Eligibility and Benefits in Advance of the Patient Visit**

Once staff obtain the information from the patient, they need to verify the patient's insurance coverage and benefits with the payer. They can either call the payer or go to the payer's Web site (if the payer makes this available and your practice has the equipment). In some markets, large medical groups have set up an electronic batch process to automate large numbers of eligibility transactions. For example, the medical group sends an electronic batch listing of all the patients it will be seeing three days from now for a payer; the payer compares that list to its eligibility database and electronically notes the status and eligibility date on file. The payer returns the list to the medical group, which electronically uploads the information into its practice management system or manually updates patients' accounts.

If resources permit, staff should conduct verification of insurance coverage for *all patients*. If there are limited resources, consider verifying Medicare patients only once a year, for example, while still verifying HMO coverage quarterly. To decide the extent to which you should plan to verify coverage, hold a meeting with the billing office to review the denials for insurance eligibility during the past six months. Understanding why your claims are being denied by your payers – whether for eligibility issues, incorrect payer or other reasons – will help you allocate your resources. For more information on managing your denials, see Chapter 8.

For patients scheduled for a service that is often not considered a benefit (such as infertility treatments), it is still necessary to verify information regarding benefits. The same holds true for any patients who indicate an insurance change or receipt of a new insurance card from their payers. Verify with the payer the scope of services covered. In particular, obtain information regarding the services that you may render to the patient. If the services are not covered, contact the patient prior to the visit. When a payer does not cover a child's immunizations, for example, explain this to the parents. This allows them to make a decision about whether to proceed with the service, and it allows you to confidently collect for the services from patients when they present for an appointment.

Many practices go beyond a simple verification of insurance and benefits and request information regarding eligibility dates, requirements for pre-authorization, deductibles, copayments, coinsurance and any other pertinent information. Develop a customized verification and benefits eligibility form (see example on page 27) based on the needs of your specialty (for example, for an obstetrics practice, determine whether amniocentesis is covered). Maintain the form electronically so that all staff can access it; at a minimum, place it in the patient's chart. This allows the practice to save precious time because nurses and referral staff will have access to this information, which will eliminate additional calls to the payer. To determine the content of your form and where to place your resources, use your denial data as your guide. You may choose to gather more or less information by payer, depending on your history of denials.

The better informed your practice is during the previsit process, the more knowledge you can impart to your patients. An informed patient base is advantageous when it comes to maximizing your collections because patients will understand their financial responsibility for the service that was rendered. Patients will be prepared to pay their portion of the bill, will know what services are covered and won't be surprised during the visit.

■ Ask Patients about Secondary Coverage
To avoid the common problems associated with coordination of benefits (COB) issues, ask patients for both primary and secondary insurance. In addition, ask questions about the existence of secondary coverage when you verify insurance. Many payers, particularly Medicare, have additional coverage listed in their beneficiary databases.

■ Set Expectations Regarding Patient Financial Responsibility
The patient collections process can begin long before the patient arrives at your office. Communicate the importance of your patients' financial responsibility in your practice brochure and Web site. During the appointment reminder call, remind patients of their time-of-service responsibility (for example, copayment), as well as a prior balance they may have on their account. A staff member should review the appointment schedule several days prior to the date of service, alert front-office staff to patients with problem accounts and identify payments owed. Most practice management systems today offer some sort of flag or alert system so you can identify those patients needing financial counseling. A better performing practice has access to and knowledge of the patient's account and copies of the explanation of benefits forms (EOBs) in question at the front office so it can keep the patient fully informed and increase the likelihood of payment. These processes can enhance cash flow, improve patient service and education, and reduce the cost of attempting to collect from the patient after the visit.

■ Develop a Written Financial Policy
A financial policy provides the details of your expectations – in writing. The following are examples of financial policies and the operational questions you should ask yourself (and answer!) as part of each policy:

Policy: Copayments are required at time of service.
- Will we turn away a new patient who does not pay the copayment upon visit arrival?
- Will we continue to schedule return visits if a patient owes the copayment?
- When will we collect the copayment (before or after the visit)?

Policy: Referrals are required for the specialty practice.
- Will we require the physician referral before the patient can schedule an appointment? Will we obtain the referral before the patient arrives for the appointment?
- Will we reschedule a patient who does not provide a referral?

Policy: Prior balances must be paid in 30 days unless a signed payment plan has been executed.
- Who will identify prior balances and remind the patient? Will we schedule appointments for patients who owe prior balances or fail to pay pursuant to their agreed-upon payment plan?

Policy: We will educate patients about their responsibility to pay.
- When? On the telephone during appointment scheduling, at check-in, at checkout or during the visit?
- Will we follow a different process for (1) new patients, (2) urgent visits and (3) elective services?

Other financial questions to ask:

- If we are not participating with the patient's payer, will we see the patient? What financial arrangements must we follow? (We recommend registering the patient as self-pay and collecting the money before the visit.)
- What patient behavior is unacceptable and will cause us to discharge a patient from our practice? What process will we follow to discharge a patient?
- Will our practice adopt a charity care policy? How will we implement it?
- Will we give uninsured patients who are below a predetermined income level a discount if they make payment at the time of service? Who will address their questions about payment if they ask at the front office? What language or scripting will we use to communicate this policy?
- What is our policy regarding payment plans?

     Will our practice charge additional fees, such as interest on past-due balances? Copayment rebilling fee? Pass-through of the collection agency fee to the patient?

As you can see from the examples above, your financial policy needs to include implementation guidelines so staff understand the action they should take and know how to respond to circumstances that may arise.

Make sure you have only one financial policy for the practice, not separate financial policies for each physician in the practice. You cannot require copayments on Mondays but ignore time-of-service collections on Thursdays because different physicians work in the office on those days. Identify several physicians to draft the practice's financial policy, obtain approval through your normal governance channels, then communicate this to every physician and staff member. Write it down and review it at least once a year.

Once you have developed a clear financial policy, share it with patients. Depending on your practice's preference, you can communicate your financial policies to new patients by mailing a brochure prior to the first appointment. Alternatively, a staff member can meet with all new patients when they present for appointments to review the important elements. Many medical practices ask patients to sign a financial policy agreement. Remind return patients during appointment calls or appointment reminder calls that appropriate payment is required at the time of service.

Process Referrals and Authorizations

In addition to evaluating the patient's financial responsibility, review the appointment schedule to determine if the patient is scheduled for a service that requires a referral or authorization. Process all referrals and authorizations in a timely manner. Most payers do not retroactively pay for services that require approval, except in true emergency situations. Use automated referral processing systems when payers make them available. Vigilance during the previsit process is critical to maximize your payments for these services.

Tool 1: Previsit Checklist (see next page)
To assist medical practices in conducting the previsit functions, we have provided a previsit checklist. This tool is intended to be a template only; we encourage you to customize the form for your use.

> ### ▮ Develop a Guide to Payers
>
> Create a payer guide or insurance plan summary sheet and give it to the practice sites as well as to the billing staff. A typical guide includes an outline of the requirements for each of the major payer contracts, with specific items such as the need for pre-authorization, specified laboratory, copayment level, formulary, telephone number of provider relations department and other pertinent information related to referrals. Many practices have placed this information on a secure Web site or local area network for access throughout the practice.

Tool 2: Payer Guide (see pages 20 and 21)
We have provided an example of a payer guide that can be constructed for each of your payers. This type of guide details the pertinent information required by all staff regarding payer-specific issues.

TOOL
1 PREVISIT CHECKLIST

Date of service _____

Patient's name _____

Account number _____

Staff member completing form/date of completion _____ _/_/_

Signatures needed from patient:

☐ New patient – all registration forms
☐ Change of insurance – all insurance forms
☐ Noncovered services waiver form
☐ Advanced beneficiary notice (ABN) (Medicare only)
☐ Consent for treatment
☐ Medical history
☐ Financial policy
☐ Other _____

Information required from patient:

☐ Copy of insurance card
☐ Copy of driver's license/other identification
☐ Other_____

Insurance verification complete and documented? Y / N If N, please address: _____
Benefits eligibility complete and documented? Y / N If N, please address: _____
Referrals secured? Y / N If N, please address: _____
Should patient be requested to meet with the financial counselor? Y / N

Collection of payments at the visit:

$ -	Copayment
$ -	Co-insurance
$ -	Payment on deductible
$ -	Payment plan
$ -	Payment on account
$ -	Other

Notes: _____
_____

TOOL 2 | **PAYER GUIDE**

Last Updated:

Payer's logo	**Payer's Name**	**Financial Class ##**
	Payer's Web site address	
	*Include notes about this payer not mentioned elsewhere.	

PRODUCTS	REFERRAL/AUTHORIZATION	CONTRACTS/CONTRACT DATES

PRODUCTS / **REFERRAL/AUTHORIZATION**

Product A	Yes	
Product B	Yes	SEE BACK FOR
Product C Open Access	No	MORE
Product D Opt-out	No	INFORMATION

CONTRACTS/CONTRACT DATES
- Primary Care (6/01/04)
- Specialist/Tertiary Care (06/01/05)
- Hospital A (10/1/04)
- Hospital B (6/01/04)
- Hospital C (10/07/05)

REFERRAL LENGTH
- Up to 3 visits per referral
- Valid for 60 days from the date of issue
- Exceptions to 60-day window (unless otherwise noted)
  - Allergists (1 year)
  - Hematologists (1 year)
  - Oncologists (1 year)

LAB-OUTPATIENT SERVICES
Lab X: 800-xxx-xxxx
- Lab X requisition forms including the patient's ID# must be used when ordering lab tests or referring a member to a draw station

IMPORTANT PHONE NUMBERS/WEB SITES

Eligibility	800-xxx-xxxx
Precertification/Admission	800-xxx-xxxx
Provider Relations	800-xxx-xxxx
Customer Service	800-xxx-xxxx
Case Management	800-xxx-xxxx
Care Management (authorizations, etc.)	800-xxx-xxxx
Claims	800-xxx-xxxx
Web Access	

RADIOLOGY-OUTPATIENT SERVICES
Imaging Center: xxx-xxx-xxxx
Any designated health care provider
- Patients referred to an approved radiology facility require a script from the referring physician

---

Include image of insurance card Front

PCP name will be on the card.

Claims Address
Street
City, State, Zip

Certificate Numbers
Certificate number begins with xxx followed by numbers. Some ID cards may not have an alpha prefix. This indicates that the claims are handled outside the Payer X Program.

Include image of insurance card Back

Payer's logo	Payer's name	Financial class ##

GENERAL REFERRAL REQUIREMENTS (Office)
All office visits to a participating specialist require a referral (*Outpatient authorization requirement: any service provided in a setting other than a physician office [regulated hospital space])

Services NOT requiring a referral:
- Routine and non-routine services provided by a participating OB/GYN for care performed in office setting
- Routine and non-routine services provided at a participating freestanding radiology facility listed in the payer's directory
- Routine vision exams by participating optometrists
- Mental health/substance abuse services, provided/coordinated by _____
- Services provided by a specialist to members with Payer's Opt-out Open Access
- Visits to a participating urgent care center
- Services provided by a participating provider while the member is an inpatient

Note: Additional authorization of ancillary services and a more limited 90-day authorization period may apply if services are performed in a hospital-based clinic. The rendering physician must identify the number of visits within the 90-day period to be utilized.

Long-standing referrals:
- Members are allowed up to one year of unlimited visits if **all** of the following criteria are met:
  - member has life-threatening, degenerative, chronic and/or disabling condition or disease requiring specialized medical care;
  - member's PCP determines in consultation with the specialist that the member needs continuing specialized care; and
  - the specialist has expertise in treating the patient's condition and is a participating provider.

AUTHORIZATION REQUIREMENTS (Admitting provider required to obtain authorization at least 5 days prior to admission/outpatient service)

Services that require authorization:
- Any services provided in a setting other than a physician's office (regulated hospital-based clinics), except for lab and radiology facilities
- All hospital admissions or outpatient/ambulatory care procedures
- All diagnostic or preoperative testing in a hospital setting
- Chemotherapy or intravenous therapy in a setting other than a practitioner's office and billed by a provider other than the practitioner
- DME for a diagnosis other than asthma or diabetes and when provided by a contracted vendor
- Prosthetics and orthotics when provided by a contracted vendor
- Follow-up care provided by a non-participating practitioner following discharge from the hospital
- Radiation oncology, except when performed at a contracted freestanding center
- The following services:
  - Hemodialysis
  - Home health care
  - Nutritional services
  - Hospice care
  - Treatment of infertility

Notes: The patient must meet the Payer's eligibility requirements and services must be covered under the patient's health benefit plan for an authorization to be valid.

SPECIAL INSTRUCTIONS:

Claims filing limits
- 6 months from the date of service

Claims appeals
- 6 months from the date of denial

Emergency admissions
- Contact members PCP or Specialist
- Hospital should contact

Provider numbers
- Listed in Dictionary #

Physical therapy
PT Practice: xxx-xxx-xxxx

Behavioral xxx-xxx-xxxx

Vision
Mandated provider for routine vision:
xxx-xxx-xxxx
Mandated provider for non-routine services:
- Any participating provider

Payer Guides are published by Management Team and can be obtained by calling xxx-xxx-xxxx
Source: University Physicians Inc., Practice Operations, 2003; Sample payer guide with specific payer blinded. Reprinted with permission.

Performance Workload Ranges — THE PREVISIT PROCESS

The performance workload ranges for the previsit functions that we typically expect are provided below. The ability to perform within these ranges may vary due to internal practice-specific factors (such as facility layout, telephone system and practice management system). The workload ranges are based on a staff member performing these functions approximately seven hours of productive time per day (allowing one hour for breaks, interruptions and other downtime). Note that the workload ranges reflect *quantitative* performance levels. *Qualitative* performance – accuracy, completeness, appropriateness and quality of these functions – should also be measured. When issues of quantity versus quality arise, we strongly recommend that quality be emphasized, even if the performance workload ranges for a particular function need to be relaxed from these levels.

Appointment Scheduling

Appointment scheduling with patient demographics only:

$\qquad$ 70 – 120 calls/day $\qquad$ 10 – 17 calls/hour

Appointment scheduling with full registration:

$\qquad$ 50 – 75 calls/day $\qquad$ 7 – 11 calls/hour

Previsit registration with insurance verification:

$\qquad$ 60 – 80 patients/day $\qquad$ 8 – 12 patients/hour

Error rates of patient demographic and insurance information:

$\qquad$ < 2 percent

© 2004 Walker, Larch, Woodcock: Day-to-Day Practice Operations. *Reprinted with permission.*

⚠ Practice Blunder — THE PREVISIT PROCESS

With too few staff members at the front office, Practice Blunder barely has enough time to get the patient's name during the scheduling call, let alone any information regarding insurance. When patients arrive, Practice Blunder has a sign that reads, "Please take a number and be seated. You will be called in the order of arrival." The patient then takes a number from a number machine (similar to those in postal offices or ice cream parlors) and sits down in the reception area. The staff then overhead pages the patient to the front desk to complete the required forms and to verify insurance. Staff collect patient demographic and insurance forms throughout the day and give them to a charge entry employee the next day to input to the practice management system.

The front-office staff cannot check in the patients fast enough, so the nurses begin to pull patients from the check-in line out of frustration. Although the practice may have saved money by understaffing the front office, services are often billed directly to patients out of error. Frustrated patients call to ask why their insurance was not billed.

Practice Blunder is proud of the fact that it asks front-office staff to personally correct errors involving insurance and demographic information. It captures errors by front-office staff and communicates these errors to the individual employee responsible for the error, requiring him/her to personally correct the error. By the time most of the front-office staff find time to attend to their errors, the payers' filing deadlines for submission of claims have passed!

Case Exercises

1. What processes could Practice Blunder better accomplish before the patient visit?
2. Can you recommend a better check-in process for Practice Blunder?
3. Should registration be processed by batching work or processing work in real time? Why?
4. Can you recommend a better process for correcting registration errors?
5. How could training be improved for the front-office staff?
6. Does Practice Blunder need to consider its front-office staffing? How should Practice Blunder analyze its staffing needs?

Policies and Procedures | THE PREVISIT PROCESS

At the end of each chapter we provide policies and procedures to assist you in developing a policy and procedure manual for your practice. Below are three policies specific to the previsit process.

POLICY 1 Patient Registration

Policy: Demographic and insurance information will be collected from all patients, and it will be verified prior to or at the time of the scheduled appointment.

Procedures:

1. Any patient being seen must be registered in our practice management system. This ensures that pertinent patient demographic and insurance data is captured in the system for the purposes of billing, contracting and data analysis.

2. A new patient may pre-register at the practice by telephoning the office or by presenting at the office for purposes of scheduling an appointment. At this time, the following minimal demographic and insurance information will be collected by the practice staff:

   - Patient name*;
   - Patient address*;
   - Home, work, and cellular telephone number(s) (Home*);
   - E-mail address;
   - Date of birth*;
   - Social Security number;
   - Primary insurance name*;
   - Policy and group number(s)*;
   - Guarantor name*; and
   - Guarantor address.

   * If time does not permit collection of all this data, a telephone registration may be completed with this minimal information.

3. The scheduler/receptionist should assure that all available information has been collected before the patient/guarantor ends the telephone conversation or leaves the office.

4. All new patients will be given, sent or directed to the practice Web site to download a new patient information packet that will include:

- Practice brochure;
- The practice no-show policy;
- The practice financial policy; and
- New patient registration form.

5. Three days prior to the appointment, all patient registration information will be reviewed. If information is missing, the patient will be contacted regarding the missing information. The insurance will be verified with the payer, and based on a review of the nature of the appointment benefits eligibility will be conducted. If coverage and/or benefits eligibility cannot be verified, the patient will be contacted by telephone 48 hours prior to the appointment (combine this call with the appointment reminder call). The patient will be informed that coverage could not be verified, and that the visit will be considered self-pay unless the patient chooses to present additional information regarding his/her coverage.

A new patient will be fully registered 24 hours prior to the visit.

POLICY 2 Practice Brochure

Policy: All new patients will be presented with a practice brochure that describes the practice's policies and procedures relevant to patients.

Procedures:

1. The practice brochure will include the following information:

   - Practice's mission/vision statement;
   - Office hours;
   - Emergencies;
   - Protocols, including telephone number, for appointment scheduling, test results and prescription refills;
   - Specialty information;
   - Personal and professional information regarding physicians and other providers;
   - Directions to practice or map;
   - Referral to specialty care (if applicable);
   - Financial policy, to include the telephone number of person to call regarding billing questions;
   - Pertinent telephone numbers; and
   - Termination of services.

2. If a new patient appointment is made for more than one week from the current date, the practice brochure will be mailed to the patient. If the patient does not receive a practice brochure in the mail, it will be presented to the patient at the first appointment.

3. At their first visit, new patients will be asked to sign a form stating, "I received the practice's brochure and understand the financial policies."

Best Practices: What else can you do?

You should feature your practice's brochure prominently on your practice's Web site.

POLICY 3 **Insurance Verification**

Policy: It is the policy of the practice that insurance coverage and benefits eligibility will be verified with the insurance company for all new patients, patients indicating changes in coverage and high-dollar procedures or services, including all inpatient services.

Procedures:

1. All new patient accounts and accounts with information changes noted will be pulled three days prior to the appointment date.

2. For each account, the insurance company will be contacted to verify coverage and benefits eligibility via Internet, or telephone.

3. The insurance verification form will be completed for each account. (If possible, a screen should be added to practice management system to allow collection of information online.)

4. If insurance or benefits for the services scheduled to be rendered cannot be verified, staff will contact the patient immediately to inform him/her of the situation and request coverage information. If coverage is not available, staff will inform the patient of his/her responsibility to pay for the services rendered during the appointment. If the patient chooses, the appointment may be rescheduled.

Insurance Verification

Patient name: Date of verification:

Patient telephone number: Date of birth:

Social Security number: Doctor the patient is seeing:

Appointment time and date: Chief complaint:

Primary insurance company: Network:

PCP (if in an HMO or POS plan):   Name of insured person:

Relationship to patient: Insured's date of birth:

Insured's Social Security number: Employer:

Effective date:

Person contacted: Telephone number/extension:

Who is covered under this plan?

Are there other insurance(s) listed?

Send claim to: Group number:

Policy number: Copayment:

Deductible: Co-insurance:

For family:

For individual:

Policy coverage notes: Lab and X-ray:

Immunizations: Well visits:

Referral required?   Other:

CHAPTER 3

POTHOLE 2:
The Patient Check-in Process

The front-office staff control financial viability and access to the practice. We are well beyond expecting these employees to just smile and be nice. Their ability to obtain and translate patient information accurately and efficiently is vital to ensuring that billing is conducted *right the first time*.

In this chapter, we cover:

- Time-of-service collections
- Automated receipt processes
- System updates in real time
- Waiver forms
- Referral and pre-authorization confirmation
- Feedback to front-end billing staff

Is a happy patient a paying patient? Certainly, patients make their unhappiness known if the billing and collection process presents obstacles for them. The front-office staff are the first opportunity for your practice to make a good impression. Their knowledge of the billing and collection process, their ability to clearly explain the financial policy to the patient and to define patient expectations, and their skill in accurately obtaining and recording data are critical to a streamlined billing and collection process.

The previsit process initiates the patient to your practice; when the patient arrives at the office, you will complete the registration function. Present patients with all relevant paperwork – to include forms to capture updates to the patient's demographic and insurance information, as well as notification of new or revised practice policies. Obtain the necessary signatures, copy or scan insurance and identification cards and request payment. You may also direct patients to complete medical history forms. After the paperwork is completed, notify the clinical staff that the patient is ready to be seen.

If your practice did not have the opportunity to conduct any previsit processes, verify insurance coverage and benefits eligibility as the patient is completing the paperwork and reviewing the practice's financial policy. Obtain or confirm referrals and authorizations.

If the patient is not physically present during the registration process (for example, for hospital services and hospital-based specialties), obtain registration information from the most trusted source, normally the hospital's registration system. Conduct the rest of the registration process – to include insurance verification, benefits eligibility and referral processing – prior to charge entry.

To ensure efficient and effective check-in processes, we present proven strategies to enhance your revenue cycle.

Advanced Practices | THE PATIENT CHECK-IN PROCESS

■ **Create a Unified Team between the Front-office Staff and Billing Staff**
Many better performing practices create a formal reporting relationship between the front-office staff and the billing office. They recognize the importance of the check-in function for reimbursement. This tends to reduce the turf issues between front-end and back-end billing staff that some practices experience. If a practice does not institute this type of reporting relationship, it should develop clear performance expectations for the front-office staff regarding timeliness and accuracy of data to ensure attention to billing and collection functions. At a minimum, the front-office staff and the billing staff need to realize that they are part of the same team. Written job descriptions and team goals can help make that point.

■ **Report Error Rates to the Front-office Staff**
Report error rates involving inaccurate or incomplete demographic and insurance information to staff on a regular basis. Some of these errors may be "subscriber not enrolled on the date of service" or "subscriber not identified." Many practices require front-office staff to correct the error as a learning opportunity; if no one tells the staff that errors are being made, they have no opportunity to improve their performance. However, the timeliness of this correction needs to be monitored. Communicating errors should be a training tool so that staff can recognize their errors and avoid repeating their mistakes. The tools below will help you audit your front-desk performance and report errors to the staff so that they can improve front-end billing performance for the future.

Tool 3: Front-desk Audit Tool
This tool provides a systematic process for reviewing the work of the front-office staff involved in key front-end billing functions. We recommend that your practice conduct audits for both new and recurring staff on a regular basis. Many practices have elected to audit the front-desk staff quarterly because of the need to keep current on changing payer information, practice management system modules and other similar developments.

TOOL
3 FRONT-DESK AUDIT TOOL

Level: 1 = Needs improvement; 2 = Meets expectations; 3 = Above expectations	Level
Previsit	
Does practice prepare prior to visit and flag information to update forms as needed?	
Does practice have current list of insurance plans and critical plan elements to ensure compliance?	
Does practice communicate electronically with payers for eligibility and authorization?	
Does practice verify eligibility prior to every visit/procedure?	
Does practice verify insurance for new patients and those with procedures?	
Does practice verify insurance at least annually for all patients?	
Does practice obtain pre-authorization and referrals as needed for all services?	
Does practice capture the referring physician for each service?	
Do charge tickets reflect updated procedure and diagnosis codes?	
Patient check-in/reception	
Does practice review all scheduled patient accounts for prior balances prior to appointments and issue reminders?	
Does practice attempt to collect all prior balances at time of service?	
Does practice collect copayments required at time of service?	

Patient check-in/reception (continued)	Level
Does practice collect co-insurance and deductible at time of service?	
Does practice verify that HIPAA signature is on file?	
Does practice initiate waiver forms for patient signature?	
Does practice verify demographic and insurance information on all patients and provide real-time updates?	
Do office staff have easy access to equipment to perform their duties, e.g., copier, fax, scanner?	
Does practice obtain a copy of insurance card at time of visit?	
Does practice date the insurance card that is copied?	
Is scanning technology employed?	
Does practice offer credit and debit cards as payment options?	
Does practice give a stamped self-addressed envelope to patients who do not pay at time of service and follow up?	
Does practice initiate a receipt for payment (preferably electronic receipt)?	
Is the receptionist prepared for patients to check in with prompts to collect copayment or account balance and obtain waiver forms?	
Would the patient be likely to agree that his/her privacy and confidentiality were protected?	
Is the patient asked to provide information s/he has already provided to another source?	
Are staff trained to discuss financial issues with the patient?	

Patient exit/departure	
Does the patient understand the referral process and any required prior authorization for referral services?	
Is the patient offered a follow-up appointment when applicable?	
Does the provider complete charge ticket in a timely, accurate fashion?	

Charge entry	
Is charge entry conducted within 24 hours of date of service?	
Does practice have cash controls in place to ensure all money is accounted for each day?	
Is charge entry reconciled to appropriate source documents?	
Does practice complete requests for information to central billing office within 24 hours of request?	

Tool 4: Front-desk Monthly Denial Report

To track and report error rates incurred by front-office staff, create a spreadsheet delineating major error categories as demonstrated in the table below. You can develop data for the spreadsheet by sampling the explanation of benefits forms (EOBs) received during a one-week period for one payer only. You don't need a formal scientific sampling of the errors; if you have a problem with registration with one payer, that problem typically is also occurring with other payers. This tool is designed as an educational opportunity for front-office staff to ensure they are entering billing data right the first time.

TOOL 4   FRONT-DESK MONTHLY DENIAL REPORT

	Percent of Average Claims per Month		
Denial Reason:	Main office	Satellite office	Total
Patient not eligible on date of service	5%	2%	4%
Claim filed in error to wrong payer	4%	1%	3%
No referral	1%	5%	2%
Services not covered	1%	1%	1%
Duplicate claim	2%	2%	2%
Claim returned – need additional information	1%	0%	1%
Total Denial Rate	14%	11%	13%

Interpret the data and take action – for example:
- Satellite office has reduced its denials by improving its registration quality.
- Main office has not made progress in registration areas – more training will be held; individual registration audits will be completed this week.
- Referral management needs more attention at satellite office. Referral coordinator from main office will spend one day per week at satellite office.

© 2004 Walker, Larch, Woodcock. Reprinted with permission.

Systematically Collect Copayments at Check-in

Most medical practices have started collecting copayments *before* the patient sees the physician (when possible). Practices that have instituted this approach typically see an increase in time-of-service cash collections of 10 to 20 percent and a reduction in their cost of billing, as fewer patient statements are required and less patient follow-up is needed.

It is the patients' responsibility as beneficiaries of their insurance company to pay their copayment; your job is to facilitate the collection per the payer's rules and regulations. If patients have concerns about copayment amounts, direct them to their payers. When patients do not regularly pay their copayment amounts, they should be reported to their payers' member services as they are technically in violation of their contract. Some practices have changed the signs at the front desk from "Payment is Expected at the Time of Service. Thank you" to "Your Insurance Company Requires Us to Collect a Copayment. Thank you" to emphasize the reason the patient is required to make a copayment. Many practices provide their staff with training on collecting at time-of-service that includes role playing and brief scripts to use for different situations. Refer to Tool 5: Sample Cash-at-Time-of-Service Scripts.

Tool 5: Sample Cash-at-Time-of-Service Scripts (see next page)
Help your staff collect cash at the time of service by reviewing sample scripts with them so they know how you expect them to communicate with patients. This tool provides samples of phrases that they can use to overcome payment obstacles. Customize the tool based on your practice's preference regarding payment options and tolerance for payment delays.

■ **Systematically Collect All Patient Balances at the Patient Visit**
   Institute a policy to collect all patient balances at the time of service – to include prior patient balance, deductibles, co-insurance and fees for noncovered services – in addition to the copayment. As we shall see in a later chapter, the cost to produce a statement, mail the statement and follow up with the patient is significant. Practices that have instituted systematic review of all patient financial responsibility are able to improve their payment cycle time. Collecting patient balances at the time the patient is physically present in the office can substantially reduce billing expenditures. If the patient is unable to pay, give the patient a pre-addressed billing office envelope and establish a timeline when payment is expected. Some practices have even instituted a copayment rebilling fee of $5 to $10 if patients do not pay while they are in the practice to encourage time-of-service payments.

■ **Print the Explanation of Benefits (EOB) Form**
   For patients with prior balances due, copy or print the patient's relevant EOB(s). You can present the EOB(s) to the patient to substantiate your request for payment at the request of the payer and further your position as the patient's financial advocate.

■ **Collect Payments for Procedures and Surgeries (Non-emergent) Prior to Time of Service**
   More practices are collecting payments for procedures and surgeries *prior* to the time of service so they can capture patient payments and decrease billing costs. Patients respond well to this expectation if you present it as part of the financial policy. For example, when a medical procedure is determined to be necessary, have schedulers call the patient's insurance company to determine payment levels and

TOOL 5 SAMPLE CASH-AT-TIME-OF-SERVICE SCRIPTS

ASKING FOR PAYMENT:

"Your copayment for today's visit is $10, and you can pay that today by cash, check, credit or debit card."
This straightforward statement makes it difficult for the patient to respond any other way than how s/he will pay!

"The fee for today's services is $200. As we explained, we do not participate with your insurance carrier. You can handle payment by cash, check, credit or debit card."
State the full amount of the visit and acknowledge the fact that you know the patient was informed previously that his/her insurance was not accepted.

PHRASES TO USE WHEN THE PATIENT PRESENTS OBSTACLES:

- *Patient can't pay (for various reasons).*
  Don't say: "I want you to..."; "We require..."; "Our policy states..."

  Do say: "Here is an envelope for you to mail your payment within three days."
  "May I suggest payment by credit card, or do you have an ATM card?" "There is a convenient ATM machine *around the corner.*"
  "Okay, let's see, today is Tuesday. How much time will you need on the $200?"

- *Patient: Bill me.*
  "I wish we could, but we need you to pay today."
  "Your copayment is due at time of visit. This was explained in your insurance information, and your insurance requires us to collect the copay each time you see the doctor."

  Note: If you're collecting payment **prior to the visit** and the patient refuses to pay, determine if your physicians want the patient to be rescheduled. This will obviously depend on the specialty of your practice and the reason for the patient visit. If appropriate, state:
  "You can pay today with check or credit/debit card, or we can reschedule your visit."

- *Patient: Bill my insurance company.*
  "We will be happy to submit a claim to your insurance company for you. But the practice expects all patients to pay for services at the time they are provided if we do not participate in your insurance plan."

- *Patient: This policy doesn't make any sense.*
  "I'm sorry you feel that way. The policy is to clear up any questions that may come up about what your financial responsibility is."
  "I'll be happy to have my supervisor discuss it with you; however, I still need you to pay your copayment (or fee)."

- *Physicians or other professionals request a waiver or discount.*
  "Our physicians adopted a policy that does not allow me to waive or discount your copayment. Here is a copy for you to review. How will you be paying today?" or "I am unable to waive or discount the payment; I'll be happy to refer you to my supervisor. Here is a copy of the policy adopted by our physicians."

responsibility. Develop a worksheet that records the payer's estimated payment for the service (and the practice's agreed-upon contractual write-off) in addition to the patient's responsibility. At that time, you can make payment arrangements or establish a budget plan with the patient. If you couch this as a service to your patients, this can be a win-win for the practice from a cash-flow perspective (it also saves billing costs) and for the patient who is now informed. The following is a script used to communicate this message to the patient: "Let's determine what your insurance company will pay for this service so you will know the amount that you will need to pay prior to the procedure."

This tool is a sample of a patient financial agreement for non-emergent specialty services.

Tool 6: Patient Financial Agreement (see next page)
Once you know the clinical service that is to be performed, contact the patient's payer to find out the patient's payment responsibilities. Collect the full amount or establish a payment plan. Use this tool to record the information and to set up the payment plan in your practice management system.

▎ **Accept Credit and Debit Cards**

Accept major credit and debit cards. Be sure patients know they can pay with credit or debit cards at the time of service and include this information on their patient statements. Offering credit and debit card options increases your patient collections and lowers your billing costs. Some patients may not be able to pay more than their copayment amount in cash, but they typically have at least one credit card.

Credit cards reduce patient statements. Once the credit card has been accepted, the practice receives the entire amount. The credit card company takes over the responsibility (and the risk) for billing the patient.

Better performing practices offer patients the option of giving the practice authorization to bill their credit card for balances not paid by insurance. These amounts usually include copayments, deductibles and repeating amounts due for high-frequency services, such as physical therapy. Patients complete a form authorizing these charges, and it is kept on file in the practice. For the protection of both parties, the authorization form should include the patient's signature and date of signing, as well as the period of time the patient is authorizing the credit card to be used. Every time the card is charged, the practice should send the patient a receipt of the transaction.

PATIENT FINANCIAL AGREEMENT

Patient: _____

Guarantor/person responsible for payment: _____

Address: _____

City: _____ State: _____ Zip: _____

Home phone: _____ Business phone: _____ E-mail:_____

Service(s): _____

Fee for services rendered $ _____

Expected third-party reimbursement $ _____

Estimated insurance benefits $ _____

Estimated patient responsibility $ _____

Payment plan options:

☐   I will pay 100% of the patient responsibility portion on the first appointment.
☐   I prefer to pay 50% of the patient responsibility portion on the first appointment. The remainder to be paid within 15 days after the insurance company has paid its portion.

In the event my account becomes delinquent for a period of thirty (30) days, I hereby acknowledge that I will be immediately responsible for the balance, interest, court costs and/or attorney fees.

I hereby certify that I have read and received a copy of this statement.

This _____ day of _____ , 2 _____

Signature: _____ , Responsible Party

© 2004 Walker, Larch, Woodcock. Reprinted with permission.

■ **Use Waiver Forms**

When medical practices conduct previsit activities they are better prepared to use waiver forms. Besides Medicare's Advanced Beneficiary Notice (ABN), better performing medical practices institute waiver forms that are payer-specific to address services that may not be covered by the payer. Obtaining a waiver form, however, is only the first step. Setting up systems to collect payments in advance for noncovered or "waived" services, as discussed above, will help you collect revenue without incurring a back-end billing expense.

■ **Institute Automated Receipt Processes**

Some practice management software systems generate an automatic receipt. As staff collect payments, they post them to the practice management system in real time, and the system generates an electronic receipt to give the patient at the time of service. This provides a higher level of internal controls than a discretionary receipt process and lets staff balance cash receipts effectively. Note, however, that when staff post payments prior to charges, a reconciliation of the payment and charge is required. Typically, practice management systems can provide a report that identifies missing charges associated with a patient payment so that these can be easily resolved. Some systems are even able to find the match and auto-reconcile for you.

■ **Provide Real-Time Patient Information Updates to Your System**

Conduct real-time updates to the practice management system for insurance and demographic updates. That is, as patients provide new or updated information, key it into your practice management system without delay. Delays cause inaccurate claims and statements to be sent because the claim or the statement may be dropped before the new information is entered into the system. The more the information and paperwork is handed off to another staff member, the greater the opportunity for errors and delays.

■ **Don't Ask Patients for the Same Information More Than Once**

Patients do not need to provide the information they already supplied during the previsit process. A brief verification only is needed. Your staff can print out a "face sheet" that reports the patient's demographic and insurance information and ask the patient to review, verify and sign the form. Or they can ask, "Ms. Smith, are you still living at XYZ address?" Missing data elements should be highlighted either in the practice management system or on the patient schedule to ensure that patients are asked to provide this information at the time of the visit.

■ **Copy and Date Stamp the Insurance Card**

Unless your medical practice has a very stable patient base, review insurance cards at each patient visit. Have the staff member responsible for the registration copy or scan the card and initial and date the copy when information has changed. When you date stamp the card, you know how current the information on file is. Often a patient receives a new card from the same payer and is unaware that there was a change such as the payer address; hence the need to review insurance cards at each visit and compare the card with the information that resides on your practice management system.

■ **Verify the Patient's Identity**
Consider also requesting to copy a patient's identification card with a photograph. While most patients will hand you a driver's license, this should be voluntary. Photo identification can help you resolve data discrepancies in the information recorded on or keyed off of the registration form. The date of birth on the photo identification will help ensure that the coverage is for the correct patient. If your practice is regularly obtaining copies of photo identification, however, and is not using them, consider discontinuing this policy as it represents unnecessary work for your staff.

■ **Implement Scanning Technology**
Instead of copying the insurance and identification cards, consider purchasing scanning technology. Practices are using this cost-effective, readily available technology to scan the cards upon the patient's presentation to the practice. Using a small scanning terminal, the image of the cards is attached – in an electronic file – to the patient's account. This allows staff (front-end and back-end) and physicians to have access to this critical information without having to pull the paper copy.

Be aware that copying or scanning patients' cards offers only a record of what they presented. It does not guarantee or imply coverage. You must also verify eligibility with the payer.

■ **Verify Insurance Eligibility and Benefits (if not conducted during the previsit process)**
If you did not verify insurance before the patient presents at the office (this will happen with walk-in patients, patients who have scheduled same-day appointments for which there was no time to perform previsit verification and patients who present with an insurance change), verify the patient's insurance at check-in by either placing a telephone call to the payer to confirm coverage and benefits eligibility, or going online. Electronic access will obviously streamline this process if it is available with the payer and if your practice has the equipment. Increasingly, payers are offering insurance verification at their Web sites or Web portal. If a complete benefits eligibility is necessary, be sure you can perform it online; if not, resort to the telephone. The information is important to ensure payment, and it is worth dedicating staff resources to this function.

■ **Develop Performance Expectations for Staff Involved in Scheduling, Registration and Check-in**
Sometimes, employees of the hospital or other entity participate in your practice's scheduling, registration, and/or check-in processes, and these employees do not have a direct reporting relationship to your medical practice. If your practice relies on hospital staff or others outside of the practice to conduct the front-end billing process, establish performance expectations and communicate them to the

employer of these individuals. Make sure the staff is held accountable. You should receive error rates on a regular basis and agree on expectations for improvement. Regularly track and monitor copayment and time-of-service payment levels and give feedback to the supervisor of these staff. When you formally enter into a contract to provide these front-end billing services, include these types of performance expectations in the contract language and terms and review them annually. At a minimum, meet with the supervisors of these staff about the level of accuracy and timeliness that you are experiencing, as well as the impact of their activities on your revenue cycle.

Change Your Financial Counselor's Job Title

Although most practices call the front-office staff who are responsible for patient collections "financial counselors" or "collectors," better performing practices refer to the employees fulfilling this function as "financial advocates." This change in job title conveys to patients that the practice is their advocate with regard to the insurance company.

Performance Workload Ranges   THE PATIENT CHECK-IN PROCESS

The performance workload ranges for patient check-in that we typically expect are provided below. The ability to perform within these ranges may vary due to internal practice-specific factors (such as facility layout, telephone system and practice management system). The workload ranges are based on a staff member performing these functions approximately seven hours of productive time per day (allowing one hour for breaks, interruptions and other downtime). Note that the workload ranges reflect *quantitative* performance levels. *Qualitative* performance – accuracy, completeness, appropriateness and quality of these functions – should also be measured. When issues of quantity versus quality arise, we strongly recommend that quality be emphasized, even if the performance workload ranges for a particular function need to be relaxed from these levels.

Error rates:	< 2 percent	
Time-of-service collections:	98 percent	
Referrals:	70 – 90/day	10 – 13/hour
Checkout with scheduling, cashiering:	70 – 90/day	10 – 13/hour
Checkout with scheduling, cashiering, charge entry:	60 – 80/day	8 – 12/hour

© 2004 Walker, Larch, Woodcock: Day-to-Day Practice Operations. *Reprinted with permission.*

⚠ **Practice Blunder** THE PATIENT CHECK-IN PROCESS

Practice Blunder rarely has time to ask for copayments during the check-in process. Sometimes, the staff member who collects the patient's encounter form and schedules his/her next appointment remembers, but often it's forgotten. The telephones are ringing off the hook because there are no designated staff to answer them. To attend to the telephone calls, the front-office staff process patients through check-in and checkout as fast as they can. Practice Blunder has no financial policy, and it is well known that its billing office struggles with an increasing amount of patient collections.

Case Exercises
1. Can you recommend a different check-in process for Practice Blunder?
2. How would you develop your argument for a different check-in process?
3. How would you convince Practice Blunder to invest in its front-office staff?

Policies and Procedures | THE PATIENT CHECK-IN PROCESS

POLICY **4** Patient Check-in

Policy: Patients will check in at the front desk before they are seen by the provider to verify the registration information on file and to make time-of-service payments when appropriate.

Procedures:

1. All patients will be asked to review and correct, if necessary, the information provided on the registration form. The patient will sign the form, confirming that the information provided is complete and accurate, and return it to the front-desk staff.

2. Patients with insufficient insurance information at the time of service will be registered and billed as "patient responsible" for charges incurred.

3. Practice staff will enter any changes to demographic and insurance information into the practice management system immediately. The most current signed registration form will be filed or scanned in the patient's medical record, behind the "registration" tab.

4. New patients will be asked to provide a valid insurance card and/or identification at the time of the scheduled appointment. A photocopy or scanned image of the front and back of the card will be made and maintained.

5. If there are any changes to the registration information, a new encounter form will be printed and/or the registration information manually updated on the previously printed encounter form.

6. An encounter form will be attached to the patient chart and forwarded to the appropriate staff for treatment.

7. When the patient has completed the registration process, the patient will be arrived in the appointment scheduling system according to the practice management system protocol; or the clinical staff will otherwise be informed of the patient's arrival. This announcement may occur prior to keying in the registration information for that patient, but after the patient has completed registration responsibilities.

Best Practices: What else can you do?

Consider placing a computer kiosk where patients wait, or hand them a tablet PC and ask them to review/update their registration information. Or, register patients in the exam room and seamlessly transition into the clinical encounter.

POLICY **5** Patient Checkout

Policy: After the provider has seen the patient, the provider will indicate the services provided on the encounter form, and the patient will take the encounter form to the checkout desk where appropriate copayment or other money will be collected (if it wasn't done at check-in). The encounter form will also include provider instructions to the checkout desk regarding future appointments for the patient (or alternatively, the patient will be given a discharge flow tool with that information recorded).

Procedures:

1. At the completion of the encounter, the physician will sign and indicate the services provided and corresponding diagnosis codes on the preprinted encounter form. The timing and nature of any future appointments requested by the physician will be indicated on the encounter form.

2. At the completion of the encounter, all patients will be given a completed encounter form and will be directed to the checkout desk.

3. Practice staff will enter the charges into the practice management system, using the codes the physician indicates on the encounter form.

4. Practice staff will ask the patient for any money due for the day's services and/or for prior outstanding balances (if it wasn't done at check-in).

5. Any payments received will be indicated on the encounter form as paid as cash at time of service (or alternatively, a written or automated receipt form will be provided).

6. Any payments made will be posted in the practice management system.

7. Practice staff will schedule follow-up appointments as appropriate.

Best Practices: What else can you do?

Some practices have eliminated the checkout process, and they collect all payments at check-in. Follow-up appointments are scheduled in the clinical area by a back-office scheduler or by the medical assistant(s), located near the physicians. Encounter forms are collected in a bin in the clinical area, and routed to the billing office at the end of each clinic or to check-in/checkout staff throughout the day for keying or scanning; or, physicians enter their own charges through the electronic medical record, which interfaces with the practice management system. Better performing practices collect payments at patient check-in, retain the encounter form in the back office and give patients a discharge order sheet to take to patient checkout for return appointment, test and/or procedure scheduling.

POLICY **6** Assignment of Benefits

Policy: It is the policy of the practice that an assignment of benefits statement will be completed by all new patients and patients presenting with an insurance change.

Procedures:

The following statement will be integrated into the registration form and will be completed by new patients and patients presenting with an insurance change.

Assignment of Benefits

I hereby assign to XYZ Practice any insurance or other third-party benefits available for health care services provided to me. I understand that XYZ Practice has the right to refuse or accept assignment of such benefits. If these benefits are not assigned to XYZ Practice, I agree to forward to the practice all health insurance and other third-party payments that I receive for services rendered to me immediately upon receipt.

_____

Signature of patient/legal guardian   Date

POLICY **7** Cash Handling and Reconciliation

Policy: It is the policy of the practice that all payments collected at time of service, including balances on accounts, are accounted for and subsequently posted to patients' accounts. A "change bank" of $100 will be available for staff use in making change.

Procedures:

1. Change bank

   ▪ Each collector will be responsible for his/her change bank:
     - Cash will be in the amount of $100, in denominations of $5 and $10.
     - Each collector will reconcile at the beginning and close of their session using the reconciliation log.
     - Discrepancies will be brought to the supervisor's attention prior to using monies from the bank. If unable to reconcile and the collector begins using the bank, the discrepancy will be the responsibility of the collector currently using the bank – not that of the previous collector.
     - No patient payments will be kept in the change bank.

2. Daily patient cash/check payments received

   ▪ Each collector will be responsible for safeguarding and accounting for payments received at time of visit.
     - Cash and checks received at time of visit will be kept in a separate envelope in the drawer with the change bank – *not in the change bank.*
     - Cash and checks should not be attached to encounter form and/or left outside the drawer.
     - Checks must include the following:
       • Patient/guarantor name, address and driver's license number;
       • Today's date (date of visit);
       • Handwritten and actual dollar amount;
       • Payee (practice – not the provider);
       • Account number in the lower left side; and
       • Patient/guarantor signature

3. Receipt books

   ▪ Receipt books (numbered and in three-part) will be used as follows:
     - Patient will be provided with a receipt for their payment, noting the following information:
       • Patient name;
       • Account number;

- Today's date (date of service);
- Dollar amount received;
- What the payment was for (copayment or balance);
- Type of payment (cash, check, credit or debit card);
- Provider name; and
- Name/initials of collector.

4. Encounter form

   - Each collector is responsible for ensuring that the encounter form is complete with the following information:
     - Patient name, medical record number and type of insurance;
     - Procedure (code describing type of service);
     - Diagnosis;
     - Physician's signature; and
     - Amount and type of payment made at time of service.
   - Forms with patient payments will be separated from all other encounter forms (use of different color file folder is helpful).
   - Forms that are incomplete (e.g., lacking procedure code, diagnosis, physician signature) are separated and returned to the physician for completion.

5. Reconciliation at end of session

   - Each collector is responsible for reconciling at the end of the session by completing the following. If unable to reconcile, the collector must contact the supervisor.
     - Total the payments recorded on the encounter form— *by type of payment*, and attach calculator tapes noting if sum is cash, check, credit card, or debit card.
     - Total payments recorded on the receipt forms – in the same manner as above – and attach calculator tape.
       Note: these two tapes should match; if they do not, repeat procedure. If still unable to reconcile, notify the supervisor.
     - Complete a confirmation of batch form and prepare deposit.
     - Count the money in the cash box/envelope. It should reconcile to $100. Sign out or initial for close of session; lock box/seal envelope.

Note: Any discrepancies in the "change bank" or payments collected must be brought to the supervisor's attention. Reconciliation must be completed at the end of every workday. Repeated failures to reconcile the change bank may lead to disciplinary action for performance.

CHAPTER 4

POTHOLE 3:

The Charge Capture and Charge Entry Process

The charge capture process appears to be relatively straightforward: Perform the service and capture the fact that it was performed! Unfortunately, this process is highly error-prone in many practices. Errors in developing the fee schedule, auditing charge capture and ensuring process quality can prevent practices from effectively recording charges.

In the chapter, we discuss:

- Charge capture
- Charge entry
- Fee schedules
- Encounter forms
- Procedure and diagnosis coding
- Charge and coding audits

Charge Capture

In many practices, the *inpatient* charge capture process is poorly designed. These practices continue to rely on the old method that requires the physician to self-initiate the process by capturing the service on a card, form, hospital face sheet or some other record. Physicians are asked to remember each and every patient they see in the inpatient setting, and each and every consult and procedure they perform. As noted in the advanced practices in this chapter, many medical practices have improved revenue generation by providing staff support and process improvement for inpatient charge capture.

For *surgical procedures or office procedures*, the charge capture process typically runs more smoothly. A dictated report is often used as the source document for the charge, with physicians and/or certified coders involved in the coding process. The key to charge capture of procedure activity is to ensure that all of the procedures that have been performed and documented are billed.

For *office activity*, charge capture is usually easy if the medical practice has practice management software that integrates the patient scheduling, registration and billing processes. Typically, the encounter forms (also known as superbills, charge tickets, fee tickets or vouchers) are numbered in the system, and a missing encounter form report permits the office staff to retrace the patient visit for the day and retrieve or reconstruct the missing encounter form. One of the toughest challenges for charge capture in the outpatient setting is to ensure that ancillary services and supplies are duly accounted for.

Charge Entry

Many practices require outpatient charge entry to be performed at the location of service. They distribute this function to multiple sites if they exist. Inpatient charge entry is more typically performed in a central billing office; however, it may also be distributed to the physician's primary outpatient location, a staff member may be sent to the hospital or other site of service to capture the charges for services rendered or the function may be the responsibility of staff already at the hospital (for example, the practice employs a nurse to round with the physicians at the hospital). A number of practices have electronic access to hospital demographic and insurance information online. If this is not feasible, practice staff may ask a hospital employee to place a copy of the patient's face sheet in a designated location for pickup.

To ensure efficient and effective charge capture and charge entry processes, we present proven strategies to enhance your revenue cycle.

Advanced Practices | THE CHARGE CAPTURE AND CHARGE ENTRY PROCESS

■ **Develop a Rational Fee Schedule**
Regardless of who performs charge entry or where it is performed, be sure that the fee schedule your medical practice uses is "rationally" based – designed with a systematic framework. Many practices have established their fees based on the Resource-Based Relative Value Scale (RBRVS), which involves multiplying the total relative value units (RVUs) of the procedure code by a multiplier. Because RBRVS is the system used by the CMS to establish Medicare rates, this method of fee setting is akin to setting fees as a percent of the Medicare allowed. Most practices set their fees within a range of 200 to 400 percent of the Medicare allowed. This type of consistent approach to establishing a medical practice's fee schedule enhances your ability to analyze payer reimbursement levels, to update the fee schedule and to study budgetary impacts of reductions in reimbursement levels.

Some medical practices have decided that it is no longer worth the trouble to keep their fee schedule current. They believe their payer contracts dictate what they are paid regardless of what they charge. But almost every practice has some percentage of commercial payers that pay a percent of the charge. Even if these payers make up only 2 percent of your patient volume, your revenue performance will be healthier if you keep your fees at competitive market levels.

■ **Systematically Review and Update Your Fee Schedule**
Review your practice's fee schedule at least annually to ensure it is appropriate based on reimbursement levels, your local market and other factors. A sure means of identifying fees that are too low is to watch for EOBs in which the payers reimburse at 100 percent of the practice's charge. This should alert you that you need to update your fees.

Here is a tool to use to examine your fee schedule for update opportunity.

Tool 7: Fee Schedule Review (see page 50)
This tool is a sample of a practice that is conducting an annual review of its fee schedule. The top procedure codes – representing the majority of the practice's business – are displayed with the current fee, relevant pricing from top payers and a proposed new fee schedule for the coming year.

FEE SCHEDULE REVIEW

Services sorted by charges	CPT®*	Charges	Freq'cy	Fee	Allowed rates Payers	Proposed new fees for practice
Office/outpatient visit	99213	$591,708	8,160	$73	To be filled in for each CPT®* code for payers that make up 80% of volume	Fees will remain the same or will change based on relationship to payer-allowed amounts, RVUs or some percentage of Medicare fee schedule.
Office/outpatient visit	99214	$536,548	4,862	$110		
Subsequent hospital care	99232	$400,334	3,393	$118		
Tissue exam by pathologist	88305	$377,275	2,417	$156		
Subsequent hospital care	99231	$372,198	4,235	$88		
Emergency department visit	99285	$321,953	981	$328		
Critical care, first hour	99291	$298,026	766	$389		
Subsequent hospital care	99233	$283,936	1,680	$169		
Office consultation	99244	$238,418	980	$243		
Office/outpatient visit	99212	$220,750	4,283	$52		
MRI brain w/o and w/dye	70553	$190,699	385	$495		
Emergency department visit	99284	$187,239	789	$237		
CT abdomen w/dye	74160	$158,265	600	$264		

*Note: The data in the above table were created for example purposes only.
Current Procedural Terminology ©2003 American Medical Association (AMA). All rights reserved. CPT® is a trademark of the AMA.

▌ Capture All Charges

Office and outpatient charges: For office and outpatient activity, construct an encounter form in a way that assists the physician in capturing the appropriate procedure and diagnosis codes. Submit charges at the end of each patient visit. Where appropriate, clinical support staff should assist in ensuring all charges are captured. Your practice should schedule all encounters, to include nurse visits, walk-ins and activity at satellite clinics, in your practice management system to ensure you capture all outpatient services. Conduct daily reconciliation of any missing encounter forms. You can achieve this by using an automated reconciliation report in your practice management system, by manually comparing encounter forms to an appointment schedule and/or sign-in sheet or by using pre-numbered encounter forms. The turnaround time for this correction should be within 24 hours.

Inpatient charges: For inpatient activity, a number of medical practices have started using mobile devices such as personal digital assistants (PDAs) to assist physicians in charge capture. You can purchase charge capture software to facilitate the process, and many devices let you wirelessly download the charges directly into the practice management system. If the software is interfaced with your practice management system, this download posts the charges electronically, thereby minimizing errors and reducing lag time from date-of-service to date-of-charge entry. Other practices have developed a spreadsheet that records the patients who are on the inpatient service and prompts the physician to submit charges for his/her hospital patients. Finally, others rest the responsibility on nurses, nonphysician providers or consult secretaries deployed to the hospital with the physicians to ensure that physicians document all services performed.

All other charges: Physicians practice in multiple locations – ambulatory surgery centers, nursing homes, patients' homes and so forth. Whether your practice develops a similar manual form or deploys mobile devices with appropriate software, the key is to have a process that allows physicians to record charges without undue effort, ensures capture for all services and provides for accurate and timely submission of charges to the billing office. Some practices have also scheduled these types of services into their practice management system so that a missing reconciliation report is created to ensure these charges are captured for billing.

■ **Capture Charges for Non-operating Hours Activity**
For a consult or admission conducted in the middle of the night, many practices have instituted a telephone message line that allows physicians to simply call the line and note brief patient information. When the staff member arrives in the morning, the calls are transcribed and the appropriate research is conducted. Other practices delegate this responsibility to an existing staff member, or they have an employee travel to the hospital to review the charts of patients seen by the practice's physicians. Or, as noted above, the physician records the charges on his/her PDA.

■ **Verify Charges with Source Documents**
Practices that provide services at the hospital should request electronic access to the hospital's registration and clinical systems. Access to demographic information as well as clinical information, such as operative reports and discharge summaries, enables the practice to verify data and capture missing data as appropriate.

Verify charge capture with other source documents such as hospital reports, admission-discharge-transfer reports, operative reports, clinical databases, transcription/dictation logs and/or other physician logs. When one cardiothoracic surgery practice instituted this verification, it found that 20 percent of its charges had been missed. A cardiology practice reported that 15 percent of its cardiac catheterizations were not billed. These examples reflect significant lost revenue opportunities that you can easily avoid using a verification process.

Enter All Charges

It seems unnecessary to state that your practice should enter charges for all services provided into your practice management system. But it is necessary, based on what we have observed in practices across the United States. The reasons practices don't enter encounter forms as they are received include:

- The encounter form is incomplete;
- The physician providing the service is not credentialed with that payer; and
- The service was not documented appropriately.

For each of these situations, you need a procedure to follow. If you use a claim scrubber module, you can create claim edits which will hold your claim until the outstanding information is obtained. If the claim is unbillable, then you write off the charge with a write-off code specific to the reason (for example, no documentation or not a credentialed provider). These write-offs become data so that you can take action to improve your collections. We will discuss claim scrubbing software and adjustment codes more in later chapters, but for now the key is to follow procedures to ensure all of your charges are entered into your system.

Annually Review and Update Your Encounter Form

Procedure and diagnosis codes change annually. Update all of the documents and software that you use to capture charges on an annual basis; using invalid codes will result in denied claims.

Track When Physicians Submit Charges

Comparing the lag time between the date of service and the date the physician submits the charge lets you identify outlier behavior by physicians and/or by a particular practice location. Some practices date-stamp their documents as they are received from each physician and enter that date into their systems. They can then report actual lag time between the date of service, the date the physician submitted it and the date of entry of the charges, as well as any outstanding charges that are pending complete submission (and their dollar value). Late submission of charges not only contributes to problematic staffing workload, but to fluctuating revenue streams. Some practices find that their physicians are submitting the majority of their charges in the last few days of the month. This requires an extraordinary amount of work for the staff, and often generates staff overtime, which increases the practice's overhead. Define a cut-off date by which no more charges will be entered for that month, with all late charges entered the next month. This policy improves the quality of charge entry (because staff are not rushing to finish) without negatively impacting cash flow. It also lets your staff perform the important work of reviewing charges and claims and responding to claim edits to ensure the claims are correct the first time.

Ensure That Codes are Selected by Providers or Certified Coders
Regardless of who captures the charge and where it is performed, either the providers or a certified coder should select the appropriate procedure and diagnosis codes. The business risk is too great – for both the physician and the practice – to involve untrained staff in this process.

Locate Coders in Close Proximity to Providers
Many better performing medical practices have recognized the importance of facilitating communication between coders and providers. Thus, many medical practices are now locating the coding staff in close proximity to the physicians, either in the back office of the clinic or in hospital space where the physicians typically reside. For practices with multiple sites, the coder may travel throughout the week to each of the practice sites so that physicians can develop an effective relationship with the coder.

Audit Coding Accuracy: Initiate Peer Review
One of the most effective means of disseminating important information regarding coding practices is peer review. Physicians are able to discuss with their physician colleagues clinical findings and associated documentation and coding in a manner that is rarely equaled by nonclinical coding personnel. Quarterly prospective audits – audits performed prior to charges being submitted – should be performed for each physician involving a sampling of charts. Share the results with the physicians regularly. Consider contracting with an external reviewer with coding expertise every year or two to ensure that your practice is employing the latest industry knowledge.

Compare Your Coding Frequency with Data Sources
Compare your coding frequency with data available from CMS and other sources. Correct coding maximizes your reimbursement. The tool on the following page is a sample of a comparison of a practice's coding frequency to CMS-reported levels.

Tool 8: Comparison of Coding to CMS-reported Levels

One of the basic tools to determine whether there is an opportunity to improve coding education is to compare the practice's level of coding with external benchmarks. One of the most easily accessible benchmarks is coding data reported through CMS. An example of this type of comparison is reflected in this tool. While there may be legitimate reasons for a practice to have a different bell-shaped curve than CMS-reported levels (or other coding benchmarking tools), this simple analysis may indicate problems in the coding knowledge of physicians and nonphysician providers. Other coding benchmarks are available from medical specialty associations and the Medical Group Management Association.

TOOL
8 SAMPLE COMPARISON OF CODING TO CMS-REPORTED LEVELS

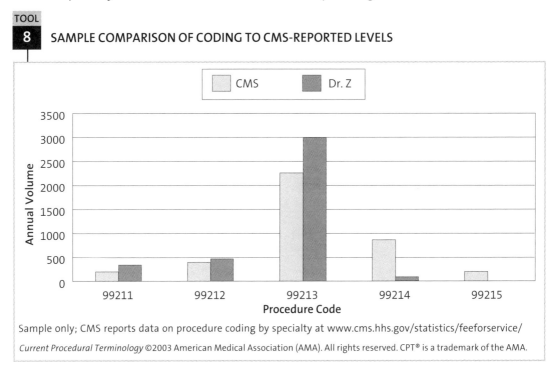

Sample only; CMS reports data on procedure coding by specialty at www.cms.hhs.gov/statistics/feeforservice/

Current Procedural Terminology ©2003 American Medical Association (AMA). All rights reserved. CPT® is a trademark of the AMA.

■ **Conduct Quality Assurance Review for New Front-office Staff**

Conduct a detailed review of the work by staff involved in scheduling and front-office activities daily for at least one month after (1) hiring a new staff member, (2) acquiring a practice or (3) opening a new practice. During this training period, the billing staff should review each encounter form and the data entered into the practice management system for accuracy of registration, collection of time-of-service payments and charge entry. While this may result in an increased workload over regular billing and collection functions for a one-month period, the opportunity to respond to and resolve data capture and charge entry problems early in the employee's tenure with the practice reduces billing rework and ensures that staff are educated to perform the work correctly and ensure a clean claim.

■ **Provide Appropriate Separation of Duties for Charge Entry and Changes to Charges**
Make sure that you have instituted appropriate internal controls for any changes to charges that are needed. Many medical practices, for example, do not permit staff who perform charge entry functions to change incorrect invoices. Instead, they institute a formal method by which charges are corrected: They designate the charge correction process to another staff member or manager. This separation of duties supports charge entry internal controls.

Performance Workload Ranges THE CHARGE CAPTURE AND CHARGE ENTRY PROCESS

The performance workload ranges for charge capture and charge entry that we typically expect are provided below. The ability to perform within these ranges may vary due to internal practice-specific factors (such as facility layout, telephone system and practice management system). The workload ranges are based on a staff member performing these functions approximately seven hours of productive time per day (allowing one hour for breaks, interruptions and other downtime). Note that the workload ranges reflect *quantitative* performance levels. *Qualitative* performance – accuracy, completeness, appropriateness and quality of these functions – should also be measured. When issues of quantity versus quality arise, we strongly recommend that quality be emphasized, even if the performance workload ranges for a particular function need to be relaxed from these levels.

Lag time from date of service to date of entry:	Office/outpatient: 24 hours Inpatient: 48 hours
Charge entry encounters (without registration):	375 – 525/day 55 – 75/hour

Note: Institute these workload ranges only if accuracy can be assured in this time frame. If not, you may increase the lag time to evaluate and remove errors. If you rely on a hospital registration system, it may be totally appropriate to suspend charges within your practice management system until the hospital patient accounts department has completed making its updates to insurance and authorizations.

© 2004 Walker, Larch, Woodcock: Day-to-Day Practice Operations. *Reprinted with permission.*

⚠ Practice Blunder THE CHARGE CAPTURE AND CHARGE ENTRY PROCESS

Practice Blunder has assigned a receptionist the task of going to the closet where the physicians' white coats are kept and rummaging in their pockets to collect the inpatient encounter forms. The receptionist must then carefully smooth out the tickets and sort them for keying. The receptionist hopes that she locates all of them, but has overheard physicians saying that their dry cleaners have complained about having to empty pockets.

Of course, not all the tickets even make it to the pockets. Many are likely left in the medical chart ... or the trash can. Without a mechanism in place to verify that all visits and consults are accounted for, Practice Blunder can only hope that most charges are in.

Case Exercises

1. Can you recommend a different charge capture process for Practice Blunder?
2. How would you justify a performance improvement initiative and any necessary resources?
3. How would you involve the physicians and billing staff in your initiative?

Policies and Procedures | THE CHARGE CAPTURE AND CHARGE ENTRY PROCESS

POLICY 8 Encounter Form Layout

Policy: It is the policy of the practice to use a well-organized encounter form (also called superbill, fee slip or charge ticket). The following standards will be applied to the development and use of the practice encounter form.

Procedures:

Encounter forms are very effective for saving time and assuring correct communication to the billing office. For best results, the encounter form should be customized to the practice, including current procedure and diagnosis codes that are frequently used by the practice.

Physicians are responsible for the selection of the procedure and diagnosis codes relevant to the billed service. To ensure appropriate reimbursement, it is imperative to design an encounter form with a layout that facilitates appropriate code selection with ease and accuracy.

The encounter form is an internal document to communicate the codes for the services rendered between the provider(s) and the billing office. It is not a substitute for the documentation of the encounter. Chart documentation to substantiate the level of service provided is crucial. Some examples of necessary documentation in the patient chart include: the level of history taken, a description of the extent of the examination, the complexity of the decision made, counseling, and the time spent with the patient.

Encounter forms can also be used as receipts for the patient, tracking documents for patient flow and/or orders, as well as communication regarding the recommended follow-up appointments for patients. If the form is to be used to capture patients' signatures as their agreement to assign their benefits to the practice, or a similar use, add a signature line for the patient. These alternative uses should be taken into account by the practice when the encounter form is developed, and consideration for ease of use and accuracy should be made.

To ensure billing of all services, sequentially number all forms to provide an audit trail for daily reconciliation (or utilize an automated encounter form tracking system provided by your practice management system).

Layout

The top of the encounter form should include information about the practice (name of practice, physicians, address and telephone number). Query the practice management system vendor for the layout that is compatible with your system. The specifications provided by the practice management system vendor for the patient's name, date of service, insurance company and other relevant information that is printed by the practice management system should be accommodated. It is preferable for this information to print together at the top or the bottom of the form, allowing the practice to utilize the remainder of the space to efficiently format coding choices.

The layout of the information regarding procedure and diagnosis codes on the encounter form should be set up in a logical order to facilitate ease of selection and immediate recognition of code selection by the provider. The subject areas should be in the same logical order as in the procedure coding books:

- Office visits;
- Consultations;
- Preventive medicine services;
- Surgical procedures;
- Pathology, laboratory;
- Injections, immunizations;
- Medical supplies; and
- Diagnosis codes.

After the code, brief descriptions (e.g., "level-1 office visit") should be provided. For procedure codes, after the description, the fee – or a blank space for the fee – should be included. (If the practice uses the encounter form as a receipt for the patient, it is recommended that fees not be preprinted on the form.) The procedure codes should be listed in the order of level where appropriate (e.g., 99211 followed by 99212, and so on). The most frequently used diagnosis codes (with appropriate level of specificity) should be included on the form. Leave room for writing in seldom-used CPT® codes[1] and modifiers as well as diagnosis codes. Use shading to highlight and/or delineate sections. Do not crowd the information. If there is too little space on the form for the practice to include all of the codes it needs to reference, print on the back of the form or maintain a listing of the codes in each exam room on a laminated piece of paper.

If the practice has multiple specialties, an encounter form should be developed and customized for each specialty (and, if appropriate, subspecialty). The layout should be consistent for all specialties to facilitate efficient processing in the billing office.

---

[1] *Current Procedural Terminology* ©2003 American Medical Association (AMA). All rights reserved. CPT® is a trademark of the AMA.

The practice should review the encounter form on an annual basis when new codes and changes to existing codes are announced. If the practice offers a new service, the encounter form should be immediately updated to reflect the codes associated with the service.

Offsite Encounter Forms

Use separate encounter forms, utilizing the same design formats, for services provided out of the office (e.g., hospital, ambulatory surgery center, nursing home, and all other locations of service). If the physician is responsible for collecting demographic and insurance information at the offsite facility, allow ample room for the information to be stamped, recorded, or attached to the encounter form. Since offsite forms may contain information for multiple dates of service, make sure that the format allows for recording multiple dates, as well as discharge and admission dates.

When the billing office receives an offsite encounter form, the patient's demographic and insurance information should be promptly reviewed. If no information can be located in the practice's registration system (e.g., the patient has never been seen in the office or by the practice before), seek assistance from the registration department of the facility at which the patient was seen. Registration information should be confirmed within 24 hours of receipt by the billing office.

For offsite encounter forms, record the proper procedure and diagnosis codes (based on the physician's level of service and diagnosis). Batch the encounter forms and route to charge entry personnel for keying. These charges will be posted within 48 hours of receipt.

These procedures assure correct and complete charge capture and provide a convenient record-keeping method with accurate communication to the billing office.

POLICY **9** Coding

Policy: The provider will completely and accurately assign procedure and diagnosis codes for every encounter at the time of service. The provider will base the codes on supporting documentation that is recorded in the patient's chart.

Procedures:

1. The provider will complete the encounter form at the time the service is rendered. This includes all services: office, inpatient visits, consultations, procedures, surgeries, and all other services.

2. Incorrect or incomplete charge documents will be returned to the provider for correction on the same date of service (or day following) so that timely charge entry can be performed.

3. The provider will indicate on the encounter form the procedure codes that reflect all services provided to the patient and the corresponding diagnosis(es). The codes will be supported by documentation in the patient's record. If multiple procedure codes are indicated, the provider will match the procedure codes to the appropriate diagnosis code(s) using a numerical method or lines.

4. According to the regulations that govern procedure codes for professional services, diagnosis "rule outs" will not be permitted. A diagnosis must be made and coded based on information available and symptoms presented. If an encounter form is received in the billing office containing a rule out, it will be resubmitted to the provider for correct coding.

5. The accuracy of charge coding and medical record documentation will be regularly reviewed. Providers with a coding error rate of greater than five percent will be subject to training at the discretion of the medical director.

6. The timeliness of charge coding will be tracked and regularly reviewed. Providers with a coding lag time of more than 24 hours for outpatient services and 48 hours for inpatient services will be subject to intervention and discipline at the discretion of the medical director.

POLICY **10** Charge Entry

Policy: Charges for outpatient services will be accurately posted in the billing system at the point of service and balanced at the end of the day that services are rendered.

Procedures:

1. Staff will post charges to unique batch-control groups at the time and point of service. Account representatives in each practice location will be assigned individual control groups. They will be responsible for posting the financial transactions.

2. Providers will document charges and corresponding procedure and diagnosis codes on preprinted encounter forms. These encounter forms will be created for each unique patient visit.

3. All charges will be posted to a batch control group assigned to each account representative.

4. Staff will post accurate charges to the patient account and print a receipt for the patient.

5. The account representative to whom the batch is assigned will balance each batch control group at the end of each day.

6. Staff will generate an audit report and use cash totals to balance the batch control group.

7. Staff will resolve all batches with conflicting balances immediately.

8. Staff will return encounter forms with incomplete charge data to the originating provider for completion to assure expedient billing and collection. This process must occur on the same day as the service. The practice's charge-entry suspense system will monitor return of the incomplete encounter forms sent to the providers.

POLICY **11** Data Entry

Policy: All demographic, clinical and financial data entry will occur in a timely and accurate manner.

Procedures:

1. Staff will enter data according to the following:

   - Registration and patient demographic data will be entered at the time the patient schedules the appointment;

   - Clinical data and all medical chart documentation will be recorded on the date of service; and

   - Billing and all charges, adjustments and payments will be entered into the computer within 24 hours of the date of service for outpatient activity and 48 hours for offsite services.

2. Staff must achieve a 98 percent accuracy rate for data entry. Staff not achieving this goal will be assigned to complete a day of training. If a staff member is not able to achieve accuracy during this additional training, the employee will be considered for transfer to another work area.

POLICY 12 Charge and Appointment Reconciliation

Policy: Charges for patient visits will be collected and entered throughout the day and organized by appointment time. Charges should be reconciled with the appointment schedule and sign-in sheet to ensure that all services are billed. A missing charge report will be generated to confirm that all encounter forms are included for that date of service.

Procedures:

1. Staff will generate an encounter form for all scheduled appointments. If a patient cancels or does not present for his/her visit, staff will mark this fact on the encounter form and record the information regarding the cancellation or no-show in the practice management system. If a patient walks in without a scheduled appointment, staff will generate the appointment and an encounter form at that time.

2. At the end of the day, the billing office will generate a missing charge report that will confirm all patients and charges for the day are included.

3. Staff will generate an appointment reconciliation report to compare the scheduled patients who kept their appointments to those patients with charges on their accounts.

4. All encounter forms will be sequentially numbered to provide an additional mechanism for monitoring missing forms.

5. In the event that a missing encounter form cannot be found, a supervisor must be notified. The supervisor will conduct a review of the search process, and will notify the physician immediately if the form cannot be located.

CHAPTER 5

POTHOLE 4:

The Claims Process

As we write this book, many individuals are actively working to standardize the use of the CMS 1500 claim form. The intent of the Health Insurance Portability and Accountability Act (HIPAA) Transactions and Code Sets regulation is to reduce variation in how we communicate information. Currently there are hundreds of claim formats being used across the United States in response to payer claim requirements. Standardization would greatly simplify the claims and payment process. (See Chapter 14 for more information on HIPAA.) In the meantime, we have Pothole 4, the Claims Process, to navigate.

In this chapter, we cover:

- Claims clearinghouses
- Claims review and scrubbing
- Electronic claims submission
- Suspended claims
- Secondary claims

The claims process starts with ensuring that the right information is recorded in each field consistent with the requirements for HIPAA and for each payer. The claim is then submitted, either manually or electronically, to the payer. The claim may take an indirect route to the payer by first being sent through a clearinghouse. At multiple steps along the way, quality review and edits are worked to ensure that, to the extent possible, a clean claim is submitted and the claim has successfully negotiated each step along its journey to the payer.

A claim is a request for payment form that insurance payers have agreed to accept and adjudicate for services rendered by providers. For years, medical practices recorded charges manually on this standard form. Today, practices post the charges to the patient's account in the practice management system, and the system generates a claim form that is specific to that patient's payer(s). The claims can be printed and mailed or transmitted electronically to the payer. The electronic transmission can be directed to a payer or through a clearinghouse. Whether transmitted on paper or electronically, practices can submit claims daily, weekly or as often as the practice chooses. Most practices batch their claims, combining the most recent date of service with rebills and secondary claims (further defined below). They release the batches every day or several times a week.

Rebills are claims that are being resubmitted because there was an error on the first submission. With a rebill, the practice requests a reconsideration of the original claim, or it has discovered that the original claim was never received and thus needs to be resubmitted. Rebills are different from appeals (discussed in Chapter 8) because a rebill involves resubmitting a claim accompanied by no additional explanation or supporting documentation.

Secondary claims are claims that are submitted to secondary payers. This occurs when the patient has another insurance carrier in addition to a primary insurance carrier, and the practice has agreed to submit a claim to the patient's secondary insurance company after it has received a portion of the payment from the primary insurance company. The primary payer, for example, Medicare, will either indicate on the explanation of benefits (EOB) that the claim should be printed and submitted to the secondary payer, or the primary payer will automatically "cross over" the claim. (An EOB is the payer form that accompanies the payment. On this form, important information is recorded regarding payments, denials, adjustments and reasons for particular actions taken by the payer. We discuss EOBs further in Chapter 6). If your practice is required to submit the secondary claim, you must attach the primary EOB to it. This is most frequently performed immediately after the receipt of the EOB from the primary payer because this primary EOB is readily available for duplication and attachment to the secondary claim. You print the secondary claim, attach the primary EOB and submit the documents to the secondary payer together.

If the primary payer automatically crosses over the claim to the secondary payer, in what is termed an "automatic crossover," the practice does not need to generate a secondary claim because the primary payer has already sent it. The relationship between the primary and secondary payer is referred to as the coordination of benefits (COB). It can be complex and may require communication with both payers to determine which is considered the primary payer and which is considered the secondary payer.

Whether you submit the claims manually or electronically or whether the claims are initial submissions, rebills or secondary claims, the billing staff often review the information on the claim or even hold or suspend the claim if there is a concern about the accuracy of the practice's information that is being submitted.

The billing staff may deploy technology to assist in evaluating whether claims comply with payer rules. A clearinghouse will also edit claims and report on any claims that have inaccurate or missing information. Your practice must correct and resubmit these claims.

To ensure efficient and effective claims processes, we present proven strategies to enhance your revenue cycle.

Advanced Practices | THE CLAIMS PROCESS

▌ **Make Wise Use of Your Clearinghouse**
Many medical practices submit some if not all of their claims through a clearinghouse. A clearinghouse serves as a data broker between the medical practice and the payer. Typically, the practice submits claims electronically to the clearinghouse and the clearinghouse is responsible for routing the claims to the payer. It is critical that you receive acknowledgement from the clearinghouse and the payer that your claims were received. Most clearinghouses have filters that evaluate the claims for missing information. The clearinghouse lists any rejected claims on an error report and sends the report to the practice. From either your payer or your clearinghouse you should receive acknowledgement that:

- Claims sent from your practice management system were received by the clearinghouse;

- Claims sent from clearinghouse were received by the payer; and

- Claims received by the payer were accepted into the payer's adjudication system.

At each of these stages, you should receive a number and list of claims not received and the reason. In your contracts with your clearinghouse and payers you should also require these acknowledgement reports. Figure 5.1 provides an example of these necessary acknowledgement reports.

FIGURE 5.1	The Electronic Claim Journey

	Number of claims	Date	
Claims to clearinghouse	100	15-June	
Clearinghouse acknowledges receipt	100	16-June	
Clearinghouse sends claims to payer	100	16-June	
Payer acknowledges receipt	98	18-June	2 claims hit error report – insurance number doesn't match payer format
Payer acknowledges claims hit adjudication system	92	20-June	6 claims rejected – cannot identify patient

Practice Tips: The electronic claim journey outlined above is sometimes not known by the practice. To track this claim batch, this practice would need to receive three acknowledgement reports and two error/rejected claims lists. Not all clearinghouses and payers provide timely acknowledgement reports. Few provide error/rejected reports with much detail other than number of claims received.

In this scenario, you know that eight claims will never be paid unless you take action to correct the claims and resubmit them. This is one of the reasons payers state, "We don't have a record of your claim" – and they don't in this case.

© 2004 Walker, Larch, Woodcock. Reprinted with permission.

Although the clearinghouse filtering process allows practices to correct claims before submitting them to payers, the filters are typically inadequate and mistakes are inevitable. Recent technological advances have enhanced the ability of medical practices to submit clean claims. Typically the electronic clearinghouse – and, increasingly, applications for the practice management software used by the practice – include "scrubbing" software to identify problems with claims *before* they are transmitted to the payer for adjudication. Scrubbing software helps you increase the number of clean claims you submit and thus increases the percent of claims paid correctly the first time.

In addition to using a clearinghouse, some practices relay claims directly to payers. This saves money, but it is limited to those payers that have the technology to accept a direct transmission.

▉ **Conduct a Quality Review of Claims**

Some better performing practices have found that printing and reviewing each claim (or encounter form, if reviewed prior to keying) before its submission is cost effective though resource intensive. The person assigned to review the claim is typically an insurance account representative. Reviewing the information allows the representative to recognize and fix problems that would likely result in denials. While the review of the information does take time, each denial that can be avoided represents 15 or more minutes of time saved in the future. In addition, the cash flow for the practice is improved significantly by avoiding the denial.

▉ **Hold Claims until Documentation Is Completed**

For those practices that have physician outliers in this area – physicians who do not dictate or write chart notes on a daily basis when they see the patient – the encounter forms or claims need to be held until the documentation is completed. This ensures that claims are submitted with adequate documentation that the services were performed.

▉ **Submit Claims on a Daily Basis**

Your practice should generate and submit claims on a daily basis. If you submit them once a week, it delays your payments by one to four days. Over time, this delay significantly impacts your cash flow.

▉ **Submit E-claims**

Payers are installing more sophisticated technology that lets you submit claims electronically. This saves the practice costs and typically reduces the turnaround time for payment of the claim. Figure 5.2 shows how much money a one-physician office can save by switching from paper claims to e-claims.

FIGURE 5.2	From Paper to E-Claims

One-physician office savings: 15,000 claims per year

- $1,440 claim forms (30 boxes @ $48)
- $270 envelopes (6 boxes @ $45)
- $600 on 600 long distance telephone calls to payers
- $1,110 on 3,000 stamps @ .37 (5 claims per envelope)
- $500 supplies (ink, pens, electricity, overhead)
- $11,440 salaries (20 hours per week @ $11/hour for salary and benefits)

Total: $15,360 or about $1 per claim savings

© 2004 Walker, Larch, Woodcock. Reprinted with permission.

But you must know the claim requirements and keep them current, or your claim will be denied. One practice that recently transitioned to e-claims experienced a reduced time to payment from three or four *weeks* to three or four *days*. CMS has instituted a deadline by which e-claims are expected for all Medicare and Medicaid services, and many other payers are developing systems to accept e-claims and issue electronic remittance advices. Here is a tool to help you avoid e-claim rejections.

Tool 9: E-Claims Checklist
Sending e-claims is cheaper than sending paper claims. These e-claims also get paid faster, but you need to avoid data errors. Some of the most frequent problems found in e-claims are the easiest to correct. This tool provides you with the top four reasons e-claims were rejected for one Medicare agency.

TOOL 9 E-CLAIMS CHECKLIST

- **Name mismatch:** This means the name was not entered exactly as shown on the insurance card. The name on the claim must match exactly with the payer's records.
- **Gender mismatch:** This indicates a discrepancy in the gender associated with the records of the payer and what was entered on the claim.
- **Payer insurance certificate number mismatch:** Verify that the number on the patient's insurance card exactly matches the number on the claim. Review format for all numbers/alphas (prefix/suffix).
- **Invalid assignment agreement:** Indicate your assignment choice — either assigned or nonassigned.

© 2004 Walker, Larch, Woodcock. Reprinted with permission.

■ **Keep Updated on Claim Formats**
If your practice's physicians participate in third-party contracts, you must stay current on changes from the payers. Payers communicate claim-specific changes in their newsletters and e-mails. Be sure to keep updated on these changes and communicate them to the appropriate staff involved in charge entry and claims generation.

■ **Review and Work Your Claim Edits**
Whatever method your practice chooses for reviewing the claim information prior to its submission, your practice should develop a protocol that outlines the steps and the extent to which changes or corrections of problems should be undertaken. For example, if there is a coding problem, how and to what extent does the physician who rendered the service need to be involved? Should the chart be pulled? Who

should pull the charts and how? Maintaining these protocols in writing ensures that you consider all aspects of the problem and outlines the process steps to be taken.

At the very least, you should establish required fields to ensure that all information requested by the payer is provided. Many payers will provide you with their claims specifications. There are different field requirements for paper claims and e-claims, so be sure to ask for both formats.

Work Error Reports Daily

Work your error reports and edit lists daily (including claims, remittance advice and acknowledgement reports). But don't stop there! Track the cause of the most frequent errors. Work with staff to make changes to process performance to prevent future occurrences.

Monitor Claim Filing Deadlines

Claim filing deadlines vary by payer. Currently, most payers have 45- to 90-day filing deadlines. Medicare requires submission no later than the end of the calendar year following the year in which the service was provided. (*Note:* the claim filing limit for services provided in the last three months of the year is the same as if services were provided in the subsequent year.) For example, for services rendered in March 2004, the Medicare claim must reach the payer by December 31, 2005. Most Medicaid plans follow Medicare guidelines. Make sure you know the initial claim submission filing deadline and the appeals filing deadline for all of your plans. Some states have passed managed care legislation that requires these payers to extend their claim filing time lines to six months. Your practice's revenue cycle performance will be stronger if you stay current on state legislation that affects billing and claims submission.

Know Your State's Regulations about a Clean Claim

Many states now have laws or regulations in place that help medical practices be more successful in getting paid what they are due. One area that is still evolving is the definition of a clean claim. In some state statutes, the definition of a clean claim is so vague, it provides little help to a practice. The figure on the next page outlines an example of a state's clean claim law. Contact your state MGMA or state medical society for information on your state's laws and regulations.

FIGURE 5.3	Sample Definition of Clean Claim

- **Centers for Medicare & Medicaid Services (CMS) standards for completion of a Form 1500 will be, in effect, law.**
  - Payers must accept a properly completed CMS Form 1500 "and instructions provided by CMS for use of the CMS 1500 as the sole instrument for filing claims."
  - A fully completed Form 1500 that contains all of the essential information is a clean claim, and a payer cannot demand additional information to justify payment, except as provided in the rules regarding attachments.

- **The regulations limit payers to 12 circumstances in which they can require attachments to accompany the CMS 1500 in the first instance.**
  - For example, carriers no longer will be able to routinely demand submission of office records with a claim. Now payers will be allowed to demand office records only if the claim included modifier 21 or 22, or the payer's audit of the practitioner "demonstrated a pattern of improper billing."
  - Importantly, physicians are free to supply more than the essential data elements or allowed attachments if they wish, but carriers cannot require more than the specified elements or attachments.

- **Carriers cannot use their own unique codes, or "local codes," meaning that the entire current procedural terminology (CPT®) code regime* is required.**
  - Carriers cannot require physicians "to use any code or modifier...that is different from, or in addition to, what is required under the applicable standard code set for the professional service provided," except in connection with a global contract (contract involving one payment for services of multiple practitioners).
  - With regard to physician claims, the term "applicable standard code set" is defined to mean the current version of the CPT®, "including its codes and modifiers, and codes for anesthesia services."

- **Mandatory use of the full CPT® regime and CMS standards for completion of the Form 1500 means that payers cannot ignore parts of the CPT® regime, i.e. they no longer can ignore modifiers.**
  - Importantly, the rules state that a payer may not challenge the sufficiency of a claim based on a policy or protocol "that is inconsistent with the applicable standard code set." Thus, the CPT® manual (*CPT® Current Procedural Terminology*, published by the American Medical Association) should become a standard book for claims processing.

▌ Investigate Scrubbing Software

Look into scrubbing software for your practice management system. Scrubbing software allows you to apply additional edits to the claims, giving you the chance to identify and correct the error *before* the claim is submitted. Your practice's denial data is an excellent source of edits that need to be added to the scrubbing software. If your current practice management system does not have such an application, consider maximizing the required fields on the claim forms to ensure that the claim is complete before it is transmitted. Stand-alone software that requires double key entry (once into the software for scrubbing and once into the practice management system for charge submission) is also available. Although integration with your existing system is preferable, catching the errors may be well worth the extra keying.

Finally, as noted above, some practices have recognized the value of claim scrubbing but cannot find an appropriate technological solution. Therefore, they assign staff the responsibility of manually reviewing all claims (for example, Medicare claims are reviewed by the Medicare follow-up staff). This will ensure that problems with the claims are identified and corrected before the claim goes out.

Tool 10: Clean Claims Checklist (see page 74)
This tool is a checklist to ensure your claims are clean. Completing a clean claims checklist, building edits into your practice management system and making maximum use of required fields help you submit a clean claim, requiring less rework and improving timeliness of reimbursement to your practice.

▌ **Institute an Edit Function for Paper Claims**
Consider a manual edit function for paper claims to ensure they are accurate and complete before they are mailed. In the past, many practices focused on the time it took to get claims out. But now, practices need to focus on the completeness and accuracy of the claim. As we noted earlier, it takes less time and money to correct the error before the claim is released.

Another benefit to this review of paper claims is to reduce the number of claims that go out on paper. Review your paper claims, asking, "Why does this claim have to go on paper?" Then determine how you can submit it electronically. Some practices are not aware that they can forward attachments, documentation and authorizations via fax or e-mail without sending a paper claim. Ask each of your top payers about which claims need to go on paper. Some practices are following payer claim processes that are outdated or they are duplicating automatic crossovers.

As Medicare implements an e-claims only strategy, other payers will follow, so you want to be sure you have maximized your e-claims capability.

CLEAN CLAIMS CHECKLIST

The following are common reasons that claims are not clean:

☐ **Assignment:** "Accept assignment" box checked inappropriately.

☐ **Authorization:** Claim form did not list the mandatory authorization number, or referral form is missing.

☐ **Procedure:** Invalid procedure code.

☐ **Contract number:** Subscriber's contract number missing or invalid.

☐ **Dates:** Missing or incorrect dates, such as admission and discharge dates, duplicate dates of service for same procedure code, dates of first symptom, etc.

☐ **Diagnosis:** Diagnosis code missing or invalid.

☐ **Group number:** Missing group number on claim form.

☐ **ID number:** Physician's provider ID missing on claim form.

☐ **Incorrect balance:** Incorrect balance printing on claim.

☐ **Insurance information:** Subscriber's name, gender, social security number, group and/or plan number missing or invalid. Medicare ID cannot have a space or hyphen between the numeric and alpha character. Names must appear exactly as they appear on the patient's card.

☐ **Modifiers:** Missing modifier on procedure that mandates usage of one.

☐ **Other:** Units (quantity) are incorrect and are manually changed or deleted.

☐ **Patient information:** Patient's gender missing or invalid, patient's address invalid, birth date missing, etc.

☐ **Place:** Place of service incorrect:
1. Inpatient
2. Outpatient
3. Physician's office

☐ **Provider:** Provider (physician) information missing or incorrect (for example, provider ID, license number, etc.).

☐ **Referral:** Referring physician's name and/or ID missing on claim form.

☐ **Type service:** Type of service listed incorrectly on claim form.

© 2004 Walker, Larch, Woodcock. Reprinted with permission.

▌ Review Your Clearinghouse Costs

Some medical practices have realized that the cost of using a clearinghouse is greater than the savings realized. Consequently, they are pursuing a set fee for clearinghouse activity (rather than a cost-per-claim basis) or are talking with payers about accepting direct claims transmissions. With more sophisticated scrubbing software available to medical practices, many perceive that the benefits associated with clearinghouse functions have lessened. In addition to considering a change in your clearinghouse fees, consider adding a penalty clause in case the clearinghouse does not perform its functions within certain agreed-upon parameters. If all the claims are going through the clearinghouse, all of the practice's revenue could be disrupted. Obviously we'd like the clearinghouse to share the risk and be prepared to provide the practice with compensation if cash flow is disrupted more than a certain number of days.

Work Suspended Claims

Many practice management systems are able to hold or suspend a claim to obtain additional information or verify the accuracy of information. Your practice should regularly track, resolve and release accounts put into this category. Establish thresholds to identify the number of claims in suspense and/or the dollar value of the claims in suspense. Your practice manager should monitor accounts in this category against those thresholds. When billing staff members leave the practice, be sure to check any accounts that may have been suspended and assigned to the departed staff member. Re-assign these so they are worked in a timely fashion.

Be Efficient in Processing Secondary Claims

Process as many secondary insurance claims as possible as automatic crossovers to avoid the need for manual intervention. If the payers do not permit crossovers, or if the secondary volume is otherwise high, scan all of your EOBs into a database that is accessible through your practice management software or by toggling to it from the employees' desktops. Easy access at employee workstations to print EOBs or automatically attach them to an electronic claim allows secondary claims to be processed more efficiently. You can achieve this process through a document management system.

Some payers are beginning to allow electronic submission of secondary claims. In order to provide the secondary payer with required information, you often need to modify your practice management system's claim specifications so that additional information can be provided on that claim form. (This will eliminate the need to send a copy of the primary EOB.)

Performance Workload Ranges — THE CLAIMS PROCESS

The performance workload ranges for the claims process that we typically expect are provided below. The ability to perform within these ranges may vary due to internal practice-specific factors (such as facility layout, telephone system and practice management system). The workload ranges are based on a staff member performing these functions approximately seven hours of productive time per day (allowing one hour for breaks, interruptions and other downtime). Note that the workload ranges reflect *quantitative* performance levels. *Qualitative* performance — accuracy, completeness, appropriateness and quality of these functions — should also be measured. When issues of quantity versus quality arise, we strongly recommend that quality be emphasized, even if the performance workload ranges for a particular function need to be relaxed from these levels.

Percentage of claims billed electronically:	> 75 percent (100 percent for payers who are able to accept e-claims)
Lag time from date claim posted to date claim submitted:	Same day or 24 hours
Number of claims pending on edit/ suspense report:	< 2 percent of claims

© 2004 Walker, Larch, Woodcock: Day-to-Day Practice Operations. *Reprinted with permission.*

⚠ Practice Blunder — THE CLAIMS PROCESS

Practice Blunder generates great expense when it bills claims to a patient's secondary payer. A staff member posts the primary claim payment, then simply files away the EOB. In order to bill the patient's secondary claim – just days later – another employee has to go to the file room, find and retrieve the EOB, copy the EOB, then generate the paper claim for secondary billing. This is a cumbersome process that significantly delays the billing of secondary claims.

In addition, billing staff at Practice Blunder have been instructed to put a hold on an account while they research a particular item. The hold essentially means that a claim will not be released. Unfortunately, staff do not review the suspended claims regularly, and the claims are maintained on hold status in perpetuity, causing the practice to lose money because of missed filing deadlines.

Case Exercises
1. Can you recommend a better process for Practice Blunder to submit its secondary claims?
2. Should the staff at Practice Blunder be suspending claims? Can you recommend a better process?
3. How should Practice Blunder determine which insurance is primary and which is secondary for a patient?

Policies and Procedures | THE CLAIMS PROCESS

POLICY 13 Billing Third-Party Payers

Policy: Third-party payers will be billed in a timely manner to receive timely payment for claims sent.

Procedures:

1. Staff will bill third-party payers via electronic claims service when available.

2. Third-party claims that cannot be billed electronically due to payer's inability to accept e-claims or other requirements, such as the need for attachments or for other reasons, will be billed using the standard CMS 1500 claim form.

3. Staff will generate third-party claims and forward them to payers on a daily basis to expedite reimbursement.

Every manual and automated effort will be made to eliminate errors in registration, charge coding and charge entry to ensure a clean claim and timely reimbursement.

CHAPTER 6

The Payment Posting Process

The payment posting process is one of the most frequently underrated and overlooked processes in the revenue cycle. Posting a payment is highly complex, yet rarely do we see medical practices devoting appropriate resources to this function. It is not sufficient to simply post the money received in an accurate and timely fashion. Payment posters play a key role in the revenue cycle by determining contractual and non-contractual adjustments and recognizing underpayments by a payer.

In this chapter, we cover:

- Payment posting
- Prompt payment laws
- Lockbox services
- Classification of adjustments
- Credit balances
- Insurance take-backs
- Capitation
- Payment variance

Once a practice receives payment for services, it posts the payment to the patient's account by transferring the payment reported on the explanation of benefits (EOB) form to the appropriate line item on the account. In addition to providing a check, the payer explains on its EOB form the details of the payment – and what may be further due from the patient or another responsible party, such as a secondary payer. A skilled and experienced staff member needs to read and interpret the EOB. Each payer's EOB format is different, and each one uses varying EOB remark codes. The Health Insurance Portability and Accountability Act (HIPAA) Transactions and Code Sets regulation is intended to standardize EOB content. But at the writing of this book, it appears the implementation of the HIPAA simplification features is going to take some time – possibly several years. Until those improvements are realized and/or the process is totally automated, you should employ a skilled payment poster. Payment posters need advanced education in insurance and account follow-up and should have direct access to the payers so they can ask questions about the EOB. Payment posting must be highly accurate, so your poster must be diligent. If your poster makes mistakes in posting payments, your practice may fail to appeal underpayments and to bill balances due from patients.

Lockbox Services

Many practices use lockbox services to process their payments. A lockbox service, often provided by a financial institution, receives the payments, opens the mail, copies the check and backup information, and deposits the check to the bank. Medical practices typically realize revenue associated with taking advantage of the float by accelerating the deposit. Lockbox services also provide enhanced internal controls because the practice will receive only copies of checks, not the actual checks. However, lockbox services cost money, and if there is a delay between the deposit of the funds and the posting of them, the timing can create extra work and frustrate patients. If patients sent in their payments in a timely manner, but the payments aren't posted prior to the next set of statements being released, this creates another bill – and very likely a call from an angry patient.

Contractual Adjustments

When the practice receives the payment, the EOB includes notification of the "allowance" or "allowable" per procedure code. The allowance is what the payer has agreed the service is worth. The check sometimes does not reflect that amount, because the payer often requires the patient to pay for a portion of the service in the form of a copayment or co-insurance. As we discussed in Chapter 2, a practice with a good accounts receivable process would have already determined what the patient's responsibility level is and collected it at the time of service. In addition to the allowable, the EOB also notes the amount of the contractual adjustment – which equals the charge minus the allowable. By signing an agreement with the payer, the practice has agreed to write off that difference as a contractual adjustment.

Non-contractual Adjustments

On occasion, the EOB contains no payment or only a partial payment. The EOB indicates that the payment was reduced or not paid because of a particular reason. These are called "non-contractual allowances" because they are outside of the contract that has been entered into by the medical practice and the payer. That is, your practice did not agree to accept that level of write-off. A common reason for a non-contractual allowance is that the filing deadline was missed. That means that your practice did not submit the claim for your services within the payer's designated time frame for submission of claims. Therefore, the payer is denying payment for the service.

The payer rejects or denies some claims appropriately, and you cannot appeal these. You need to research and follow up others that you can appeal. We discuss denial management further in Chapter 8. The important element to note now is that you need to capture the rejections in your practice management system and monitor them so you can take action to improve your performance.

If your practice uses adjustment codes inconsistently or inappropriately, you will not be able to determine the effectiveness of the billing process. We have often found that practices write off non-contractual adjustments incorrectly either as a contractual adjustment (confusing the legitimate contractual adjustment that has been recognized via contract terms), or as bad debt, again confusing data interpretation. These inappropriate treatments of non-contractual adjustments could mislead the practice administrator into thinking that billing and collection performance has been optimized. The practice may not be pursuing opportunities to enhance its revenue potential.

Figure 6.1 on page 82 shows three scenarios: In the first, staff have posted the adjustment codes correctly; in the following two, they have posted the codes incorrectly. Notice how much less the practice collects when staff post the adjustment incorrectly and how the net collection rate responds. Improved payment posting accuracy results in $315 more in cash and an accurate (real) net collection rate!

FIGURE 6.1	Payment Posting Scenarios

Posting Adjustment Codes: 3 Scenarios

Patient receives medical service (charge = $900)
Patient pays copayment at visit ($10)
Claim to payer goes out ($900 charge)
Explanation of Benefits (EOB)/check received for $150, but contract payment dues is $380.

Scenario 1: Payment posted correctly.

	Cash received	Contractual adjustment	Other adjustment	A/R	Formula	NCR[1]
Charge = $900				$900	$\frac{0}{900}$	0%
Patient pays copayment = $10	$10			$890	$\frac{10}{900}$	1%
Claim goes out to payer EOB received ($150 paid)	$150			$740	$\frac{10+150}{900}$	18%
Allowed amount on EOB $475 (Note: Contractual adjustment = charge - allowed)		$425		$315	$\frac{160}{900-425}$	34%
Staff notices payment is low Low payment appeal filed EOB received (remaining $230 paid)	$230			$85	$\frac{160+230}{475}$	82%
Statement to patient to collect remaining balance ($85)						
Patient pays	$85			$0	$\frac{390+85}{475}$	100%
Result	$475	$425	$0	$0		100%

Scenario 2: Payment incorrectly posted!

	Cash received	Contractual adjustment	Other adjustment	A/R	Formula	NCR
Charge = $900				$900	$\frac{0}{900}$	0%
Patient pays copayment = $10	$10			$890	$\frac{10}{900}$	1%
Claim goes to payer						
EOB received ($150 paid)	$150	$740		$0	$\frac{10+150}{900-740}$	100%
Allowed amount on EOB $475						
Staff member contractual adjusts off entire remaining balance						
Result	$160	$740	$0	$0		100%

[1]Net Collection Rate (NCR) = $\dfrac{\text{Collections} - \text{Refunds}}{\text{Charges} - \text{Contractual Adjustments} + \text{Debits} - \text{Credits} - \text{Discounts}}$

FIGURE 6.1	Payment Posting Scenarios (continued)

Scenario 3: Again, payment is posted incorrectly.

	Cash received	Contractual adjustment	Other adjustment	A/R	Formula	NCR[1]
Charge = $900				$900	$\frac{0}{900}$	0%
Patient pays copayment = $10	$10			$890	$\frac{10}{900}$	1%
Claim goes to payer						
EOB received ($150 paid)	$150			$255	$\frac{10+150}{900-475}$	38%
Allowed amount on EOB $475 (Staff posts wrong contractual)		$475				
Statement to patient ($255)	$0			$255	$\frac{160}{425}$	38%
Patient calls – payer owes more and patient refuses to pay						
18 months later – w/o bad debt — no follow-up done	$0	$0	$255	$0	$\frac{160}{425}$	38%
Result	$160	$475	$255	$0		38%

$$\text{[1] NCR} = \frac{\text{Collections} - \text{Refunds}}{\text{Charges} - \text{Contractual Adjustments} + \text{Debits} - \text{Credits} - \text{Discounts}}$$

Figure 6.1 Payment Posting Scenarios – Summary

Scenario one: Posted correctly
Result: cash received = $475
Net collection rate: 100%

Scenario two: Posted incorrectly
Result: cash received = $160
Net collection rate: 100%

Scenario three: Posted incorrectly
Result: cash received = $160
Net collection rate: 38%

Payment Variance

Are you being paid what you are due? This question is obviously critical, but the answer is not at all obvious. Some payers do not publish their fee schedules, and a practice must often estimate if the payer is paying at appropriate levels. At times, the payer reimburses at variable levels on the same procedure code due to different employer-defined plans, making an accurate estimate particularly challenging and certainly frustrating. In addition, practices often do not provide payment posters with appropriate tools to estimate if the practice is being reimbursed at the expected levels. Many payment posters are essentially eyeballing the payment on the claim and making a quick decision about whether to flag the EOB for additional internal review. If there is a payment on even one line item some payment posters consider this good enough and write off the remaining balance to a contractual adjustment.

Below we have listed examples of payment errors with an explanation of why the error may have occurred:

A procedure code for a service is reduced	Payer's claims adjudicator down-coded for lack of documentation, or does not support medical necessity, or level of procedure code is not supported for that diagnosis.
Low or no reimbursement	Provider credentialing is pending and physician is paid at nonparticipating rate.
Reimbursement is at a much reduced rate	Possible data error – compare the procedure code submitted with the code paid and what you expect to be paid.

To ensure efficient and effective payment posting processes, we present proven strategies to enhance your revenue cycle.

Advanced Practices | THE PAYMENT POSTING PROCESS

■ **Assign Payment Posting to Account Follow-up Staff**
In the past, many medical practices instituted a focused payment posting unit within their billing office. Today, with the complexities of medical insurance, better performing practices are delegating payment posting to account follow-up staff and/or assigning a dedicated payment poster to a specific payer account follow-up team. Co-locating this function with accounts receivable follow-up lets staff research and resolve the account simultaneously with payment posting because account follow-up staff are skilled in payer reimbursement strategies. It also reduces the number of process hand-offs and the cycle time to resolve payment discrepancies. The staff post the payment/denial, perform necessary follow-up, process secondary billing to payer or patient and make appropriate adjustments. These payer teams are responsible for resolving the account once the EOB has been received until the account balance is $0.

■ **Provide Tools to Payment Posters**

Give payment posters tools so they can recognize low reimbursement levels and flag accounts for appeal. For example, make sure that the maximum number of payer fee schedules are loaded into your practice management system and produce exception reports on a daily basis to recognize payments that fall outside of defined ranges.

The following checklist and audit tools will help you make sure that payment posters have the tools and education needed for this important billing function.

Tool 11: Payment Posting Performance Checklist

This tool is a checklist for payment posting to ensure that your practice has appropriately delegated the payment posting function and educated staff in this function.

TOOL
11 PAYMENT POSTING CHECKLIST

Yes	No		
___	___	1.	Are payment posters familiar with A/R follow-up and/or are payment posters assigned to payer-specific account follow-up teams?
___	___	2.	Have staff been given tools and resources so they can identify low reimbursement?
___	___	3.	Are the maximum number of payer fee schedules loaded on the practice management system?
___	___	4.	Are exception reports by payer produced daily so they can be worked?
___	___	5.	Are payments posted within 24 hours of receipt?
___	___	6.	Is there a streamlined hand-off from payment posting to billing of secondary claims?
___	___	7.	Are EOBs appropriately flagged for appeal?
___	___	8.	Are there sufficient adjustment codes for non-contractual adjustments?
___	___	9.	Do payment posters understand the use of contractual adjustment, non-contractual adjustment and bad debt codes?
___	___	10.	Is there an appropriate separation of duties between individuals who receive the mail, open the mail, post the payment, deposit the payment and reconcile bank ledgers?
___	___	11.	Are $0 payments posted and worked the day of receipt or no later than 24 hours after receipt?
___	___	12.	Is the small balance write-off set at an appropriate level (for example, lower than typical copayment levels and/or cost of claim)?
___	___	13.	When credit balances are generated are they worked the same day or no later than 60 days from the date of discovery of the problem?

Tool 12: Payment Posting Audit Tool

Payment posting accuracy and interpretation are learned over time. Managers need to perform audits to evaluate how staff are interpreting EOBs to provide ongoing feedback to staff. This tool provides a sample audit form. We recommend that you evaluate 10 payments for each existing payment poster on a quarterly basis to determine if the staff member is performing at optimal levels. We recommend weekly audits to assess the performance of new staff. An alternative strategy is to have staff audit each other and discuss results as a group. The manager will need to participate to ensure accuracy of the audit.

TOOL
12 PAYMENT POSTING AUDIT TOOL

Payment Posting Quality Review   Type of payments_____

1. Select 10 payments posted to patient accounts.
2. Review the EOB and other back-up for proper research.
3. Access the account in the billing system and review for the following errors.
4. Discuss the results of the quality review with the employee.
5. Log results into performance management file.

	1	2	3	4	5	6	7	8	9	10
Invoice number										
Applied payment to correct account										
Applied the correct payment amount										
Applied in a timely manner										
Correct paycode used										
Correct rejection code used										
Contractual adjustments made correctly										
Correct action taken on under-reimbursed procedures										
Account in appropriate payer after posting										

Comments:

Action taken on accounts:

This sample indicates payment posting performance at the following level:

____ Unsatisfactory ____ Needs improvement ____ Satisfactory ____ Exceeds expectations
____ Significantly exceeds expectations

_____   _____   _____
Supervisor's Signature   Employer's Signature   Date

▌ Institute Electronic Payment Posting

As we already discussed, payment posting is a complicated function. Interpreting EOBs and accurately posting payments requires skill and experience. More and more payers are improving their information systems to offer electronic payment remittances and funds transfer. Practices proficient with e-claims move quickly to e-remittances as the next opportunity to improve efficiency. Many national payers have offered this option to practices already. Few practices have had the technical expertise or interest to move to this newer option, but most payers are now offering training on implementing their remittance systems.

Those practices that have converted to electronic posting are realizing real savings in staff time and reduced payment error rates. Payers send an electronic file that the practice enters into its practice management system, and they transfer funds directly into the financial institution identified by the practice through electronic funds transfer (EFT). Alternatively, practices can consider scanning technology to replace manual payment posting. After mapping EOB fields to payment posting screens/fields using optical character recognition (OCR) technology, the practice scans EOBs upon receipt. Both systems require a staff member to review any error reports that kick out. For more information on these technologies, see Chapter 11.

▌ Establish Appropriate and Effective Internal Controls

A practice needs internal controls to ensure that there is appropriate management oversight in handling the receipt of funds and payment posting. If the practice is using a lockbox and/or electronically posting its payments, many internal control risks are eliminated. Better performing medical practices that don't use lockboxes ensure that internal controls are in place by having separate employees perform separate tasks. A staff member who controls both charge entry and payment posting, for example, poses a greater risk for theft or fraud, as s/he would be able to alter accounts more easily. Typically, a separation of duties is required for the following functions:

- Opening mail;
- Preparing payment posting batch;
- Posting payment;
- Deposit; and
- Bank reconciliation.

For smaller practices, separate the duties between two people but consider alternating the duties between them and/or involving physicians or managers in oversight functions.

Staff who work outside of the billing office, such as the accounting or finance staff or the practice's manager, should reconcile daily cash deposits and payment posting. Similarly, an individual who is not directly involved in the performance of these functions should verify posting and depositing levels.

■ **Safeguard Checks and Credit/Debit Card Receipts**
Immediately endorse and deposit checks daily. This may require you to develop courier services for outlying practice areas. Maintain all cash, checks and credit and debit card receipts in a locked drawer or safe until deposit.

■ **Make Sure Payers Have Updated Information on Your Practice**
When you're submitting applications to insurance companies, make sure you provide accurate information for payers to submit payment to you. If and when you move your practice or change the name of your practice, submit the new information to each payer and monitor payments carefully for at least six months to ensure that the payers acted on your change request.

■ **Actively Manage Unidentified Payments**
When you deposit checks daily, you need a separate process to record unidentified payments. Post to a separate account the checks that are unapplied or require research, and make controlled transfers of this account once you have established proper identification. Undertake a bounded search process that defines the research steps the employee should make to attempt to identify the payment. This could involve gaining access to the hospital information system, searching appropriate potential databases and communicating with the payer or patient. If your staff has followed this defined search process and the payment remains unidentifiable, prepare a refund and return the money to the payer or patient in a timely fashion. Identify and refund all monies received within 60 days.

■ **Implement Non-contractual Adjustment Codes**
To report non-contractual adjustments, and to distinguish them from the contractual adjustments, implement non-contractual adjustment codes in your practice management system. Using these codes helps you collect data and create reports that outline the level of non-contractual adjustments by category so you can intervene to resolve the problem and/or prevent its recurrence. You should post the following types of non-contractual adjustments or $0 payments into your practice management system like other payment transactions:

■ Untimely filing;
■ Lack of authorization/referral;

■ Not a covered benefit (this is sometimes billable to patient; not always an adjustment);

■ Out-of-network or non-credentialed provider;

■ Noncovered service/diagnosis;

■ Medical necessity;

■ Not eligible on date of service; and

■ All other "controllable" losses.

Investigate Insurance Take-Backs

At times, the payer withholds from a current claim a specified amount that relates to a prior claim. That is, the payer reduces the amount paid for the date of service on the current claim by a level that it deemed to be an overpayment on a prior claim. This requires the payment poster to readily identify the "take-back" and post this to the system so that both dates of service are accurately reconciled with the EOB and the payment level. Investigate the source of take-backs to ensure that the payer is consistently applying them and that they are consistent with your current contract and state law. Some states and some payer contracts limit the length of time a payer can alter a prior payment due and perform a take-back, so be sure to monitor the timeliness in case you can appeal with the payer.

Create Separate Tracking of Capitation Funds

If your practice maintains a capitated contract with a payer, delineate that book of business. You should book the revenue, but set up your practice management system to report it separately. In addition, set up your system so you can track the utilization of your capitated business without carrying the accounts receivables ad infinitum. Instead, you should book the charges to track service utilization, and write off the accounts receivable (A/R) at minimum, each month, or maintain the A/R in a separate report.

Monitor Your State's Prompt Payment Laws

Most states have passed prompt payment laws. These laws outline the maximum time allowed for payment of a clean claim. Typically, when a payer misses this payment deadline, either penalties or interest accrues and is due to the medical practice. The current problem with these laws, however, relates to the definition of a clean claim, which can vary considerably from state to state and often requires subjective interpretation. Moreover, there is no federal law related to prompt payment.

ERISA plans are often excluded from state legislation and regulations. These plans, for example, do not have to meet prompt payment guidelines. ERISA, the Employee Retirement Income Security Act of 1974, is a federal law that sets minimum standards for most voluntarily established pension and health plans in private industry to provide protection for individuals in these plans. Payer contracts will indicate whether the plan is under ERISA.

ERISA requires plans to provide participants with important information about plan features and funding. In addition, it provides fiduciary responsibilities for those who manage and control plan assets, requires plans to establish a grievance and appeals process for participants to receive benefits from their plans and gives participants the right to sue for benefits and breaches of fiduciary duty.

A Web site that informs you of your prompt payment law for your state is listed in the Additional Billing and Collection Resources section provided at the end of this book. If your state allows for remuneration for delayed payments, be sure to pursue payments owed to you, including interest.

■ **Generate and Review Payment Exception Reports**
Generate a payment exception report by payer. If a particular payer is to reimburse 80 percent of usual and customary charges, produce an exception report with reimbursement levels that fall outside of these limits. When you're armed with this data, a meeting with the payer can produce excellent results.

Tool 13: Verifying Reimbursement Level by Payer (see next page)
To ensure that your practice is being paid what it is due, analyze reimbursement levels by payer. The tool we provide on the next page is an example of this analysis. It outlines the top 25 procedure codes and reimbursement levels by the top six payers of the practice. Because of software limitations, it is rarely possible to load all of the payer fee schedules into the practice management system, thus this tool provides a systematic method to review reimbursement levels to ensure consistency with contract terms. Your practice should develop this report for the top 25 procedure codes by frequency and the top 25 procedure codes by dollar level. For more information about reimbursement management, see Chapter 13.

TOOL
13 VERIFYING REIMBURSEMENT LEVEL BY PAYER

CPT®*	Description	Practice charge	Reimbursement by Payer					
			Payer 1	Payer 2	Payer 3	Payer 4	Payer 5	Payer 6
11200	Removal of skin tags	$175.00	$70.19	$66.68	$94.76	$77.21	$73.70	$112.31
45330	Diagnostic sigmoidoscopy	$300.00	$120.23	$114.22	$162.31	$132.25	$126.24	$192.36
71010	Chest X-ray	$70.00	$27.63	$26.25	$37.30	$30.39	$29.01	$44.21
73090	X-ray exam of forearm	$71.00	$28.38	$26.96	$38.31	$31.21	$29.80	$45.40
99202	Office/outpatient visit, new	$161.00	$64.59	$58.13	$87.20	$77.51	$61.36	$103.35
99203	Office/outpatient visit, new	$240.00	$95.96	$86.36	$129.54	$115.15	$91.16	$153.53
99204	Office/outpatient visit, new	$340.00	$135.53	$121.98	$182.97	$162.64	$128.76	$216.86
99205	Office/outpatient visit, new	$430.0	$172.13	$154.91	$232.37	$206.55	$163.52	$275.40
99211	Office/outpatient visit, est.	$53.00	$21.28	$19.15	$28.73	$25.54	$20.22	$34.05
99212	Office/outpatient visit, est.	$94.00	$37.71	$33.94	$50.91	$45.25	$35.83	$60.34
99213	Office/outpatient visit, est.	$132.00	$52.65	$47.38	$71.07	$63.17	$50.01	$84.23
99214	Office/outpatient visit, est.	$205.00	$82.14	$73.93	$110.89	$98.57	$78.04	$131.43
99215	Office/outpatient visit, est.	$298.00	$119.11	$107.20	$160.79	$142.93	$113.15	$190.57
99222	Initial hospital care	$275.00	$111.27	$77.89	$150.21	$133.52	$89.01	$178.02
99223	Initial hospital care	$385.00	$154.95	$108.47	$209.18	$185.94	$123.96	$247.92
99231	Subsequent hospital care	$83.00	$33.23	$23.26	$44.86	$39.88	$26.58	$53.17
99232	Subsequent hospital care	$137.00	$54.89	$38.42	$74.10	$65.86	$43.91	$87.82
99233	Subsequent hospital care	$195.00	$78.04	$54.62	$105.35	$93.64	$62.43	$124.86
99235	Observ/hosp. same date	$455.00	$181.46	$127.02	$244.97	$217.75	$145.17	$290.34
99239	Hospital discharge day	$238.00	$95.21	$66.65	$128.53	$114.25	$76.17	$152.34
99302	Nursing facility care	$254.00	$97.82	$68.48	$132.06	$117.39	$78.26	$156.52
99303	Nursing facility care	$300.00	$120.97	$84.68	$163.31	$145.17	$96.78	$193.56
99312	Nursing facility care, subseq.	$158.00	$63.10	$44.17	$85.19	$75.72	$50.48	$100.96
99313	Nursing facility care, subseq.	$215.00	$86.25	$60.37	$116.44	$103.50	$69.00	$138.00
99316	Nursing fac. discharge day	$230.00	$91.85	$64.30	$124.00	$110.22	$73.48	$146.96

*Note: The data reflected in the above table were created for example purposes only.
Current Procedural Terminology ©2003 American Medical Association (AMA). All rights reserved. CPT® is a trademark of the AMA.

■ **Resolve Credit Balances within 60 Days**
Your practice should regularly research and resolve outstanding credit balances generated by the payment posting process. Staff can work these daily by producing an ad hoc report after they post payments; however, medical practice staff typically work a credit balance report each week to correct payment posting errors as well as ensure appropriate refunds are sent to the patient and/or payer. Many payers, in addition to the Centers for Medicare and Medicaid (CMS), are requiring medical practices to repay overpayments within a specified time period, and many legal experts have outlined an "affirmative duty" on the part of medical practices to report overpayments within a timely fashion.

A number of states have unclaimed property laws, also known as "escheats laws," that dictate how you should treat refunds that you are not able to return to the patient or payer. For example, you may owe credit balances to a patient who has relocated with no forwarding address or to a payer that is out of business. Or you may be limited in your research on the credit balance because of a practice management system conversion. Your practice should develop a policy that outlines the steps to take to resolve credit balances when these types of circumstances occur.

Before you process a refund request for a service from several years ago, it is wise to know your state's escheats law. This law sets a boundary of time that an individual or business can ask for unclaimed property. Most states vary from three to seven years; if the request is from a service dated in 1995, for example, in most states, the claim on this has already expired and you need not refund it. In other states, if you are unable to return the money but it is not yours, it becomes the state's property and you are required to return it to the state instead. This is just another good reason why timely research of credit balances is important. Discuss this with your attorney: S/he can answer your questions regarding these old refunds.

Work all credit balances daily or weekly and completely research them and return overpayments within 60 days. You can generate a daily, weekly and monthly credit balance report from most practice management systems. The payment posters can produce a daily report of credit balances that are created via the payment posting process and determine whether the credit is accurate, for example, or flag it for work. Remember that your credit balances offset your total accounts receivable. Therefore, if your credits are high, you may be understating the dollar value of your accounts receivable.

Many medical practices continue to have problems with non-governmental payers regarding correspondence about refunds. In some cases, the medical practice identifies a refund due a non-governmental payer and the payer, unable to identify the refund in its system, denies it, returning the funds to the medical practice. In other cases, the non-government payer requests money that is due from the medical practice, but when the practice writes to the payer to say "Received your request – need more details," the payer does not respond. How the medical practice eventually resolves these issues depends on your practice's business risk tolerance, legal implications related to income reporting and other similar factors. No matter what process you choose, maintain all correspondence on file.

■ **Develop a Streamlined Refund Process**
Many practices have initiated overly encumbered refund processes that involve multiple individuals and multiple steps. Better performing practices involve refund staff who investigate and approve the refund request; the checks are written in the practice's accounting office. Approval levels escalate within the practice based on dollar thresholds of the refund amount.

■ **Develop a Streamlined Process for Billing Secondary Claims and EOBs That Need Follow-up**
Practices typically assign the actual billing of secondaries to one of three different staff: payment posters, account follow-up staff or claims staff. We have seen these roles performed well by each of these staff, and your workload delegation will depend on the staffing model you elect. For purposes of this discussion, we will assume that you have delegated the billing of secondaries to the account follow-up staff.

During the payment posting process, have posters flag claims that need to be submitted to a secondary carrier. Do not send a secondary claim if it has been automatically crossed over, because the carrier has already sent it, and this will create a denial for "duplicate submission of claims." For secondary claims that didn't cross over, clerical staff should be responsible for duplicating the original EOB or printing a stored image from your document management system. These staff should give copies of the primary EOBs for secondary claim billing to the account follow-up staff for timely processing.

For $0 payments — also known as denials — payment posters should flag the entire claim or a line item(s) that needs to be researched. As the poster is posting payments, s/he enters denials into the practice management system or marks them on a copy of the EOB. At the end of each payment posting batch, submit this information to the account follow-up representatives who are responsible for researching the accounts and working them from billing system reports or the marked-up EOB. Especially for practices that do not post payments by line item (charge level), copies of the EOBs with $0 payments embedded within the EOB (where some charges have not been paid) should be given to the account follow-up staff to actively pursue these claims to determine whether the denials are appropriate. See Chapter 8 for more information about managing your denials.

Performance Workload Ranges — THE PAYMENT POSTING PROCESS

The performance workload ranges for payment posting that we typically expect are provided below. The performance workload ranges for payment posting are highly variable depending on the work functions assigned to these staff. For example, if a payment poster is also processing secondary claims, the workload range would be less than that for a payment poster who simply flags the EOBs for someone else in the billing office to work. The ability to perform within these ranges may vary due to internal practice-specific factors (such as facility layout, telephone system and practice management system). The workload ranges are based on a staff member performing these functions approximately seven hours of productive time per day (allowing one hour for breaks, interruptions and other downtime). Note that the workload ranges reflect *quantitative* performance levels. *Qualitative* performance – accuracy, completeness, appropriateness and quality of these functions – should also be measured. When issues of quantity versus quality arise, we strongly recommend that quality be emphasized, even if the performance workload ranges for a particular function need to be relaxed from these levels.

Transactions posted manually (payments/adjustments):	525 – 875/day	75 – 125/hour
Lag time from payment receipt to posting:	Same day or within 24 hours	
Refunds researched and processed:	70 – 90/day	10 – 13/hour
Identification and return of unidentified or overpayment funds:		Within 60 days
Write-off due to untimely filing:		0 percent
Credit balances as a percent of A/R:		< 2 percent

⚠ Practice Blunder THE PAYMENT POSTING PROCESS

Practice Blunder diligently records its non-contractual adjustments. Unfortunately, these data are not used to effect change to current processes to prevent lost revenue to the practice. In this practice, $325,000 was written off in one year due to lack of referral or authorization and to missed filing deadlines. The good news is that staff know how much they wrote off; the bad news is that no one in the practice took any action to reduce or eliminate its occurrence.

Practice Blunder also does not have sufficient staff working the credit balance report. Consequently, $500,000 in credit balances has accumulated. This is a significant sum if these are true credit balances and the amount is owed to the payer and/or to the patient. This could also mean that Practice Blunder is out of compliance with payer or contract rules. Moreover, the practice does not recognize that the credit balance offsets its accounts receivable amount.

Case Exercises

1. Can you recommend to Practice Blunder a process that will improve the practice's non-contractual adjustments?
2. How can Practice Blunder justify its performance improvement initiative? Are there any necessary resources to improve payment posting?
3. Should Practice Blunder be concerned about its credit balances? Why?
4. If the total current A/R report at Practice Blunder indicates $2 million, what is the true A/R?
5. Can you recommend a process to resolve Practice Blunder's credit balances?

Policies and Procedures | THE PAYMENT POSTING PROCESS

POLICY 14 Credit Balances

Policy: Establish and define standard guidelines for the timely resolution of credit balances and unidentified accounts. Failure to notify patients and/or payers of an overpayment within a reasonable period of time could be interpreted as an intentional attempt to conceal the overpayment.

Procedures:

1. It is our policy to resolve credit balances and to process refunds to patients and third-party payers in a timely and accurate manner.

2. Each practice location or specialty must have internal controls in place to detect and prevent inappropriate or unauthorized refunds.

3. Credits must be researched and monies due returned within 60 days of credit creation.

4. Unidentified accounts should be used only as a temporary holding area for unidentified cash and should be closed out monthly.

CHAPTER 7

POTHOLE 6:

The Account Follow-up Process

Account follow-up is pursuing an outstanding claim to ensure that the practice receives payment. One would think this process would be easy, but unfortunately it is more like a complicated puzzle. You need to investigate where the claim is, determine its status, then follow a well-defined strategy to ensure that the claim is adjudicated and paid.

In this chapter, we discuss:

- Open claims follow-up
- Account follow-up structure
- Account follow-up strategies
- Small balance adjustments

Once claims are sent, one of four events typically occurs:

The claim is paid appropriately: This is obviously the preferred option for the medical practice. The practice submits the claim and receives the expected level of reimbursement.

The claim is paid incorrectly: Sometimes the payer will adjudicate the claim for payment but the payment will be incorrect. The payment may be too much, creating a refund (discussed in Chapter 6), or it may be too little. If the claim is underpaid, follow-up is necessary to understand the cause of the mispayment and to direct the carrier to adjudicate it correctly.

The claim is denied: Whether the denial is due to payer error or practice error, the billing staff needs to actively pursue the denial, potentially appealing it. We will discuss this further in Chapter 8.

The claim is unpaid and resides in limbo: This is often the most frustrating scenario, and it is why we recommend that staff follow accounts every 30 to 45 days to determine the status of the claim. An "open" claim occurs because the patient provided the staff with the incorrect insurance information, staff keyed the patient's information in incorrectly, the payer lost the claim or the payer chose to hold the claim for manual review or for another reason (often unknown to the practice). If these open claims are not pursued, they can lead to write-offs due to untimely filing.

If the claim is denied, unpaid or paid incorrectly, the practice should follow up with the payer regarding the account. Working accounts requires diligent, energetic staff and a streamlined process.

To ensure efficient and effective account follow-up processes, we present proven strategies below to enhance your revenue cycle.

Advanced Practices | THE ACCOUNT FOLLOW-UP PROCESS

■ **Prioritize Account Follow-up**
Account follow-up work must be divided up between (1) those accounts for which you have received no response from the payer and (2) those accounts for which you have a response but more work is indicated. You should prioritize "no response" accounts receivable (A/R) – normally reported from your practice management system in an open claims report – by date of service and dollar amount. Prioritize A/R requiring more work by the date the explanation of benefits (EOB) was received and by the payer. Filing deadlines for appeals are very short. You will improve results by focusing staff on those accounts with short appeal time lines. No one wants to

spend a lot of time putting together an appeal only to realize it is past the filing deadline and the rework was wasted effort. Work insurance and patient correspondence as they arrive – the correspondence may supply the new information you need without requiring you to initiate communication with the patient or payer.

■ **Ensure Timely Account Follow-up**
Ensure that staff work accounts every 30 to 45 days. Use account notes and an automated tickler system to develop a queuing strategy that prompts additional follow-up action.

■ **Follow Up on All Open Claims**
Most practice management systems can run an "open claims" report, which shows all those claims that are pending – claims that have been sent but not yet paid or denied. Better performing practices work the open claims report at 30 to 45 days. If state laws allow for collection of lost interest on these claims, particularly if the payer did not attend to a batch of clean claims, pursue remuneration.

Avoid "lost" claims by following up with the payer within a defined period if no correspondence has been received regarding the claim. If a payer is notorious for asserting that it does not receive claims, send claims via certified mail or drive the claims to the office of the payer and ask for a signed receipt. Some practices are hiring minimum wage employees simply to contact the payer to determine whether the claim has been received and/or to look up the claim on the payer's Web site to determine receipt if this function is available. A sample of an open claim follow-up script to use is provided in Figure 7.1.

FIGURE 7.1　Insurance Follow-up Script

A simple approach, but effective!

"Have you received the xyz claim from us?"
      If NO, resubmit today.
      If YES, ask:
            "When was the check cut for the claim?"
            "When should we expect to receive payment for the claim?"

      If NO check has been cut, ask:
            "What information do you need from us to process the payment?"
      LOG your notes.
      END CALL.

Performance standard: 30 claims per hour; 200+ claims per day

Note: Actual workload will depend on payer cooperation.

Although these measures may appear dramatic and they consume valuable employee time and money, some practices have found that these steps are the only way they can ensure payment. Evaluate what percent of your claims seem to be lost or never paid and calculate the value of collecting on those claims. This will help you decide how best to use your time and resources for claims follow-up.

Do Not Automatically Rebill Accounts

Automatic rebilling can lead to (1) allegations of duplicate billing and (2) denials due to duplicate claims, which then requires manual posting and staff research time. Do not automatically rebill accounts when you haven't received communication from the payer; investigate the account status and take action on the claim.

Clean Up Your Accounts Receivables

Absent well formulated reasoning, accounts that are more than one year old should not be on the A/R. Some exceptions to this rule are workers' compensation, auto accident claims and some legal cases. We recommend that you classify this exception A/R separately so that the medical practice can manage and monitor active accounts. Including these outstanding account levels in your current A/R days can mask the actual billing and collection success on current activity. Your oldest A/R may include only a few complicated, time-consuming accounts that are going to take another four to six months to resolve. Consider handling these unusual accounts by re-categorizing them to improve the accuracy of your A/R performance measures. Don't let a few outliers alter your true performance.

Identify a Small Balance Adjustment

There is no current industry standard regarding the level of a small balance account write-off; the level tends to fluctuate depending on whether you are in a primary care or specialty care practice. Clearly, if your practice's copayment levels are routinely $5, then you may not want to initiate a small balance write-off at this level. The typical range for small balance write-offs is $4.99 to $9.99. Run a report showing patient responsibility and look at the frequency of balances at the low end. This will help you target what is a small account balance for your practice.

Organize Account Follow-up Staff by Payer

Your staff should organize follow-up work by payer unless there is a compelling reason otherwise (which could include a surgeon providing unique services that require in-depth understanding to work the claims). If the practice is large, consider organizing the staff by specialty and then by payer. Advantages of a payer-focused strategy include the following:

- Development of relationship with payers;
- Development of local experts in the practice to correspond with payers;
- Increased focus on follow-up activity; and
- Assessment of staff productivity on follow-up efforts.

Determine Staffing per Payer by Assigning Weights

If your practice assigns staff members by payer, it is important to recognize that payers require different levels of effort. Assign a score of 1 to Medicare and weight each other payer according to the level of work it requires as compared with Medicare. For example, you may contract with an HMO that has aggressive reimbursement policies and a high denial rate. The weight you assign to account follow-up for this HMO is 3 because those accounts require three times the amount of effort – and staff – as Medicare. Staff your account follow-up according to the volume of claims per payer and the weights. Review volume and weights on an annual basis.

Define Account Follow-up Strategies by Payer

How and when you follow up on an outstanding invoice varies depending on the payer. Each payer requires specific strategies and techniques. The more you understand the payer, the better prepared you are to define your follow-up strategies. Here are some ideas for your follow-up team to consider:

Medicare: Medicare is typically the fastest payer. If you send your claim electronically and it is correct the first time, you can receive payment in 14 days. If a Medicare claim is denied, your appeal will also move quickly unless it involves review of physician documentation or substantiating medical necessity. Thus, account follow-up on Medicare claims can result in quick cash.

Medicaid: This payer can also be fast but is usually one of your lowest payments per procedure code. Experience tells us that Medicaid appeals do not happen as quickly as the claims process.

Commercial payers: This includes many different types of companies. The reimbursement rate is often good but the timeliness of those payments can be fast or very slow. Make sure you follow up on no-response claims – the higher reimbursement from this type of payer makes it a priority.

HMOs: Additional administrative requirements such as referrals and authorizations make it more difficult to bill claims correctly the first time. It also takes the payer longer to pay or deny your claim. Claim filing limits and appeal filing limits are often the shortest in this payer type.

Workers' compensation: There is unanimous agreement that this is one of the slowest parts of your A/R to collect. Once you know the patient may have been involved in a work-related injury, you need to step up the effort to ensure you capture all of the necessary information. Be prepared for this part of your A/R to take the longest to resolve.

Auto accidents: The other part of your A/R that rivals workers' compensation is auto accidents. It is imperative that staff follow-up to obtain the third party responsible. Staff need to understand that some of these accounts will result in legal action and time lines will be extended. Accounts receivable balances associated with auto accident claims can be very large in some specialties, thus these specialties typically have older A/R.

Tool 14: Sorting Your Outstanding A/R – Ways to Prioritize Your A/R Efforts

To improve the effectiveness of your insurance account follow-up, report your outstanding A/R in several different ways. This will help you identify where you need to target account follow-up efforts. It is no longer acceptable to work accounts only by account number or patient name. Most practices have limited staff resources. If you initially focus on those accounts with the highest outstanding balances, you will realize a higher return on investment for those staff costs. This tool identifies the critical sorts that help target your A/R follow-up.

TOOL 14   SORTING YOUR OUTSTANDING A/R — WAYS TO PRIORITIZE YOUR A/R EFFORTS

- Sort by balance due (highest to lowest)
  - Create dollar buckets that fit for your specialty ($3,000+, $2,000–2,999, $1000–1,999, $500–999, $100–499, $50–99, $10–49)
- Sort by account type, payer type/plan
- Sort by date claim submitted or date of service
- Sort by age of account
  - Create age buckets (120+ days, 90–119, 60–89, 30–59, current)
- Sort insurance accounts from patient collections

■ **Educate Staff to Follow a Systematic, Bounded Process**
Staff members involved in follow-up activity should be following similar protocols for account follow-up. The process should be bounded, meaning that when the process for follow-up does not yield the expected information, the employee should know exactly what to do rather than invent a process to handle a particular account. Staff should know when and how to contact a payer and when to escalate issues within the payer's hierarchy and within the practice's management team.

■ **Develop a Systematic Follow-up Process with a Payer**
Establish a method of corresponding with the payer to follow up on accounts. Many practices have scheduled weekly telephone meetings with their major payers' provider representatives to follow up on outstanding accounts rather than be limited to a specific number of accounts per telephone call or fax inquiry. Developing a relationship with the payer enhances efficiency and speeds up account follow-up activity. Many payers are now offering claims status access via a Web site. Refer to the Payer Collection Checklist below to identify successful techniques to collect from payers.

Tool 15: Payer Collection Checklist
This tool outlines successful techniques to collect from payers.

TOOL 15 PAYER COLLECTION CHECKLIST

☐ Develop staff experience by payer.
☐ Use your practice management system to identify underpaid or inaccurate remittances.
☐ Require physicians to help with payer meetings and communications.
☐ Escalate issues within payer's hierarchy to ensure it knows you will appeal denied claims and pursue accounts due.
☐ Automate communication and inquiries to payers through template letters.
☐ Establish collector performance measures:
  – Number of claims/day
  – Dollars collected
  – Age of outstanding accounts
☐ Follow up on unpaid claims over 120 days.
☐ Initiate a routine feedback loop to the front-end staff to inform them of denial trends and engage them in correcting claims.

■ **Use the Internet to Check for Payer Updates**

Medicare and state Medicaid Web sites are excellent resources for payer updates. Other payers also may have established Web sites for communication purposes. Assign one of your staff to "surf" payer Web sites and report to the entire team any new features or e-commerce offerings.

■ **Transfer the Account to Patient Responsibility**

If you do not participate with a patient's insurance company, but choose to file the claim as a courtesy to the patient, follow up on the claim within 45 days. Most practices continue to file claims as a courtesy to their patients, and 45 days allows the payer ample time to adjudicate the claim. Furthermore, experience has shown that less effort is required to pursue payment from a payer versus a patient. However, if 45 days have passed without payment, it's appropriate to transfer the balance to patient responsibility.

■ **Resolve "Information Requested from Patient"**

If a payer indicates that payment is being held for information from a patient, contact the patient immediately. When possible, initiate a three-way conference call with the patient, the payer and your billing staff. Ask the payer to request the information, the patient to respond, then follow this transfer of information with an inquiry as to when to expect payment on your claim. If a conference call is not possible, send a standard letter template to the patient informing him/her that the payer needs information. If the patient does not supply the information within 30 days, transfer the account to patient responsibility (provided this is consistent with your contract terms).

Performance Workload Ranges THE ACCOUNT FOLLOW-UP PROCESS

The performance workload ranges for account follow-up that we typically expect are provided below. The ability to perform within these ranges may vary due to internal practice-specific factors (such as facility layout, telephone system and practice management system). The workload ranges are based on a staff member performing these functions approximately seven hours of productive time per day (allowing one hour for breaks, interruptions and other downtime). Note that the workload ranges reflect *quantitative* performance levels. *Qualitative* performance – accuracy, completeness, appropriateness and quality of these functions – should also be measured. When issues of quantity versus quality arise, we strongly recommend that quality be emphasized, even if the performance workload ranges for a particular function need to be relaxed from these levels.

Given the diverse responsibilities of an insurance follow-up staff member, we have presented the workload expectations for account follow-up based on activity. Staffing depends on the volume and level of follow-up needed; if claims are paid without the need for extensive follow-up, staffing levels will be minimal.

Account action and notes:	Every 30 – 45 days
Research correspondence* and resolve by telephone:	5 – 10 minutes/account; 6 – 12/hour
Research correspondence* and resolve by appeal:	15 – 20 minutes/account; 3 – 4/hour
Check status of claim (telephone or online) and rebill:	1 – 5 minutes/account; 12 – 60/hour

*Includes reviewing the correspondence from payer that shows the denial and/or underpayment, identifying the cause of the denial or underpayment, pulling medical documentation and/or other support and developing a case for reconsideration of payment.

Based on the above performance workload range, you can estimate the number of accounts that a staff member can follow up. For example, assuming that one-third of the staff member's time is devoted to account research and resolution by telephone, one-third is devoted to account research and resolution by appeal and one-third is spent checking on claim status and rebilling, one staff member can follow up approximately 110 accounts per day during a seven-hour productive day.[1]

Automation, such as electronic access to payers, medical documentation and payer reimbursement policies, can increase the performance workload ranges required for account follow-up even further.

[1]Computation: 7-hour productive day: 2.33 staff hours performing work at 9 accounts per hour = 20.97 accounts. 2.33 hours performing work at 3.5 accounts per hour = 8.15 accounts. 2.33 hours performing work that at 36 accounts per hour = 83.88 accounts. Account total: 113.

© 2004 Walker, Larch, Woodcock: Day-to-Day Practice Operations. *Reprinted with permission.*

⚠ Practice Blunder THE ACCOUNT FOLLOW-UP PROCESS

Practice Blunder has delegated account follow-up to one employee. Every month its practice management system creates a 600-page accounts receivable report in alphabetical order by patient last name. The employee works as much of the report as s/he can before the next month's report is provided. Upon receiving the next month's report, s/he again works the report in alphabetical order! The accounts for patients with last names beginning with the letters L through Z are never touched.

Case Exercises
1. What new process should Practice Blunder adopt for account follow-up?
2. What performance measures should Practice Blunder use to monitor outcomes for account follow-up?
3. If Practice Blunder undertakes a process improvement initiative, how can it justify a new process that may include additional resources?
4. What steps can Practice Blunder take in the front-end billing process to reduce the workload of account follow-up?

Policies and Procedures | THE ACCOUNT FOLLOW-UP PROCESS

POLICY 15 Insurance Follow-up

Policy: The billing office will be responsible for timely follow-up on monies owed to the practice from payers.

Procedures:

Reports will be generated from the practice management system to ensure timely payment.

1. For denied or pending claims, the following actions will be taken based on the denial code indicated on the explanation of benefits or remittance:

    a. If the patient is not eligible for benefits, or if the service is not a covered benefit, the balance will be transferred immediately to self-pay;

    b. If additional information is required, the claim will be resent with the appropriate information or attachments; or

    c. If demographic information or policy numbers are incomplete or inaccurate, the patient will be called to obtain valid data. This updated information will be immediately entered into the computer and a rebill will be requested.

2. The following schedule will be followed to assure consistent follow-up:

    a. **30 to 45 days after date of service:**
        1. Confirm receipt of payment.
        2. If no payment, contact the payer to determine claim status on-line or by telephone.
        3. If claim was filed as courtesy to payer with which you have no contract, transfer the financial responsibility to the patient.
        4. Determine the following:
            - Expected date of payment; and
            - Reason for denial or claim hold
        5. Assemble any documentation requested to adjudicate the claim and rebill if necessary.

    b. **60 days after date of service:**
        1. Confirm receipt of payment.
        2. If no payment, contact the payer to determine claim status on-line or by telephone.

3. Determine the following:
   - Expected date of payment; and
   - Reason for continued denial or claim hold
4. Assemble any documentation requested to adjudicate the claim and rebill if necessary.
5. Notify patient of claim status and solicit his/her assistance with the payer (see Patient Information Request Form provided on the next page).
6. Notify patient that the balance due will be charged to patient, due in 30 days, if the contract with the payer in question allows it.

c. **90 days after date of service:**
   1. Confirm receipt of payment.
      - If no payment, contact the payer to determine claim status on-line or by telephone.
   2. Determine the following:
      - Expected date of payment; and
      - Reason for continued denial or claim hold.
   3. Assemble any documentation requested to adjudicate the claim and rebill if necessary.
   4. Contact the patient by telephone and request his/her assistance immediately; if possible, conduct a three-way conference call.
   5. Summarize your efforts to follow-up on this claim in a letter, and bill patient for balance due, if the contract with the payer in question allows it.

d. **120 days after date of service:**
   1. Confirm receipt of payment.
   2. If no payment, contact the payer to determine claim status by telephone. Request to speak with a supervisor, outlining your efforts to date to follow-up on this claim.
   3. Determine the following:
      - Expected date of payment; and
      - Reason for continued denial or claim hold
   4. Assemble any documentation requested to adjudicate the claim and rebill if necessary.

e. **150 days after date of service:**
   1. Confirm receipt of payment.
   2. If no payment, document your efforts to date. Give the document to the treating physician with your recommendation(s) regarding follow-up activity. See "150-day Outstanding Balance Follow-up Form" (provided on page 110).

Patient Information Request Form

Date of notice: _____

Patient's name: _____

Patient's account number: _____

Date of service: _____

Physician: _____

Amount due: _____

____ Your insurance company is requesting accident details.

____ Your insurance company is requesting student status.

____ Your insurance company processed your claim out of network. It does not have a primary care physician (PCP) on file for you.

____ Your insurance company needs a completed claim form signed by the guarantor of your policy.

____ Your insurance company was unable to identify the insured/policy holder with the information in our records.

____ Your insurance company is requesting pre-existing information for this diagnosis.

____ Please provide us with a copy of your insurance card. (Please mail or fax it to my attention at xxx-xxx-xxxx.)

____ Your insurance company is requesting additional information. Please contact it immediately.

____ Your insurance company needs_____.

Please respond within ten (10) days, or you may be responsible for your bill. Please contact me if you have any questions.

Sincerely,

Name of patient account representative

150-day Outstanding Balance Follow-up Form

Date of notice: _____

Patient's name: _____

Patient's account number: _____

Date of service: _____

Physician: _____

Services rendered: _____

Amount of claim: _____

Record of follow-up activity on this claim:

Activity / Date: _____

Activity / Date: _____

Activity / Date: _____

Activity / Date: _____

(Please attach all relevant documents, including appeal letters and other record of communication with the payer.)

I recommend one of the following:

☐ All efforts to pursue payment have failed. Please contact the medical director. (Write name and telephone number.)

☐ All efforts to pursue payment have failed. Because of _____ (e.g., incomplete documentation, etc.), I recommend that we write off this claim.

☐ I have made the above efforts to request reconsideration of this claim (e.g., documentation of appeal letters). Please recommend further actions that I can pursue (e.g., supporting medical literature) and/or a statement from you regarding this/these service(s).

Billing staff signature: _____ Date: _____

Supervisor's approval: _____ Date: _____

☐ *I have read, audited and agree with the account representative's recommendations.*

☐ *I have read, audited and disagree with the account representative's recommendations. Please take the following actions:*

_____

_____

POLICY **16** Small Balance Adjustments

Policy: Patient account balances equal to or less than $4.99 will be written off if the account meets certain criteria.

Procedures:

1. Small balances are amounts equal to or less than $4.99 that would cost more to bill for the balance than the value of the balance.

2. If the account balance meets all of the following criteria, the account will be written off:

   - Less than or equal to $4.99;
   - Over 120 days old;
   - There are no insurance due balances; and
   - There is no violation of a contractual obligation to continue collection.*

3. On a monthly basis a report will be generated to identify accounts that meet these criteria. The account representative will review the list for appropriate criteria and authorize the monthly write-off.

4. The small balance adjustment will be conducted automatically by the practice management system, as directed by the account representative.

*It is of note that the Centers for Medicare & Medicaid (CMS) defines a "reasonable" collections effort as follows:

"When a provider claims Medicare bad debts in 120 days or less from the first bill, the provider must be prepared to demonstrate that the debts were 'actually worthless.' The provider, in all cases, must be able to support that it pursued reasonable collection efforts." "A provider may claim Medicare bad debts under Section 310, presumption of uncollectibility, if after reasonable and customary attempts to collect a bill, the debt remains unpaid more than 120 days from the date the first bill is mailed to the beneficiary unless there is reason to believe that the debt is collectable for example, the beneficiary is currently making payments on account, or has currently promised to pay the debt. Sound business judgment established that there was no likelihood of recovery at any time in the future."

Source: 42 C.F.R., Sections 413.80 and 310, Provider Reimbursement Manual, Part I.

CHAPTER 8

POTHOLE 7:
The Denial Management Process

I n the previous potholes, we highlighted important strategies to ensure your claims are received by the payers and do not remain unpaid or in limbo. Now we'll focus on those claims that the payer denies. Understanding the cause of claim denials and actively working denials are critically important to ensure appropriate reimbursement for services rendered. Computers, not people, look at the claims, so there's no wiggle room. Your staff must complete the claims absolutely correctly.

In this chapter, we discuss:

- Reasons for denied claims
- Denial management strategies
- Appeals process
- Payer meetings

Common Practice Errors That Cause Denials

Common practice errors that contribute to denials and problematic reimbursement are outlined in the table below:

Insurance correspondence language	Translation
■ Coverage not in effect at time of service; ■ Our records indicate patient is enrolled with Medicaid. Please bill Medicaid first; ■ Patient is covered by another insurance that is primary; or ■ Charges were incurred after patient's cancellation date with plan.	The patient's insurance coverage was not verified prior to service (the patient may have switched jobs, lost coverage or listed wrong payer, or the practice may have collected incorrect information from patient or failed to obtain all payers). The practice failed to note the termination date.
■ No referral in our system; or ■ Date of service not within referral time period.	The primary care physician did not send referral to payer, or the valid referral period was exceeded.
■ Charge not covered by subscriber's benefit plan.	The practice failed to verify coverage for such services as annual physicals.
■ Claim lacks information needed for adjudication.	Data – Social Security number, plan ID number, practice ID number, UPIN – are missing.
■ Incomplete/invalid patient procedure or diagnosis codes.	The encounter form is outdated: Deleted codes are still on the form, descriptions are not valid, extra digits are needed for diagnosis. There is a coding problem: invalid linkages of procedure and diagnosis data.
■ Lack of patient's date of illness/injury; ■ Age conflict with reported diagnosis; ■ Incorrect gender; ■ Capitated services billed in error; ■ Modifiers used incorrectly; or ■ Place of service (location) errors.	Data entry errors or omissions are made at charge capture or charge entry.

Reasons for Denied Claims

Medical practices need to post claim denials on the patient's account in their practice management systems and report errors to staff at the front desk and the billing office so that errors are not repeated. We have outlined major reasons for claim denial below:

- Registration error;
- Insurance verification not performed;
- Charge entry error;
- Referrals and pre-authorizations not processed;
- Duplicate billing;
- Lack of medical necessity;
- Documentation to support the claim is required; and
- Codes have been bundled – editing system, modifier problems.

The Payer's Point of View

To the payer, working paper and electronic claims involves many steps and handoffs. Within seconds, the decision is made to send the claim to medical review, down-code the claim, submit partial payment, pay the claim or deny it entirely. Anything that a practice can do to complete the claim form correctly ensures that the payer handles its claims appropriately. Any omission or error means your claim is not a clean claim and will go into a review status where it will remain for an indeterminate length of time as shown in Figure 8.1.

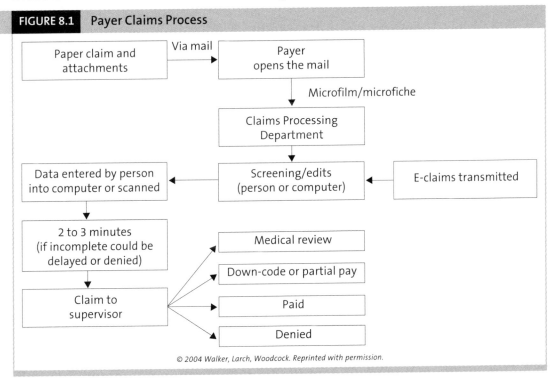

FIGURE 8.1   Payer Claims Process

© 2004 Walker, Larch, Woodcock. Reprinted with permission.

When a payer starts denying more and more claims, this can be a signal that it's in financial trouble. While the prompt payment laws in some states may help assure quick payment, the practice must monitor the timeliness of payments to avoid lost revenue associated with a payer that has closed its doors (and the potential legal challenges and patient service impacts this represents).

To ensure an efficient and effective denial management process, we present proven strategies to enhance your revenue cycle.

Advanced Practices | THE DENIAL MANAGEMENT PROCESS

■ **Measure Denial Data and Take Action**
Less than 5 percent of claims should be denied on first submission. Measure the following denial data for your practice on a quarterly basis – if not more frequently – and *take action* to reduce or eliminate the reason for the denial. Prioritize your tasks. First tackle those areas that your practice can improve, then devote your time to payer errors.

Track the following denial data:

- Percent of claims denied on initial submission;
- Number of denials and dollar value of denials;
- Top 10 reasons claims are denied;
- Percent of denied claims that are reworked;
- Time lag between date of denial received and date the appeal was sent out;
- Percent and dollars of reworked denied claims that are paid; and
- Percent and dollars of the denials that are written off.

Collect the denial data so you can sort it by the following categories: provider, specialty, location, payer, procedure, diagnosis code and reason for denial.

The two tools we provide below will help you track denial activity and graph your denial trends so you can prevent and/or appeal denials in your practice.

Tool 16: Insurance Rejection Log

We have provided an insurance denial log to help you start tracking denials. We recommend that you track each payer for a one-week period. This one-week snapshot will identify the top denial opportunities in your practice. Take action immediately to determine the originating cause and eliminate the denials.

TOOL
16   INSURANCE REJECTION LOG

To start, create this log in a spreadsheet, and track one week of EOBs for one payer.

Payer:					Claim Denial Categories									
Physician	Patient #	Proc. code	Location	Charge	Not eligible	Incorrect payer	Referral authorization	Charge entry	Patient information	Credent-ialing	Bundled	Not covered	Duplicates	Medical necessity
TOTALS ($'s and count)														

© 2004 Walker, Larch, Woodcock. Reprinted with permission.

A large multispecialty practice used this tool and identified the top three reasons for denial. They were (1) patient not eligible on date of service, (2) no referral/pre-authorization obtained and (3) incorrect payer was billed. All of the reasons fell under the control of the medical practice; consequently, the practice took steps to resolve the cause of the problems. In one year, this practice cut its claims denial rate by 50 percent!

Tool 17: Graph of Denial Trends

We have provided a sample denial graph that you can use to initiate your denial analysis. By analyzing the data in graphical form, you can identify causes of denials and track performance over time to determine what action you should take. Trend the denials by major payer, major originating cause and location of service.

TOOL
17 **GRAPH OF DENIAL TRENDS**

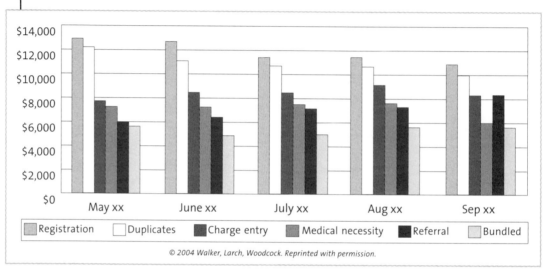

© 2004 Walker, Larch, Woodcock. Reprinted with permission.

◼ Understand the Payer's Reimbursement Policies

Some payers publish guidelines regarding reimbursement. Medicare calls its published guidelines "National Coverage Decisions," and each intermediary can also decide on local medical review policies, or LMRPs. Be sure staff understand the guidelines. If Medicare, for example, has determined that it will not provide payment for a certain service because it has decided that it is not medically necessary, then it is not worth your staff time and effort to appeal the denial. Knowing all of your payer's policies regarding reimbursement is critical in order to recognize the following:

- ◼ When financial responsibility can be shifted to patients – preferably at the time the service is rendered – if the payer contract permits it;
- ◼ Where staff resources should be allocated to gain the greatest return on investment;
- ◼ When services are bundled into payment for the primary procedure; and
- ◼ When the practice should evaluate whether it can continue to provide a service if it is not reimbursable.

■ **Decide if a Denial Is Inevitable**

Knowing the payer's reimbursement policy will help you know when a denial is likely and what kind of information you can provide to get it paid. If a denial is inevitable, print the initial claim to paper and attach a letter of support for your claim. Examples include, but are not limited to, unlisted procedure codes, unspecified diagnosis codes, multiple procedures, complex surgeries and other extenuating circumstances. Some claims scrubbing software modules allow custom edits for this purpose.

■ **Rework Appealable Claims**

Track all denials and rework appealable claims promptly. Review the top 10 denials for your major payers, identify which denials are appealable and define the actions necessary to appeal effectively. When it's possible, insert automatic write-offs of denials that you can't appeal in your practice management system. Track this activity by payer.

If you can appeal a denial, the success of that appeal depends on additional information that was not included in the initial submission. Most denial management is labor intensive and error prone. Staff spend days finding and copying documents, and this creates further delays for the practice's cash flow. You need to identify ways to automate the work effort. Some ideas to consider:

- Develop appeal letter templates for the most common denial reasons.
- Scan operative reports, office notes and other documentation to access this information easily; attach these documents to the appeal letter.
- Obtain access to the hospital's information system so you can easily pull supporting documentation, such as discharge summaries and operative reports.
- Use medical literature and your specialty society's Web site to obtain information about treatment protocols, clinical practice guidelines and policy statements to supplement appeals regarding denials for medical necessity.
- Assign different types of appeals to different staff so they can develop an expertise in that area or with that payer. Then rotate staff every six months to provide cross training and development.

Track your appeals through the practice management system, institute an automated calendar function or print a copy of the appeal and file it in a tickler file in date order so you can review it for action and resolution in 30 days.

■ **Organize Denial Follow-up Activity**

As we mentioned above, it is important to consider speed and efficiency when you're developing denial follow-up procedures. Below are key denial appeal follow-up techniques that should streamline the process:

Sort by reason and route to appropriate person: For example, if a claim is denied because no referring physician was provided, forward the list of claims denied for that reason to your medical records area, as staff will need to pull the medical chart and identify the referring physician's name.

Prioritize by payer with the shortest deadline, then dollar amount: Your priority is the denied claims with the shortest time to appeal and the highest dollar value.

Create a list of the payer's appeal deadlines: They typically vary from 45 days from date of denial to six months.

Develop a dedicated appeals team: Some practices have identified staff members to handle all appeals, while other staff focus on accounts in limbo. This ensures that an appeals team is focused on meeting appeal filing deadlines.

Establish a written protocol for appeals: These include sample letters.

Investigate appeals software tools as an option: Key functions to look for include integration with the existing practice management system and minimal disruption from day-to-day operations.

■ **Use Denial Data to Redesign Billing Processes**

According to the Advisory Board Company, approximately 90 percent of denials are preventable, and 67 percent of denials are recoverable.[1] While it is very important to your practice that you prevent denials from happening, when they do happen, you must appeal to recover the money due your physicians. Use denial data to redesign your revenue cycle.

Ask the following question: What is the source of the denial? If the source rests with the practice, fix the cause of the denial. It sounds easy, but it often requires significant operational change. If the cause is attributed to the payer and it occurs routinely, escalate denials within the payer's structure. Adding billing staff to rework denied claims over and over again is not as good an investment as adding a staff member at the front desk to reduce errors that are causing the denials. Any time you can eliminate a denial cause, the claim will be paid the first time and the cost to rework the denied claim will be eliminated.

---

[1] The Advisory Board Company as reported in "CFO Leadership Strategies for Managing Denied Claims," a Third Millennium Healthcare Systems white paper.

■ **Calculate Your Cost of Rework**

You can easily compute the total cost of rework for your medical practice. For example, let's assume that a medical practice files 1,000 claims each month and has a 20 percent denial rate. Let's also assume that the rework cost per claim is $25 (the typical cost for medical practices). The calculation for the cost of rework would be $25 x 200 claims = $5,000. Note that this cost is inclusive of the cost of lost interest earnings on the payment and additional costs of process inefficiency that hinders optimal performance. Determine the cost to rework a claim for your own practice, then calculate your total cost of rework by multiplying it by denied claims volume. This calculation can help you determine the resources you need to allocate so you can reduce your claim denials. You cannot reduce this amount until you know and act on the originating cause of the denial. In most cases, the cost of rework exceeds the cost to improve the process and prevent the denial in the first place.

■ **Appeal Denials**

Absent a clearly understood reason for a denial, or a lack of ability to support your original claim (for example, no documentation exists for the service), appeal your denials. When your claim appeal efforts are not successful, move to a formal appeals process. A formal appeals process is structured within each third-party payer organization. Providers and patients can submit appeals for treatment or reimbursement decisions. There are usually several levels of appeal:

Urgent review: If the payer denies authorization for treatment or post-treatment, a practice needs to request an immediate telephone consultation.

Level 1 appeal: The first appeal goes to the reviewer or clerk who initially denied the claim. S/he looks at any additional records submitted and claims submitted. You should request a quick response (within 24 hours).

Level 2 appeal: This usually involves a physician/medical director at the payer organization and may include a telephone conversation with the provider.

Level 3 appeal: This level of review involves an appeals committee or board. Board members review the documents and actions in the appeal process thus far. This may be the last stop, unless your payer contract includes an arbitration clause or an additional level of appeal. There may be different contacts and/or addresses for each level of appeal. Be sure to check with the payer to determine the correct channels of communication for the appeal process.

There is a right way and a wrong way to submit an appeal. The wrong way is to resubmit a claim without explaining why it should be reconsidered for payment. Following are sample appeal letters you can revise as appropriate for your practice.

Tools 18 and 19: Sample Appeal Letters – General and Specific

We have provided sample appeal letters for your use. These letters outline the specifics of the matter under appeal and provide an opportunity for your medical practice to state its case succinctly and clearly. Where possible, use the specific wording from the payer's written or electronic publications.

TOOL
18 SAMPLE APPEAL LETTER — GENERAL

To: _____   Re: Insured _____
                                          Invoice/claim number: _____

We are requesting a review of the claim above. A signed release form from your insured is enclosed allowing you to communicate directly with our office.

When reviewing, please consider these facts and circumstances:
1._____
2._____

The enclosed [_____] report(s) support our position. We appreciate your prompt attention.

Sincerely,
Account Representative

© 2004 Walker, Larch, Woodcock. Reprinted with permission.

SAMPLE APPEAL LETTER — SPECIFIC

To Whom It May Concern:

Thank you for the opportunity to submit this denied claim for reconsideration of payment. We are contacting you about the services rendered to [details about the patient's name, date of service and services rendered].

Scenario 1: Medical necessity

Your company defines "medical necessity" to your beneficiaries as "a course of treatment seen as the most helpful for the specific health symptoms you are experiencing. The course of treatment is determined jointly by you, your health professional and XYZ HealthCare. This course of treatment strives to provide you with the best care in the most appropriate setting."

The services rendered were medically necessary for this patient. The medical literature (which is attached) supports the rendering of this service in the setting in which it was rendered. Indeed, the services provided were the "course of treatment which was the most helpful for [patient's name] health symptoms" in the "most appropriate setting."

In addition to Dr. [name of treating physician], the physician who referred the patient to our practice supported our treatment decision. His/her letter of support is attached.

We believe that the service did meet your criteria for medical necessity, and is supported by other professionals in the field, as well as the patient's primary care physician.

Scenario 2: Retroactive denial of benefits

Your company retroactively denied the services rendered to this patient in your correspondence of [date of denial].

The services were authorized by [contact name and extension number] on [date and time]. Our record of the discussion is attached.

Dr. [name of treating physician] relied on your authorization to provide the services to [patient's name] on [date of service]. Under the doctrine of Promissory Estoppel, which allows recovery on a promise made, when the reliance on the promise was reasonable, and the promisee [the treating physician] relied on it to his/her detriment, we request payment for these services. We relied on your authorization to our detriment.

Scenario 3: Coding/Modifier

Your company denied the procedure as bundled into the primary procedure. According to the source of authority for procedure codes, the American Medical Association, the [quote directly from the AMA]. The copy of the AMA's statement regarding this service is attached. This service is not bundled into the primary service, and payment in full is expected.

Thank you for your reconsideration.

Note: The sample appeal letters do not guarantee payment; they are offered as exhibits only.

■ **Escalate Denials or Other Payer Issues if Necessary**
If the payer's formal appeals process is not effective, there are other ways to escalate denials in the payer's structure. Start with the claims office of the payer with whom you contracted, then systematically move to provider relations, contracts office, nurse manager, medical director and, if necessary, the executive office (chief operating officer and chief executive officer). Other external resources that may be of assistance to a medical practice in getting the payer's attention include:

■ State insurance commissioner;
■ State attorney general, state senators and representatives;
■ State MGMA affiliated organizations; and/or
■ County/state medical society.

Escalate from calls to letters to in-person meetings. A practice can ask its legal counsel to get involved. The patient should be copied on all correspondence, as the patient may be able to provide additional leverage with the payer. One practice determined that it could not afford the $850 round-trip ticket to fly a physician to the main office of the payer, yet it had $40,000 in outstanding claims with this payer! Clearly a trip may be worth the effort and expense – you typically do not have to make these trips more than once.

■ **Schedule Routine Meetings with Top Payers**
Meet with your top five payers on a routine basis. Discuss the timing of payments, confusing denials and other issues. Develop effective relationships with the payers throughout the year rather than simply meeting with them for contract renegotiation.

■ **Maintain Records of Inappropriate Denials**
Keep a folder for each of your top five payers. Place copies of inappropriate denials in the folders. Use the information as an agenda item in your routine meeting with your provider representative. This does not replace the claim appeals process that should be followed as usual – it is an extra step to focus the payer on key issues. Use actual examples, instead of spoken anecdotes or general complaints, to focus the payer on your concerns.

Compare your denial rate by payer. This will help identify those payers who deny your claims at a higher rate than payers of similar types. Tool 20 will help you monitor payer denial activity.

Tool 20: Use of Denial Data to Compare Payers

This tool provides a succinct way of seeing payer-specific denial data. Calculate your claim rejections as a percent of total claims submitted or total encounters for each payer. Monitoring and comparing the frequency of payer denials provides a statistical measure that you can share with payers at the time of contract negotiation or in regular meetings with the payer to improve practice-payer interactions and revenue for your practice. In this example, the practice experiences the lowest denial rate from Payer 2 and the highest from Payer 4.

TOOL 20 USE OF DENIAL DATA TO COMPARE PAYERS

Specialty	Third-party Payer Denials					
	Payer 1	Payer 2	Payer 3	Payer 4	Payer 5	Payer 6
1	90	43	49	23	32	63
2	27	4	16	12	22	21
3	28	8	8	8	6	10
4	119	233	121	73	101	573
5	19	0	0	2	7	2
6	175	56	71	54	113	124
7	6	1	10	29	11	35
8	16	19	2	14	13	22
9	8	1	5	6	5	11
10	220	64	187	49	65	65
11	0	0	0	0	0	0
12	2	0	0	0	10	5
13	9	4	11	9	16	5
14	1	42	7	12	20	20
15	1,609	563	1,038	44	106	133
16	0	0	0	5	78	18
17	13	8	19	23	125	60
18	547	182	173	204	446	498
19	49	91	38	42	109	103
20	55	8	27	12	27	97
21	699	154	106	56	13	32
Total denials (3 months)	3,692	1,481	1,888	677	1,325	1,897
Total encounters (3 months)	12,625	25,886	7,542	2,110	6,215	9,410
Denials as a % of encounters	29%	6%	25%	32%	21%	20%

© 2004 Walker, Larch, Woodcock. Reprinted with permission.

Performance Workload Ranges   THE DENIAL MANAGEMENT PROCESS

The performance workload ranges provided in Chapter 7 also apply to denial management.

⚠ Practice Blunder   THE DENIAL MANAGEMENT PROCESS

When explanation of benefits (EOB) forms come in with $0 payments, Practice Blunder's staff incorrectly writes them off as contractual adjustments or administrative adjustments such as bad debt. This prevents the practice from appealing inappropriate denials or understanding the reason the claims are denied. Clearly, this approach also prevents Practice Blunder from collecting revenue owed to it.

Case Exercises:
1. Can you recommend a better denial management process for Practice Blunder?
2. How should Practice Blunder track and report its denials?
3. How can Practice Blunder justify its performance improvement initiatives and any necessary resources to improve denial management?

CHAPTER 9

The Patient Collections Process

The last pothole on the road to getting paid involves payments due from patients. It is important that you perform follow-up in a timely fashion, communicating clearly to the patient, as the longer these balances stay in the accounts receivables, the harder it will be to collect. In Chapter 2, we covered patient collections when the patient is physically present in your office. In this chapter, we focus on patient collections – any and all residual payments that are owed by the patient or guarantor. Perhaps you failed to collect payment when the patient visited the office, the payer transferred part of the balance to patient responsibility, or the patient is uninsured and responsible for the entire balance.

In this chapter, we cover:

- The collection cycle
- Collections policies
- Patient correspondence
- Returned mail
- Payment plans
- Collection agencies
- Patient statements

The patient collections process involves submitting statements to patients to collect what they owe on the bill and then taking appropriate steps to ensure that payment has been received. Typically, practices send the statements to patients after both the primary and secondary insurance have paid their portions of the bill. The statement informs the patient of the activity that has occurred on the account and the account balance that is the patient's responsibility. Once the account transfers to a self-pay status, staff need to exert systematic and diligent efforts to follow up with the patient, or "self pay" quickly degenerates to "zero pay."

To ensure an efficient and effective patient collections process, we present proven strategies to enhance your revenue cycle.

Advanced Practices | THE PATIENT COLLECTIONS PROCESS

■ **Establish a Collections Cycle That Works for You and Your Patients**
Determine how aggressively you will pursue patient balances. Given the small profit margin available in most practices, collecting every dollar may be critical to the survival of your practice. Some specialties (for example, psychiatry and oncology) may decide for clinical reasons to collect balances from patients only face to face or only for large balances and not to use a collection agency. Other practices send a specific number of statements, place a set number of telephone calls and/or send a series of letters to patients. Below are three examples of a patient collection time line. Collection Policy A incurs significant time delays, while Collection Policy C represents the shortest time to send the account to collections. Define your patient collection policy – not necessarily policy A, B or C – but be sure you have one for your practice and apply it consistently.

Collection Policy A
Three statements sent to patient when patient responsibility is determined (after insurance is billed or no insurance). (Lapsed time: 90 to 120 days)

Next 14 days:	Letter #1 is sent
Next 14 days:	Telephone contact #1 is attempted
Next 14 days:	Letter #2 is sent
Next 14 days:	Request for approval for outside collection is sent to physician
Next 14 days:	Account sent to collections

Lapsed time: 160 to 190 days

Collection Policy B

Two statements sent to patient when patient responsibility is determined (after insurance is billed or there is no insurance). (Lapsed time: 25 to 50 days)

Next 14 days: Telephone contact #1 is attempted

Next 14 days: Statement #3 is sent to patient, telephone contact #2 attempted, collection letter #1 sent, pre-approval from physician to send account to collections

Next 14 days: Collection letter #2 sent

Next 10 days: Account sent to collections

Lapsed time: 77 to 102 days

Collection Policy C

One statement sent to patient.

Next 45 days: Three attempts to reach patient by telephone over a five-day period

Certified letter with 10 days to respond

Account sent to collections

Lapsed time: 60 days

■ **Set Protocols for Patient Follow-up**

Do not simply follow up accounts in alphabetical order by the last name of your patients. Prioritize the accounts based on the date of service and the dollar balance, with queuing strategies that alert staff to these levels. Your practice management system should have a reminder flag or a tickler system your staff can use.

It is important to identify the best staff member to make collection calls and to have telephone scripts s/he can follow. The Fair Debt Collections Practices Act (FDCPA), as well as other federal and state laws, have been designed to protect consumers from particular debt collection activities, and your practice should consult these sources to determine the appropriate follow-up methods. Although the FDCPA applies to third-party collection companies (to include collection agencies), the act outlines fair and reasonable processes for collection activities.

To ensure that your collection style and your patient satisfaction goals are in sync, create a collection code of ethics for the staff to follow. A sample code of ethics is shown in Figure 9.1 on the next page.

FIGURE 9.1   Sample Collection Code of Ethics

- Medical groups should fully explain the terms of any collection transaction to their patients.

- Bills should be sent as soon as possible after the billing cycle ends.

- Calls or correspondence from a patient claiming a billing error should be acknowledged promptly.

- Collection practices should be based on the presumption that every patient/guarantor intends to pay and would pay if able.

- Patient complaints concerning collection practices should be investigated immediately.

- Patients who show a sincere desire to pay their debts should be offered, if necessary, extended payment schedules, financing arrangements or similar methods that would help re-establish solvency.

- If the patient does not respond to an offer to help make alternative arrangements, the collector should explain the seriousness of the continuing delinquency and advise the patient regarding courses of action.

- Telephone calls must be placed between hours of 8:00 a.m. and 9:00 p.m. in the patient's time zone.

- Outside collection agencies, attorneys and other agents employed to collect delinquent accounts should be furnished with written instructions on how patients are to be approached and which collection practices are and are not sanctioned.

Source: Financial Management for Medical Groups by Ernest J. Pavlock, Ph.D., CPA. Adapted with permission from the MGMA Center for Research, 104 Inverness Terrace East, Englewood, Colorado 80112-5306; 303.799.1111. www.mgma.com. © 2000.

▌ Establish Protocols for Payment Plans

Outline your willingness to negotiate patient payment plans in your financial policy. Your practice needs a policy that includes acceptable payment thresholds. For example, if the account balance is from $10 to $499, then 50 percent could be paid in the first month, with 25 percent in the second month and the remaining 25 percent in the third month. Your goal should be to collect all balances in three months or less. Monthly payment amounts should never be less than your cost of billing. Following are examples of a budget plan and a payment plan agreement that you can customize for your practice.

Tools 21 and 22: Budget Plan and Payment Plan Agreement (see below and page 132)
We have provided a formal budget plan as a tool for patient account follow-up. The budget plan outlines required reimbursement based on dollar thresholds of amounts owed to the practice. Your practice should immediately contact the patient in the event the patient does not make timely payments consistent with the budget plan arrangement. Create a budget plan tool and policy that staff have the authority to implement. The practice manager or physician should not have to approve every call to a patient and every negotiated budget/payment plan.

TOOL
21 BUDGET PLAN

Amount Due per Month — Payment Schedule

Account Balance	Standard Negotiated Time Allowance				Supervisor Approval	
Operative range	Preferred 3 months	4 months	5 months	6 months	Minimum acceptable	Calculated months
$5.00–$24.99	Full				OK	0
$25.00–$50.99	Full				$25.00	2
$51.00–$150.99	$50.00	$37.50	$30.00	$25.00	$25.00	6
$151.00–$250.99	$83.33	$62.50	$50.00	$41.67	$35.00	7
$251.00–$500.99	$166.67	$125.00	$100.00	$83.33	$60.00	8
$501.00–$750.99	$250.00	$187.50	$150.00	$125.00	$90.00	8
$751.00–$1,000.99	$333.33	$250.00	$200.00	$166.67	$125.00	8
$1,001-00–$1,500.99	$500.00	$375.00	$300.00	$250.00	$175.00	8
$1,501.00–$2,000.99	$666.67	$500.00	$400.00	$333.33	$200.00	10
$2,001.00–$2,500.00	$833.33	$625.00	$500.00	$416.67	$250.00	10
If amount is greater than $2,500.00, refer to practice manager.						12

© 2004 Walker, Larch, Woodcock. Reprinted with permission.

PAYMENT PLAN AGREEMENT

I have reviewed all charges for services rendered. My balance of $_____ to my knowledge is correct. Although I have been encouraged to pay the entire balance in full, I have elected to make monthly payments as outlined below.

Beginning Balance:	$_____	**Date of Service:** _____
Number of monthly payments:	_____	Amount of each payment: $_____
Today's payment:	$_____	Today's date: _____
Next payment date:	_____	

I understand my account will be considered delinquent if my scheduled payment is more than four days late. I understand that I may be legally responsible for all collection costs involved with the collection of this account including all court costs, reasonable attorney fees and all other expenses incurred with collection if I default on this agreement. I further understand that failure to meet the prescribed payment schedule can result in listing of this debt with local, regional and national credit reporting agencies, and it may have a negative effect on the granting of future credit.

I have read the above description of the arrangement and agree to its terms.

Patient name: _____   Account #: _____

Patient signature: _____   Date: _____

_____   Date: _____
Authorizing signature and title for the practice

■ Develop a Relationship with a Financier of Medical Services

There are many financial institutions that offer financing for patients. Let your patients know about this option. Some large medical practices serve as the conduit for these relationships by facilitating the patient's loan application process.

■ Collect When the Patient Is in the Office

As we mentioned in an earlier chapter, in order to ensure timely reimbursement and reduce the cost of billing, your practice should collect patient balances including co-insurance and deductibles, in addition to copayments, when the patient is physically present in the office. If patients cannot pay at the time of service, send them home with a self-addressed envelope to return their payment to the practice by a set deadline.

■ **Follow Up on All Patient Correspondence**
Patients may respond to statements by paying the balance due, providing additional insurance information, providing credit/debit card information or clarifying previous information provided. Make sure that staff incorporate information provided by the patient into your practice management system before the next statement mailing cycle.

■ **Process Returned Mail within 48 Hours**
Review returned mail no later than 48 hours after it arrives to ensure that the mail is not returned again in the following billing cycle. The longer the delay is in attempting to locate a patient, the harder the chances of collecting the balance due. You may want to consider subscribing to some Internet search tools to identify addresses for patients with high account balances. Also, cellular telephone numbers can often be more valuable in locating patients than an address or home telephone number.

■ **Get the Patient Involved to Help You**
If the claim is clean and the payer has not paid, send the patient a letter indicating that his/her insurance company has not paid. Ask your patients to contact the insurance company regarding the delay, or to contact you if your practice billed the incorrect insurance company.

■ **Track the Volume of Statements That Your Practice Sends to a Patient**
The number of statements that you mail to a patient should be consistent with your collections policy. The majority of practices do not send a patient statement until after they have billed insurance and received a payment or an indication from the payer that the patient is responsible for the charges. This minimizes the cost to the practice related to statement mailing as well as the telephone inquiries associated with these statements. Some practices have created a fictitious patient account with the manager's address so the manager will receive the same mailings as the patients receive. Then the manager can track the performance of statement mailing.

■ **Show Patients How to Read the Patient Statement**
Provide an instructional notice that explains how to read the patient statement. Present the notice to new patients, send it with the statement or include text on the bottom or back of statements to be sure patients understand it and to minimize questions about bills. If patients are likely to receive more than one bill (for example, hospital, ancillary, etc.), explain that in the beginning to minimize confusion (and possibly reduce telephone calls). One of the easiest ways to determine if you need

to improve your statements is to ask your staff, physicians and patients to read a statement and see how well they understand it.

■ **Maximize the Use of Statement Notes to Communicate with Patients**
Use patient statement notes as a method to communicate with patients rather than initiating formal letters. This reduces the patient inquiries to the billing office as well as billing expenditures. Refer to the tool below for tips to improve statement messages.

Tool 23: Sample Statement Notes

Incorporate notes on statements to communicate with patients and to avoid the cost of mailing a separate letter. This tool provides samples of notes that can be placed on patient statements to enhance communication with patients regarding their balance due.

TOOL 23 SAMPLE STATEMENT NOTES

- Your insurance company has paid its share of your bill. This statement is for the amount due from you.

- In order to process your claim, your insurance company needs information. Please call the company or send us payment now.

- Account seriously overdue. Please send payment immediately.

- The bank has returned your check marked "insufficient funds." Please call today!

- No payment has been received from your insurance company. This amount is now due from you.

- Can we help you? We can make payment arrangements with you to help clear up your balance. Please call or stop in today.

- Second notice: Your account is past due. Please pay today. If you have paid, please disregard this notice.

- Thank you for your last payment. Your next installment of $ _____ is now due.

© 2004 Walker, Larch, Woodcock. Reprinted with permission.

■ **Use Colored Paper for Your Final Letter**
Print your final collections letter on orange paper and place it in an orange envelope that reads "FINAL NOTICE." This bright color signals an alarm, and is more effective at getting a patient's attention than a regular envelope and letter.

■ **Offer Online Patient Bill Paying**
Some practices offer their patients an online patient statement option. On their Web sites, they provide information on insurance, billing policies, answers to frequently asked questions and resources to help patients manage their health care billing. In addition, practices are starting to offer e-statements, which allow patients to access their account 24 hours a day, seven days a week. They can view their account

balances, update insurance information, ask and answer questions, and pay bills online.

Patients are interested in this option because:

It is convenient: Patients can view account information on all recent encounters with open balances in a consolidated, simplified format. They can pay bills anytime and anywhere.

Patients can get help easily: They can send an e-mail to ask about their account, update their mailing address or update insurance information online. They can find answers to the most frequently asked questions about medical billing.

It is secure and private: Access to financial account information is limited to authorized individuals only. Sophisticated encryption technology protects account information.

Patients can learn more about billing: Patients can learn how to appeal an insurance denial, shop for insurance and organize medical bills all online.

▌ Establish a Billing E-mail for Your Practice

A number of practices are establishing separate e-mail addresses to correspond with patients regarding billing issues. Some practices send their patients one statement that notifies them of this resource and they conduct further correspondence — including reminders of patient payment plans and other functions — electronically. Correspondence with the patient is faster and the practice saves money.

▌ Collect Cellular Telephone Numbers from Patients

As cellular telephones replace home and even work telephone numbers, this information can be vital to your practice during the collections process. Collect patients' cellular telephone numbers when you register them to give your practice a more effective means of communicating with the patient during the collections process.

▌ Research Coverage for Self-Pay Patients

If collection efforts are failing and the registration process was compromised (for example, the patient presented through the emergency department), query the Medicaid eligibility database for said patients, as well as the hospital's registration system. The patient may have become Medicaid eligible since your initial query. If you determine s/he is covered, submit the claim immediately.

■ **Report Bad Debt to the Credit Bureau(s)**
Your practice can sign up as a business with one of the credit bureaus (e.g., Equifax, Transunion or Experion). As a participating business, you can report bad debt to the agency. The debt will reside on the patient's credit report. Communicating your ability to report bad debt to a credit bureau can be a useful collections tool in your financial collections letter. Often, patients' concern about credit bureau reporting prompts them to contact you to make payment.

■ **Develop and Use a Charity Care Policy**
Develop a charity care policy. For patients experiencing financial hardship, offer a discount under your charity care policy. The policy should define the financial need that meets your criteria of charity, as well as the document(s) that you will collect to prove it. The policy must be consistently applied. For a sample policy, please see the financial hardship policy at the end of this chapter.

Regarding patients who are insured but cannot afford to pay their portion of the balance, the American Medical Association (AMA) offers some recommendations. "In some cases, financial hardship may deter patients from seeking necessary care if they would be responsible for a copayment for the care. Physicians commonly forgive or waive copayments to facilitate patient access to needed medical care. When a copayment is a barrier to needed care because of financial hardship, physicians should forgive or waive the copayment. ... Physicians should be aware that waiver of copayments may violate the policies of some insurers, both public and private; other insurers may permit forgiveness or waiver if they are aware of the reasons for the forgiveness or waiver. Routine forgiveness or waiver of copayments may constitute fraud under state and federal law. Physicians should ensure that their policies on copayments are consistent with applicable law and with the requirements of their agreements with insurers."[1]

Further, the Office of the Inspector General advises, "One important exception to the prohibition against waiving copayments and deductibles is that providers, practitioners or suppliers may forgive the copayment in consideration of a particular patient's financial hardship. This hardship exception, however, must not be used routinely; it should be used occasionally to address the special financial needs of a particular patient. Except in such special cases, a good faith effort to collect deductibles and copayments must be made."[2]

---

[1] Policy E-6.12. Forgiveness or Waiver of Insurance Copayments. Chicago: American Medical Association; issued 1993 June. Available from: www.ama-assn.org.

[2] Special Fraud Alert: Routine Waiver of Copayments or Deductibles Under Medicare Part B. Washington: U.S. Department of Health and Human Services, Office of Inspector General; [issued 1991 May; published in the *Federal Register*, 1994, Dec 19]. Available from: http://oig.hhs.gov/fraud/fraudalerts.html.

■ **Use a Collection Agency**

Include in your financial policy a decision about whether and when you will send patient accounts to an external collection agency. Although medical practices have traditionally used collection agencies after exhausting all internal collection efforts, many practices are attempting alternative arrangements. The role of a collection agency falls into one of the following three categories, for which we have presented average costs:

All patient collections: When an account becomes the responsibility of a patient, the practice transfers the balance to the agency to collect. The average cost is 10 to 15 percent of collections.

Pre-collect process: After a practice has sent an account through the practice's collection cycle (for example, three statements have been sent to the patient), it transfers the account to the agency to send out one final correspondence before the collection agency takes over all collection efforts on the account. The average cost is $2 to $3 per account.

Bad debt: After the practice has exhausted all internal collection efforts, the practice writes the account balance off the accounts receivable (A/R) as bad debt, and transfers all responsibility for collections to the agency. The average cost is 15 to 30 percent of collections.

Collection recovery percentages fall dramatically as time increases before the collection agency takes over. Recovery rates for outstanding accounts in the 90-day category are 50 percent of the gross charge, declining to 11 percent when accounts are more than one year old.[1] The industry standard for the recovery of medical accounts from collection agencies is 15 to 17 percent;[2] however, your results may vary based on the age of the accounts at the time you place them with the collection agency.

■ **Obtain Physician Approval to Send an Account to Collections (if required) without Delaying Its Move to the Collection Agency**

If physicians elect to review and approve patient accounts before staff send them to a collection agency, provide the list to them as you start your final in-house collections effort. This way, the physician approval does not delay the time the account is sent to collections. Not all practices require physician approval. Those that do typically state that if the physician has not responded within a defined time period (for example, 10 days) the account will be automatically forwarded to the collection agency.

[1] Blount LL, Waters, JM. *Mastering the Reimbursement Process.* 3rd ed. Chicago (IL): American Medical Association; 2001. 396p.
[2] © 2004 Walker, Larch, Woodcock: *Day-to-Day Practice Operations.* Reprinted with permission.

■ **Establish Contracts with Two Collection Agencies**
If you set up contracts with two collection agencies, you will be able to compare performance levels, and this will place your practice in a stronger contract negotiating position with both agencies. Measure and monitor recovery rates between the two agencies and watch performance over time.

■ **Establish Appropriate Internal Controls for Collection Agency Funds**
For payments on charges that have been written off, you can choose to either post the payments net of the collection fee (if applicable), or post the payments received in full and record any collection fees as an expense. Obtain your accountant's advice about handling the expensing of these collection fees. Regardless of how you choose to post the monies recovered by the collection agency, be careful to separate duties and maintain internal controls to ensure appropriate oversight of collection agency accounts.

■ **Charge Billing Fees to Patients Who Don't Pay in a Timely Manner**
Pass the collection agency fee onto the patient. That is, charge the patient the collection agency fee that the medical practice must pay the agency. You may charge patients this fee only if you informed them of it previously. You can include it in the financial policy you provide to each patient. Medical practices often pursue additional charges, including (1) finance charges, (2) rebilling fees and (3) fees for failure to pay at time of service. Again, you must inform the patient previously of the fees, and the fees must represent a cost that can be justified as reasonable and appropriate. But before you implement these fees, evaluate the downside to charging these types of fees and perform a cost/benefit analysis. These fees may hurt patient relations or create perceptions of an aggressive financial focus by the medical practice – without any positive impact.

The AMA has published the following position on this issue: "Although harsh or commercial collection practices are discouraged in the practice of medicine, a physician who has experienced problems with delinquent accounts may properly choose to request that payment be made at the time of treatment or add interest or other reasonable charges to delinquent account. The patient must be notified in advance of the interest or other reasonable finance or service charges by such means as the posting of a notice in the physician's waiting room, the distribution of leaflets describing the office billing practices, and appropriate notations on the billing statement. The physician must comply with state and federal laws and regulations applicable to the imposition of such charges. Physicians are encouraged to review their accounting/collection policies to ensure that no patient's account is sent to collection without the physician's knowledge. Physicians who choose to add an interest or finance charge to accounts not paid within a reasonable time are encouraged to use compassion and discretion in hardship cases."[1]

Make It Easy for Patients to Pay You

When patients are on a payment plan, many practices continue to send statements to the patient, incurring statement preparation and mailing costs. More advanced practices facilitate receipt of these funds by providing coupon books to patients. As we discussed earlier in this book, many practices are setting up e-mail correspondence between the patient and the practice so the practice can submit payment reminders in electronic format.

Include Billing Service Questions on Patient Satisfaction Instruments

Include questions on patient satisfaction surveys or in patient focus groups that are directly related to the billing process to determine the patient's perceptions of (1) service quality, (2) clarity of the patient statement, (3) courtesy of staff and (4) access to the billing office. Initiate improvements where indicated.

Maintain a Record of Patient Inquiries and Disposition

Many practices use automated processes such as databases or spreadsheets to document and track patient inquiries and their resolution and disposition. They review this record periodically to discuss trends, identify opportunities for process improvement and ensure equitable treatment. If patients keep calling with a particular question, you can fix your process and avoid the repeated calls. Communication from patients, particularly billing calls, exhausts staff members. We have overheard one too many conversations in which the patient states in frustration, "This isn't the right insurance! I handed my new card to the front office. Why didn't they get it right?!" A better performing billing office has a negligible amount of billing inquiries from patients because (1) patients understand their statements and (2) the statements are accurate. In other words, there is no reason for the patient to call. A sample call log is presented in the tool below.

Tool 24: Billing Inquiry Calls (see page 140)

This tool provides an easy way to record billing inquiry calls. Evaluate calls each week, looking for opportunities to reduce inbound telephone demand from patients. For example, if a trend shows that patients are calling to ask if their secondary insurance paid on the claim before submitting a patient payment for the account balance, you may want to restructure the patient statements to record primary and secondary billing status.

---

[1] Policy E-6.08. Interest Charges and Finance Charges. Chicago: American Medical Association; issued 1994 June. Available from: www.ama-assn.org.

TOOL
24 BILLING INQUIRY CALLS

Date:
Operator's name:

Nature of call (brief description)

	Name/account	Brief description	Resolution
1			
2			
3			
4			
5			

Action:
1. Evaluate log every week.
2. Determine trends regarding issues that could be fixed.
3. Establish an action plan and implement a solution to the problems — to avoid future calls.

■ **Identify Focused Staff for Patient Inquiry Management**

Designate a small number of employees who are responsible for patient inquiry, rather than distributing this function among all billing staff. Patient inquiries often take precedence over other critical billing functions, such as account follow-up activity (a ringing telephone is hard to ignore). In smaller practices where billing staff are more multitasked, assign telephone responsibility in two-hour segments to staff, rotating this function among employees throughout the day. But be sure to focus on the cause of the calls – and attempt to prevent them from occurring in the first place – instead of simply allocating more staff to the problem.

Performance Workload Ranges   THE PATIENT COLLECTIONS PROCESS

The performance workload ranges for patient collections that we typically expect are provided below. The ability to perform within these ranges may vary due to internal practice-specific factors (such as facility layout, telephone system and practice management system). The workload ranges are based on a staff member performing these functions approximately seven hours of productive time per day (allowing one hour for breaks, interruptions and other downtime). Note that the workload ranges reflect *quantitative* performance levels. *Qualitative* performance – accuracy, completeness, appropriateness and quality of these functions – should also be measured. When issues of quantity versus quality arise, we strongly recommend that quality be emphasized, even if the performance workload ranges for a particular function need to be relaxed from these levels.

Self-pay follow-up:	70 – 90/day	10 – 13/hour
Correspondence processed:	90 – 105/day	13 – 15/hour
Patient billing inquiries:	125 – 140/day	15 – 18/hour
Responding to patient billing inquiries:	Within 24 hours	

© 2004 Walker, Larch, Woodcock: Day-to-Day Practice Operations. Reprinted with permission.

⚠ Practice Blunder   THE PATIENT COLLECTIONS PROCESS

Practice Blunder does not have an established payment plan policy. Each employee can enter into an agreement with patients to establish a payment plan that is "reasonable." As a result, the employees have been setting up arrangements that are not equitable from patient to patient. In addition the practice does not receive payment in a timely fashion. One ridiculous payment arrangement Practice Blunder made was to accept $5 per month to pay off a $1,000 balance. How many months would this take? Two hundred months, or 17 years!

Practice Blunder also does not regularly monitor the number of patient statements mailed to the patient. The practice sent 26 statements to a patient who had an account balance of $6.38.

Case Exercises
1. Can you recommend a better patient collections process for Practice Blunder?
2. What is the risk to Practice Blunder if it maintains its current payment plan arrangements?
3. What is the cost to Practice Blunder to maintain its current statement process?
4. How can Practice Blunder justify a patient collections performance improvement initiative and any necessary resources?

Policies and Procedures | THE PATIENT COLLECTIONS PROCESS

POLICY **17** Budget Plan

Policy: An account representative can create a budget plan and payment schedule for a patient with a qualified outstanding balance.

Procedures:

1. Patients are encouraged to pay in full; however, if they are unable, a budget plan can be created to pay the outstanding balance over time. Any persons trained and authorized by the billing office can set up a budget plan.

2. The patient's account must be at a minimum balance greater than $50. If the balance is equal to or less than $150, it must be paid within three months; if greater than $150, within six months. Individual payments must be greater than $25 per payment period.

3. Budget plans are set up in the billing system. Upon establishing a budget plan, the system automatically generates a confirmation letter stating the patient's commitment to pay. In addition to the letter, the system generates a series of "coupons" that can be used by the patient to pay. Each coupon will have the amount and due date for every payment.

4. A specific account representative is assigned to follow up on delinquent budget plan accounts. Delinquent budget plan accounts are reviewed every week. A listing of delinquent (over 30 days since last payment) budget plan accounts will be printed each week.

5. Patients with delinquent accounts are given one month to make up the missed payment. If they fail to meet this schedule, the account will no longer be eligible for a budget plan, and the practice expects it to be paid in full. If the account is over 120 days old, it is made eligible for collection agency turnover. A standard letter is sent informing the patient of the change in the account status.

POLICY 18 Collection Agency

Policy: If a patient balance remains after patient balance follow-up, a minimum of 120 days has passed from date of posting, and it is determined that the patient balance will not be written off, the account will be turned over to a collection agency.

Procedures:

1. Patient balances will be considered for collection if the following are applicable:

    a. Patient balance is not paid in full;
    b. Patient balance exceeds the "automatic small balance adjustment amount;" and
    c. Patient does not comply with the payment plan or has failed to meet other commitments regarding his/her account balance made to the collection staff.

2. The practice management system will be configured to generate patient statements with progressively urgent statement (dunning) messages. The patient will be notified of the impending collection via collection notice and final notice letters.

3. If a patient balance is considered to be uncollectible after thorough follow-up, according to the amount of the patient balance, it will be considered for referral to a collection agency.

4. A list of patient accounts will be generated and forwarded to the agency. The list will include the data necessary for the collection agency to set up an account on its system for the patient.

5. _____ will be responsible for preparing patient accounts that will be turned over to a collection agency.

6. Prior to turning accounts over to collection, _____ will notify the appropriate provider of the account status using the form provided below.

7. If the provider has not responded within 10 days of the collection approval request, the account will be turned over to a collection agency in accordance with the practice's financial policy.

8. Any patient account balances transferred to a collection agency will be written off the accounts receivable using a bad-debt adjustment code. The patient will be

notified in writing via certified mail that s/he has been discharged from the practice. Appropriate time to find a new provider will be accommodated by the practice.

9. The patient account will be flagged as bad debt. This flag will be apparent when a patient attempts to schedule an appointment. The patient will be reminded that s/he has been discharged from the practice, and an appointment will not be scheduled until payment is received. Services will be denied except in the case of an emergency.

Collection Agency Accounts

Account number: _____

Patient name: _____

Follow-up attempted: _____

Reason for referral to agency: _____

Billing office staff signature: _____

Date: _____

If the provider does not wish the account to be referred to collection, the account information will be forwarded to _____, who will confer with the provider to determine the appropriate action to be taken. The account will be sent to collection or written off using the appropriate adjustment code.

Best Practices: What else can you do?

☐ *As mentioned earlier in the text, practices are shortening their collection cycles, and often the minimum days to collection agency transfer are much lower than 120 days.*

☐ *Most collection agencies can accept an electronic file and eliminate any paper production.*

☐ *Your practice should track recovery rates by agency and by time elapsed from transfer of account.*

☐ *Meet with your collection agency to determine what other measures you can take to improve your collections process.*

POLICY **19** Patient Correspondence

Policy: Written, telephone, or electronic (e.g., e-mail) correspondence from patients will be directed to the billing office for expedient follow-up and resolution.

Procedures:

1. The mail clerk will direct all written correspondence regarding patient billing to the billing office. The telephone operator will direct all calls regarding patient billing to the billing office.

2. Written and electronic inquiries will be directed to the staff member assigned to the payer type for the patient represented in the inquiry and/or to the staff member assigned to self-pay accounts. Telephone calls will be routed to the staff member(s) assigned to the phones for the day. Telephone duty will be rotated among staff members. No fewer than two staff members will be assigned to telephone duty, except under extenuating circumstances. Staff will be available from 8:30 to 4:30 p.m. daily to answer billing questions.

3. All inquiries will be documented in the patient's account to assure a mechanism for logging and tracking follow-up and resolution.

4. Guarantors of the account will be contacted within 48 hours to establish direct communication and inform them of the resolution process and procedures.

5. Pending inquiries will be reviewed on a weekly basis and staff members will follow up on the status to assure expedient resolution.

6. Consistent communication will be maintained with the patient or guarantor to convey steps being taken to resolve the issue.

7. Periodically, audits of communications from patients will be made to identify opportunities for performance improvement, such as registration accuracy. Logs will be provided to staff to track communication.

POLICY **20** Financial Hardship

Policy: Patients are expected to pay for services rendered. The practice will assist patients who indicate they are unable to meet their financial obligations resulting from care provided by our practice. Patients may be determined as eligible for partial-to-full discounts using the current poverty guidelines issued by the state.

Procedures:

1. Exclusions from this policy are:
   - Medical care defined as not medically necessary (cosmetic surgery, for example).
   - Services rendered to persons who are eligible, but have not applied for, medical insurance or assistance programs sponsored by federal, state or local government.

2. Financial hardship/charity care may be extended to those who qualify for **all four** of these reasons:

   a. The patient is not eligible for Medicaid, or is pending Medicaid approval;
   b. It is determined that the patient is unable to pay for services provided;
   c. The patient is unable to accept an installment payment arrangement; and
   d. The patient agrees to make payment at the time the discount is granted.

   For patients who identify themselves or who are identified by practice staff to be considered for financial hardship/charity care, staff will obtain financial information from the patient. Presumptive eligibility can be based on the patient's current status with state agencies [e.g., Food Stamp Program, Women, Infants and Children (WIC), etc.]. If such eligibility is not applicable, staff will ask patients to submit a copy of their last two paycheck stubs, current year federal 1040 tax return, and unemployment benefits check stubs (if applicable). The practice will assist patients as much as possible to compile their information.

3. The billing staff will determine eligibility for financial hardship or charity care. Discounts on charges will be calculated as follows:

Percent of state* poverty level	Discount
300%	30%
200%	50%
100%	75%
<100	100%

(*Figures shown are for example only; you can also use federal guidelines published by the U.S. Department of Health and Human Services.)

An adjustment code will be assigned to each level of discount.

4. The granting of the discount will be noted in the patient's account; however, the patient's account status will never be permanently designated as charity care or financial hardship. Staff will review the patient's status on a regular schedule.

POLICY 21 Bad Address

Policy: The billing staff will attempt to determine the reason for bad address information resulting in returned mail, and will obtain correct information for rebilling.

Procedures:

1. Staff will attempt to verify current address by investigating the patient's demographic information maintained in the medical record, the patient registration form and/or a thorough Internet search. Staff will contact the patient at all numbers (and e-mail address, if noted) listed on the registration form, and will call the emergency contact(s) listed by the patient to attempt to secure a current address.

2. If all efforts to secure a current address fail and the account becomes past due, the account may be referred to a credit bureau for additional information or may be referred to a collection agency.

3. All correspondence returned with a current address from the U.S. Postal Service will be immediately entered onto the patient's account on the information system and in the medical record, and a new statement will be sent to the patient.

4. Accounts with inaccurate address information will be flagged with an appropriate message to assure that no further correspondence is sent and that the patient address issue is immediately apparent if the patient attempts to schedule an appointment.

5. A subsequent appointment will not be scheduled for this patient (unless urgent or emergency services are required) until the balance is cleared and the deficient information is updated.

CHAPTER 10

Rightsizing the Billing Office

The key to an effective staffing organizational structure for the billing office is to recognize the end-to-end process required for the revenue cycle and to ensure that you can measure and monitor the hand-offs and performance outcomes at each step in the process.

Ask yourself four key questions when you are rightsizing the billing office:

- Do we have the right number of staff?
- Are they doing the right things?
- Are they able to devote sufficient time to their major tasks?
- Are staff members attending to the full revenue cycle?

Staffing levels vary based on productivity, payer mix, technology and other factors specific to each medical practice. If physicians are producing significantly above the industry average in volume, we would expect billing to be staffed at higher levels to reflect this enhanced productivity.

In this chapter, we provide insights into:

- Staffing the billing office
- Organizational structure
- Training and competency
- Incentive plans
- Communication strategies

Staffing the Billing Office

Many medical practices focus on claim denials by allocating additional staffing resources. Their motto seems to be "Just add one more person to fix the problem." The following case example depicts a scenario found in many medical practices.

Case Study: Staffing Strategies

Medical Practice Anywhere has the following claims track record:

100,000 claims per year submitted
20,000 claims per year (20 percent) denied due to the following reasons:

- 5,000 due to lack of insurance verification;
- 7,500 because diagnosis does not support medical necessity;
- 5,000 due to invalid procedure/diagnosis codes; and
- 2,500 because of various other reasons.

Should the practice add more staff to rework the denied claims based upon this case example? Many practices do. But we strongly recommend that a practice allocate resources to diagnose and treat the disease, not the symptom. That is, rather than add more employees to work a complex or broken process, identify the causes of the denials and correct them before you submit the claim. In this case study, you could choose to add or identify a staff member to perform insurance verification for every patient. Or you could bring in a coding specialist to review and update encounter forms and show how proper coding can reduce denials due to medical necessity.

Rightsizing staff in the billing office involves much more than simply adding staff to fix the problem. In rightsizing staff, we are looking for the right number of staff who are performing the right tasks and processes to enable a streamlined revenue cycle. The optimal staffing for back-end billing is approximately one staff member per 10,000 claims. If you have 100,000 annual claims in your practice, you should have approximately 10 full time equivalent (FTE) staff involved in back-end billing functions.[1]

---

[1] © 2004 Walker, Larch, Woodcock: *Day-to-Day Practice Operations*. Reprinted with permission.

The steps associated with rightsizing the billing office follow:

1. Determine how your staff spend their time.
2. Compare overall staffing with available benchmarks.
3. Determine benchmark measure of choice and identify specific full-time equivalent (FTE) levels required for tasks.
4. Identify performance workload ranges and compare these with suggested ranges to determine if there is opportunity for change.

If the performance is substandard, rather than have more staff involved in checking and re-checking work, train staff and provide them with additional tools and resources so they can perform at a high quality.

We now provide an example of rightsizing the billing office.

Step 1: Determine How Your Staff Spend Their Time

Have staff members estimate the number of hours devoted per day to particular tasks. Total the hours of all staff members and calculate the FTE levels associated with major billing and collection functions. Determine the hours that your staff spend on (1) insurance denial and follow-up, (2) patient inquiries and follow-up, (3) credit resolution, (4) payment posting and cash management, (5) claims and (6) other (including clerical support). To assist with this project, consider contacting the industrial engineering department of your local university and ask if a student is available to do the study for you.

Medical Practice Anywhere		
Major billing function	Hours/ week	FTE
Insurance follow-up	80	2.00
Patient follow-up	80	2.00
Refund processing	20	.50
Payment posting	60	1.50
Claims/statement generation	30	.75
Management and other	40	1.00
Total	310	7.75
Total annual claims		**100,000**

Step 2: Compare Overall Staffing with Available Benchmarks

Staffing indicators	Medical Practice Anywhere	Benchmark*
Billing FTE per 100,000 claims	7.75	10.00
Claims per biller	12,903	10,000

Source: © 2004 Walker, Larch, Woodcock. Reprinted with permission.

In this table, we have made a comparison of staffing per 100,000 claims. This is a better measure for comparison purposes than other available measures such as staffing per FTE physician or provider. Whether the claim is for $100 or $1,000, similar billing functions are required to capture the charge, enter the charge into the system, follow up on the account and post the payment.

Based on the above data, Medical Practice Anywhere has a total of 7.75 staff involved in billing functions compared with the benchmark of 10.00 staff. You should ask a number of questions at this stage in the rightsizing process: Is the medical practice outperforming benchmark levels by having lower billing staff but more productive ones? Or does the medical practice perhaps have insufficient staff to carry out billing functions in an optimal fashion?

For a more detailed staffing analysis, benchmark your billing staff by function, as demonstrated in the table below.

Step 3: Determine Benchmark Measure of Choice and Identify Specific FTE Levels Required for Tasks

Function	Medical Practice Anywhere			National benchmark*
	Hours/ week	FTE	FTE per 100,000 claims	FTE per 100,000 claims
Insurance denial and follow-up	80	2.00	2.00	4.15
Patient inquiries and follow-up	80	2.00	2.00	1.61
Credit resolution	20	.50	.50	.53
Payment posting/cash management	60	1.50	1.50	1.61
Claims	30	.75	.75	.93
Other	40	1.00	1.00	1.26
Total	310	7.75	7.75	10.05

© 2004 University HealthSystem Consortium–Association of American Medical Colleges Faculty Practice Solutions Center. Reprinted with permission. Figures include staff and management by function.

These staffing analyses can assist Medical Practice Anywhere in identifying areas in which resources may be allocated differently than they are at peer practices. These benchmarks will not provide Medical Practice Anywhere all of the answers to its staffing questions, but they will give the practice the data to determine where to carefully analyze and identify areas for improvement.

Step 4: Identify Performance Workload Ranges and Compare Staff Activity with the Ranges to Determine Areas of Opportunity

Like Medical Practice Anywhere, your practice has questions about the opportunity for improvement. In order to analyze this opportunity, we have provided three examples of Step 4 below. They reflect a comparison of a medical practice's actual performance workload ranges with that of expected workload ranges. Performing this type of analysis lets you question the current process that has been deployed, identify issues that may be associated with problem payers, provide educational opportunities for staff, pursue technological advances or take other action that may improve the staff's ability to perform within the expected workload range. Questions that you should ask for each of these examples include:

- Why are the staff performing at levels that vary from the expected range?
- Is there opportunity to improve the performance workload?
- How much are staff multitasking in this process? Is that impacting their efficiency in performing this function?
- What is different about our medical practice that others may not experience? (There may be valid reasons for a billing office that appears to be overstaffed. If, for example, one of your primary payers is workers' compensation, which requires medical documentation at periodic intervals and other in-depth manual intervention, your billing office may require more staffing resources for billing and collection processes.)
- Are the work processes the staff following encumbered or streamlined?
- Should we explore how other practices perform this function so we can see new ways to improve the process?

Answering these questions will help you review the tools and resources provided to the staff and the current processes established for this particular billing function. Conduct this type of analysis for each function of the billing and collection process to find areas where you can streamline the process.

Example 1:	**Payment posting**
Expectation:	525 – 875 transactions/day
Actual observed:	125 average transactions/day
Staff utilization:	14 – 24%

© 2004 Walker, Larch, Woodcock. *Reprinted with permission.*

In this example, when the practice asked itself why the staff was performing at a utilization level less than 25 percent for payment posting, the medical practice was able to see the impact of a policy decision it had made. The practice let each of the practice sites and specialties maintain their own database in the practice management system. Consequently, the payment posters had to post to 40 different databases. When you make analyses at this level, the financial impact of the policy decision is readily apparent.

Example 2:	**Insurance follow-up**
Expectation:	110 accounts/day*
Actual observed:	30 – 40 accounts/day
Staff utilization:	27 – 36%

© 2004 Walker, Larch, Woodcock. *Reprinted with permission.*

*Assumes a seven-hour productive day. It also assumes that one-third of the staff member's time is devoted to account research and resolution by telephone, one-third is devoted to account research and resolution by appeal and one-third is spent checking on claims status (by telephone or online) and rebilling the claim.

Again, when the practice asked why the actual performance workload ranges were low, it realized that the A/R for this medical practice was extremely dated. Many of the accounts were older than two years. The practice decided to declare some of the old A/R dead and to keep up with the newer accounts. When the practice implemented this decision, it recognized not only an improvement in staff morale but also an improvement in revenue, as staff were able to collect quickly on current account balances rather than waste time on accounts that had a very low probability of success.

Example 3:	**Patient inquiries regarding statements**
Expectation:	125 – 140 patient inquiries/day
Actual observed:	75 average patient inquiries/day
Staff utilization:	54 – 60%

© 2004 Walker, Larch, Woodcock. *Reprinted with permission.*

In this medical practice, all of the billing staff were responsible for answering the telephone whenever they could. Whoever was available to pick up the telephone did so. After performing this analysis, the practice determined that a focused unit to manage the patient inquiries would enhance staff productivity. In addition, the medical practice has decided to publish an e-mail account to permit patients to correspond with the practice electronically when they have questions about their accounts.

You can also use the performance workload ranges to determine the staff hours needed to perform billing functions and/or to correct past problem performance. The two examples that follow demonstrate the use of performance workload ranges to determine the estimated time to complete two critical billing functions.

Example 4:	**How long should it take to work the credit balance report?**
Expectation:	70 – 90 accounts/day
Basis of expectation:	Time to review account, investigate account, obtain explanation of benefits (EOB), copy backup, prepare refund request
Current state:	2,500 accounts in credit balance status
Calculation:	2,500/70 = 36 days;
	2,500/90 = 28 days
Range:	28 – 36 days

Conclusion: It would take 1.00 FTE working 1.27 to 1.64 months to completely resolve 2,500 accounts that are in credit balance status.

© 2004 Walker, Larch, Woodcock. Reprinted with permission.

Example 5:	**How many staff are needed to work a 600-page outstanding accounts receivable report?**
Expectation:	100 – 120 accounts/day fully worked
Assumptions:	Each page of the outstanding A/R report has 20 accounts. Fifty pages of the report reflect accounts in a current status (0 – 30 days), which do not need to be worked yet. Therefore, the number of accounts that need to be worked is 600 X 20 = 12,000 – 1,000 (50 X 20) = 11,000 accounts. All accounts should be fully worked within a one-month period.
Calculation:	11,000/100 = 110 days;
	11,000/120 = 92 days
Range:	92 – 110 days

Conclusion: To work the accounts in a one-month period, divide the numbers in the range by 22 working days. This example requires 4.18 to 5.00 staff FTE.

© 2004 Walker, Larch, Woodcock. Reprinted with permission.

Throughout this book, we have provided performance workload ranges by staff activity. Figure 10.1 is a summary of these ranges. These ranges can be helpful in determining opportunities for improvement, as well as analyzing your staffing needs.

As noted previously, the ability to perform within these ranges may vary due to internal practice-specific factors (such as facility layout, telephone system and practice management system). The workload ranges are based on a staff member peforming these functions approximately seven hours of productive time per day (allowing one hour for breaks, interruptions and other downtime). Note that the workload ranges reflect quantitative performance levels. It should be recognized that qualitative performance – accuracy, completeness, appropriateness and quality of these functions – should also be measured. When issues of quantity versus quality arise, we strongly recommend that quality be emphasized, even if the performance workload ranges for a particular function need to be relaxed from these levels.

FIGURE 10.1 Performance Workload Ranges by Activity		
Staff activities	**Per day**	**Per hour**
Appointment scheduling with patient demographics only	70 – 120	10 – 17
Appointment scheduling with full registration	50 – 75	7 – 11
Previsit registration with insurance verification	60 – 80	8 – 12
Referrals	70 – 90	10 – 13
Checkout with scheduling and cashiering	70 – 90	10 – 13
Checkout with scheduling cashiering and charge entry	60 – 80	8 – 12
Charge entry encounters (without registration)	375 – 525	55 – 75
Transactions (payment/adjustment) posted manually	525 – 875	75 – 125
Refunds researched and processed	70 – 90	10 – 13
Account follow-up research correspondence and resolve by phone	n/a	6 – 12
Account follow-up research correspondence and resolve by appeal	n/a	3 – 4
Account follow-up claims status check and rebill	n/a	12 – 60
Account follow-up, equal combination of above three activities	110	n/a
Self-pay follow-up	70 – 90	10 – 13
Self-pay correspondence processed and resolved	90 – 105	13 – 15
Patient billing inquiries	125 – 140	15 – 18

© 2004 Walker, Larch, Woodcock. Reprinted with permission.

Organizational Structures for the Billing Office

The next three figures outline different types of organizational structures for the billing office. The key to each of these formal structures is to have discrete billing and collection functions assigned to specific individuals so that you can establish and monitor accountabilities and performance expectations. When practices attempt to multitask staff, there is a tendency for tasks and responsibilities to fall through the cracks because no one person is responsible for the performance of a specific function.

We offer these organizational charts to give the reader examples of different typologies. Each of the organizations has established specific roles and responsibilities in the area of charge entry, account follow-up, reimbursement management and data controls. These typologies also reflect the importance of separation of duties to permit adequate internal controls.

Structure A outlines a billing office organization that small medical practices frequently adopt. We address the delineation of work functions and separation of duties through the formation of four separate units within the billing office: (1) data control, (2) charge entry and registration, (3) account follow-up and (4) coding and compliance. In this example, we identify leads for each of the first three units, with the billing office manager involved in coding and compliance functions.

FIGURE 10.2 **Billing Office Organizational Structure A**

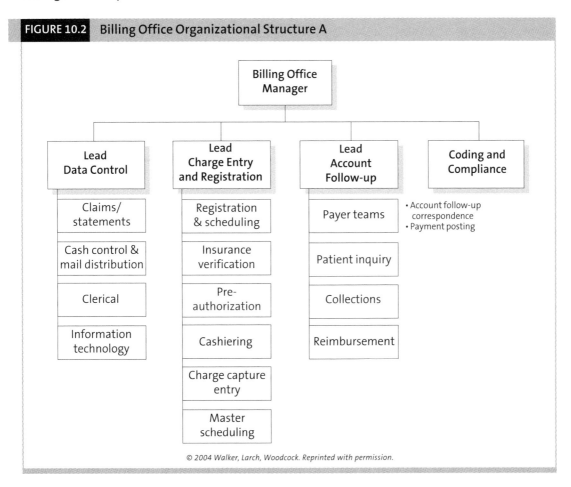

© 2004 Walker, Larch, Woodcock. Reprinted with permission.

We recommend structure B for a medium-sized medical practice. The billing manager works actively with an assistant manager in leading and directing five separate work units: (1) data control, (2) insurance billing/follow-up, (3) collections, (4) patient relations and (5) audit and compliance. Front-office staff involved in patient scheduling and patient check-in have a dotted-line reporting relationship to the assistant manager in the billing office. We have delineated an educational and training function, with the billing manager leading educational efforts.

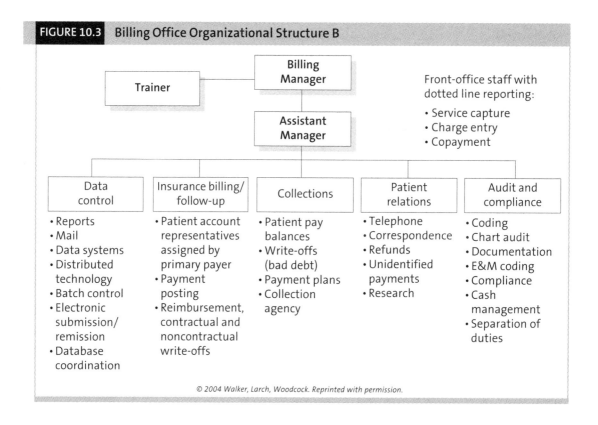

FIGURE 10.3 Billing Office Organizational Structure B

© 2004 Walker, Larch, Woodcock. Reprinted with permission.

The final example of billing office organization is often in place in large, multisite practices. In this structure, each of the practice sites has a billing lead position responsible for overseeing the billing and collection functions – patient scheduling, registration, cashiering and charge entry – performed at the site. These individuals have a dotted-line reporting relationship with the training and compliance office and serve as liaisons between the billing office and the practice sites. Within the central billing office, account follow-up and data control units provide separation of duties and permit oversight of focused roles and responsibilities.

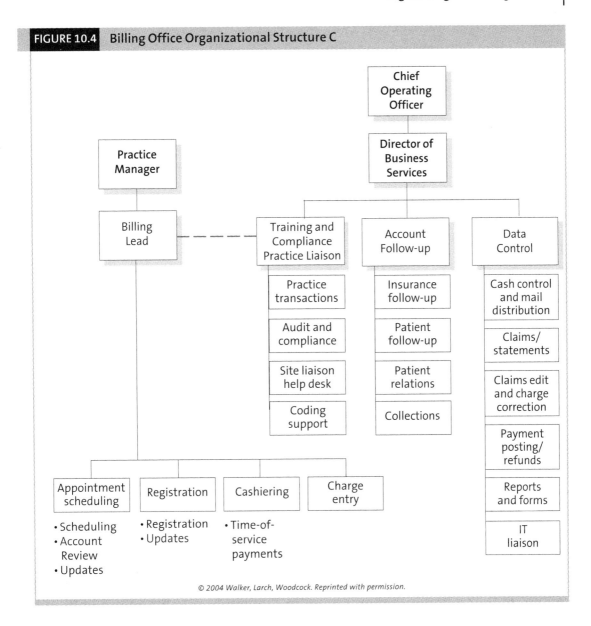

FIGURE 10.4   Billing Office Organizational Structure C

© 2004 Walker, Larch, Woodcock. Reprinted with permission.

Staff Training and Competency

If the local job market makes it difficult to recruit well-trained and knowledgeable staff, you will need to conduct internal training to develop competent employees. Ongoing education is necessary as well because third-party policies change rapidly.

Develop a formal training program for each functional area. Conduct competency assessments for any individuals who have access to your practice management system to ensure they know their assigned duties and responsibilities. Schedule regular, continuing updates in the form of seminars, tools, reading material, staff meetings and assignments to make sure employees are keeping up-to-date.

Conduct formal competency assessments before an employee uses the practice management software with "live" data. An untrained payment poster can wreak havoc on a system by inadvertently creating credit balances, selecting improper adjustment codes and failing to flag EOBs for appeal, requiring a great deal of time to reconstruct accounts on the system. An untrained employee performing patient check-in can select an improper payer for the patient, fail to recognize the need for pre-authorization and fail to collect time-of-service copayments, creating rework and escalating the cost of billing.

Conduct competency assessments at periodic intervals for current staff, not just new staff. Changes in billing and collection regulations, changes to practice management software and applications and changes to payer requirements underline the need to provide ongoing competency assessments.

You can obtain competency exams for billing and collection activities from a number of sources: These are included in the resource list at the end of this text. The following tools are examples of competency assessments for payment posting, general insurance and insurance card knowledge.

Tools 25, 26, 27: Sample Competency Assessments (see pages 163-164)
We have provided examples of competency assessments for critical functions in billing and collection to assist the medical practice in designing its own assessment instruments. These instruments will ensure that staff have the knowledge and understanding of key workload components.

COMPETENCY ASSESSMENT: CHARGE ENTRY

Demonstrate the following activities involved in the charge entry process:

	Competency Level	
	Satisfactory	Unsatisfactory
1. Creating invoices	_____	_____
2. Interpreting the encounter form	_____	_____
3. Posting office/outpatient charges	_____	_____
4. Posting inpatient charges	_____	_____
5. Linking procedure and diagnosis codes	_____	_____
6. Printing and balancing charge summaries	_____	_____

© 2004 Walker, Larch, Woodcock. Reprinted with permission.

COMPETENCY ASSESSMENT: PAYMENT POSTING

Demonstrate the following activities involved in the payment posting:

	Competency Level	
	Satisfactory	Unsatisfactory
1. Posting from EOBs	_____	_____
2. Posting patient payments	_____	_____
3. Posting insurance take-backs	_____	_____
4. Creating and posting refunds	_____	_____
5. Determining adjustment codes	_____	_____
6. Flagging EOBs for secondary billing	_____	_____
7. Flagging EOBs for $0 or low payment	_____	_____
8. Printing and balancing receipt summaries	_____	_____

© 2004 Walker, Larch, Woodcock. Reprinted with permission.

27 COMPETENCY ASSESSMENT: INSURANCE KNOWLEDGE

Demonstrate the following activities requiring general insurance knowledge:

	Competency Level	
	Satisfactory	Unsatisfactory
1. Insurance types and products	_____	_____
2. Determining eligibility	_____	_____
3. Determining primary/secondary coverage	_____	_____
4. Determing copayments, deductibles, coinsurance	_____	_____
5. Identifying when waivers are needed	_____	_____
6. Prior authorization – how and when needed	_____	_____
7. Interpreting an insurance card	_____	_____
8. Explaining a statement to a patient	_____	_____

© 2004 Walker, Larch, Woodcock. Reprinted with permission.

Accountability for Results

The key to performance management of billing and collection staff is holding individuals accountable for results. When staff are multitasking, you will have a difficult time assessing who is responsible for specific functions, problems or stellar results. By developing a performance management process that takes into account performance outcomes as well as specific functions and tasks, you can focus on accountability for performance.

Managing performance involves not only a job description outlining functions and tasks, but the outcomes expected of the staff member. You can include the performance workload ranges in the performance management process, holding staff accountable for this quantity of work. More importantly, assess the qualitative indicators related to accuracy of work functions. You can do this using a sampling of a staff member's work product. For example, you can assess the workload accuracy of a payment poster via a sampling of EOBs throughout the month. You can assess the workload accuracy of a staff member responsible for registration information relative to claim edits and claim denials. Include these types of performance indicators as a formal part of the performance management process. It is, after all, *performance outcomes* that your medical practice needs to ensure efficient and effective billing and collection.

Consider implementing specific performance indicators per employee as part of the performance management process. Track statistics by employee weekly via user codes. Some common indicators include the following:

- Dollars collected by payer according to collector responsibility;
- Aged A/R by payer;
- Percentage of receivables by payer over 120 days;
- Write-offs by category; and
- Bad debt percentage by collector responsibility.

Incentive Compensation Plans

A number of medical practices have established incentive compensation plans for billing staff. These plans have tended to focus on only one or a select few measures in the billing and collections process. For example, a popular incentive plan rewards billing staff for enhancing collections by 2 to 5 percent. Unfortunately, this type of incentive plan has drawbacks as staff may set aside other important billing and collection tasks if the aim is solely to enhance short-term collection performance.

Another type of incentive plan for billing staff consists of a collection of measures at the individual, team, specialty and/or practice level. Here are two examples of these types of incentive plans:

Incentive Plan 1

Billing staff are eligible to receive both individual and group performance bonuses for a total of $200 per quarter. Each quarter, $100 is available for *individual performance*. It is awarded for the following performance outcomes:

- Days in A/R is less than 55 on the account for which the staff member is responsible (here's where there may be some variance depending on your specialty and/or payer);

- Percent of A/R greater than 120 days is less than 10 percent on the account for which the staff member is responsible (again, perhaps there will be some variance depending on your specialty and/or payer); and

- A review of 10 sample accounts pulled at random results in 100 percent of accounts appropriately worked and documented.

In addition, another $100 is available each quarter based on *group or team* performance. The performance outcomes for this portion of the incentive include:

- Days in A/R is less than 55 (at the group or team level);

- Percent of A/R greater than 120 days is less than 10 percent (at the group or team level); and

- Cash collections are greater than $500,000 (the dollar threshold obviously depends on your medical practice).

As demonstrated in this example, a combination of individual and group or team incentive is used to provide financial recognition and rewards for billing and collection performance outcomes.

Incentive Plan 2

In this plan, individuals are able to earn up to 10 percent of their gross salary each year based on individual, team and practice goals.

- Sixty percent of the plan is tied to the individual's performance based on his/her job-specific competencies; the practice identifies individual goals at the beginning of the year. Based on the *individual's performance*, the employee can earn 0 to 6 percent of his/her gross salary. The employee must attain a minimum level of individual performance before s/he is eligible for the team or total practice incentive.

- The *team (or specialty) incentive* is 30 percent of the bonus plan and is tied to team collections, percent of claims suspended on edit list, charge entry lag and percent of A/R over 90 days. These elements are weighted in importance. The team incentive criteria are not tied together, so a staff member can be eligible for a portion of the team incentive if the charge entry lag hits the target and none of the other targets are reached.

- The final goal measures a performance outcome that is *practice-wide*: The incentive payment equals 10 percent of the potential incentive. In this example, the practice-wide incentive is total practice collections – because the practice has to collect enough cash to fund the incentive pool. The practice-wide goal is a stretch goal for the entire group and is not always reached.

Ask a number of questions when you're developing an incentive plan for billing and collection staff. These include:

Who to reward? Because the entire revenue cycle involves all levels of the organization, who should be included in the incentive plan?

Reward individual or team/unit performance? Should individuals be incentivized for their own work or should the performance of the overall team or unit be the focus for the incentive? Or both?

Reward short-term or long-term goals? Should the medical practice incentivize monthly performance, or should it take a more long-term view of performance?

Provide financial or nonfinancial rewards? Are there ways to reward our employees – and motivate them – that don't involve money?

Staff Communication Strategies

Involve staff in problem-solving and decision-making regarding billing and collection functions and tasks. Encourage staff to bring suggestions for resolution along with the problem. Share information with staff — A/R status, payment posting status, copayment collection percentages, insurance snapshots, credentialing status, payer updates and more.

Hold weekly meetings with all staff, including the billing staff. Use these meetings to educate staff on specific billing issues and to share key data related to performance expectations involving the entire revenue cycle. Share data from front-end and back-end billing functions with all staff so they can see their performance in relation to their peers and manage their workload with appropriate priorities. To keep up with policies and procedures, review a billing policy or procedure each week to (1) maintain knowledge currency among staff and (2) update the policy consistent with changes in regulatory guidelines and/or local policies and procedures.

In medical practices that have actively engaged staff in process improvement efforts and in leading change, staff can cite current performance of billing outcomes. For example, they know the current dollars outstanding or the percent of A/R greater than 120 days. Share this type of data routinely and identify action items, the responsible party and deadlines to ensure staff resolve the problems and achieve expected performance outcomes.

As we discussed in this chapter, your staff need to be actively engaged in your billing and collection operation. You need the right staff doing the right things in order to achieve optimal revenue performance. Ongoing education, communication and competency assessments ensure that staff have the knowledge and tools to perform the key functions of your revenue cycle.

CHAPTER 11

Leveraging Technology in the Billing Office

Technology offers a wealth of opportunities to save staff time and financial resources in the billing office. At the heart of technology lies the practice management system, but you can harness additional automation to assist managers and staff in ensuring timeliness and accuracy in professional fee billing. In this chapter we discuss the key features of practice management systems and explore technology to enhance the efficiency and effectiveness of your revenue cycle.

In this chapter, we cover:

- Practice management systems
- Electronic funds transfer and payment posting
- Document management
- Additional technology to enhance your revenue cycle
- Information technology support
- Information technology priority and action list

Practice Management Systems

A practice management system is the information technology hardware and software that a medical practice uses to capture registration and insurance information and to conduct billing and collections, along with a number of other operational applications. Integrating billing and collection with other critical patient flow and business of medicine processes is necessary to ensure a streamlined and effective billing and collection process.

There are major differences between practice management systems. Initiate a formal request for proposal when you're seeking a new practice management system to ensure that a number of options are considered for the practice.

Key features of a practice management system include:

- Hardware capacity and upgradability;

- Software functions (capitation support, referrals/authorizations, provider file maintenance claims management, claims scrubbing, accounts receivable management, collections management, expected fee schedule, productivity tracking, report-writer and data access);

- Operational systems applications (medical record tracking, laboratory ordering and reporting, appointment scheduling, electronic medical record, radiology and imaging ordering and reporting, prescription ordering and reporting, chart label generation, address label generation, credit card verification, electronic mail, clinical data transmission);
  - interface capability, with order entry or other hospital systems;
  - software design;
  - integrated systems;
  - security hierarchy;
  - data entry management;
  - online help functions;
  - user-defined options;
  - vendor support;
  - management reporting; and
  - storage (scanning of EOBs or storing on CD-ROM, local area network [LAN] or secure Web site)

Electronic Funds Transfer and Payment Posting

Processing checks manually can take hours, if not days, even in the most efficient billing offices. It often involves copying every check for internal controls and having someone drive to the bank to deliver the checks in the middle of the day. This staff time is costly, and may be unnecessary if your insurance carriers offer electronic funds transfer (EFT).

EFT means that the insurance carrier directly transmits the funds it owes you to your bank account. Instead of a live check, the carrier sends along a "remittance advice" – a document that lets you know how much has been deposited and to what accounts the money belongs. It eliminates internal control concerns because you're not dealing with a live check, and it's faster cash flow than you can handle with your daily bank run.

Just as manually processing checks is time consuming and inefficient, so is the manual posting of payments, and in the latter case, a single incorrect keystroke can mean a tremendous amount of staff time to research and fix the error. This process must be done with complete accuracy, yet this is where new – and untrained – billing office staff normally start. Given that they are under pressure to key as many payments as possible, the environment breeds mistakes.

Automate the payment posting process with electronic payment remittance (EPR). EPR posts the payments in your practice management system for you, eliminating manual payment posting altogether. Any payments that are not posted in your system automatically, for whatever reason, are reported to you so that you can manually review them. Manual payment posting can take a staff member an entire day, but with EPR the process takes less than an hour. Only a small portion of commercial carriers offer this, but many Medicare and Medicaid intermediaries have used it with success. Try combining it with EFT, and you'll have your payments posted and your money in the bank without anyone lifting a finger.

Document Management

You can save staff time and overhead by better managing the mounds of paperwork handled by the billing office every day. Access to electronic records through an electronic medical record (EMR) or a document management system allows you to store and query the document – or the image of it – electronically. That is, you don't need the actual paper.

Here are a few ideas for using the technology:

- Scan every patient's insurance card at registration. Set up your EMR or document imaging system to attach the electronic image of the cards to the patient's account. The billing office can access the image without having to pull the patient's chart to find the photocopy of the card (satellite offices can review it also). Unless it's integrated in your EMR, you'll need to buy a terminal and software, but it's quite inexpensive. Or your practice management system vendor might include this in your system.

- Better performing billing offices appeal denied claims, and they include in each appeal a copy of the documentation of the encounter. Instead of searching medical records for operative reports or office notes, scan them into your document management system or pull them from your EMR.

- If your practice submits secondary claims, you're pulling the primary EOBs to attach to the secondary. Instead, scan them and find them electronically.

- If you have mounds of paper related to referrals and authorizations, try integrating them into your EMR or document management system. Instead of an elaborate filing system, scan in the completed referral or authorization paperwork or design a template to capture the information in your EMR. When a claim needs an authorization number, find it in your EMR or document management system instead of a filing cabinet.

- If your carriers don't offer EPR, you could consider a sophisticated document management solution to eliminate manual payment posting. Scan each explanation of benefits (EOB) into a template (based on the layout of the payer's EOB) that you've programmed to integrate with the payment posting process of your practice management system, and post the payments automatically.

- If you have a high volume of calls from patients about their accounts, or patients asking for copies of their statements at tax time, consider scanning your patient statements.

- Scan encounter forms or post charges directly into your EMR — interface with your practice management system to post the charges without any manual intervention.

Of course, you can scan any piece of paper in your office, so the sky's the limit. If scanning registration forms or surgery schedules would help, go for it.

Additional Technology to Enhance Your Revenue Cycle

A number of electronic tools and information systems can make your office more efficient.

Staff Performance Management

Before you lose money because of an overwhelmed or uneducated staff, integrate employee performance measurements into your practice management system. Most systems have the technology, but often don't use it because supervisors find it cumbersome and meddlesome. Yet it's often easy to use and truly beneficial for the supervision of employee performance. The technology can track data by employee, including volume of accounts worked.

Online Statements

Paper patient statements normally cost 40 to 55 cents to generate and mail, and that can add up quickly. Online statements or e-mailing them costs a fraction of that amount, and can improve your cash flow. Consider online statements in a secure area of your Web site. Include in your Health Insurance Portability and Accountability Act (HIPAA) or registration forms a paragraph, with which your patients can mark their agreement, regarding your new paperless statements. You should continue sending paper statements to those patients who balk, but you'll be surprised at how many love the service. Go one step further and accept payment via your Web site with a secure credit card transaction.

Contract Compliance

If you're relying on your payment posters to see if you've been paid correctly, we can guarantee that your system isn't working very well. Because the majority of practices are dealing with more than 50 payers' fee schedules and reimbursement policies, and hundreds of procedure codes, it's impossible to memorize them all. Underpayments are a serious risk and there is software available that will match actual payments against projected payments. Ask your vendor about its ability to help you identify underpayments and explore contract compliance software that can be integrated into your practice management system.

Scrubbing

As we discussed previously, there are automated systems employed by the payers that scrub your claims as they come in the payer's door. Insurance carriers use sophisticated technology to edit the claims before adding human edits to them. After the encounters have all been coded, scrubbing software – either stand-alone or integrated with your practice management system – uses logic to indicate which codes are wrong or not billable. Instead of waiting until the claim comes back as denied by the payer, edit your claims yourself. Given the complexities of all of the edits now employed by insurance carriers, you won't catch all of the problems, but catching just one will leave you better off.

Denial Management

Use automated standard appeal letters that allow your billers to easily describe the specifics of the claim you're appealing. If you don't want to purchase expensive software, set up the templates in a word processing program. Instead of keeping a manual calendar for a reminder about when the appeal was sent or when payment is expected, use the calendar function of your software.

Interactive Voice Response (IVR)

Traditionally used exclusively by telemarketers, IVR technology is now being deployed to manage patient collections. Instead of spending hours of staff time just to reach patients' answering machines, an IVR system can automatically dial number after number. When a patient picks up, the call can be transferred automatically to a biller to handle the call.

Referrals and Authorizations

If you accept referrals or authorizations from a referral source, put your referral forms on a CD-ROM, and drop it by your referring physicians' offices. Ask them to complete the form each time they refer a patient (thus saving you a lot of work) and e-mail it via a secure link to you. If patients are added to your schedule during the day and need an authorization, send an internal e-mail to all staff involved, including the billing office or staff who will process the referral or authorization. Attach the particulars about the patient's account and flag the e-mail as important; then let the authorization process begin.

Reporting

If you're tired of getting incomplete reports from your practice management system, or need information that your practice management system simply isn't designed to give you, there are software applications that can interface with your system to extract data and allow you to manipulate the data in a form that you can use. You can create custom reports without waiting weeks for your vendor to get to your request – as well as avoiding the expense of it. Most extract the data to a spreadsheet program such as Microsoft® Excel or a database program like Microsoft® Access. Some practice management systems embed this feature in their software, or you can invest in stand-alone products.

Charge Capture and Coding

As the coding rules have become more complex, there are more electronic tools on the market to help practices muddle through the madness. Use one of the many software programs for coding and charge capture on a personal digital assistant (PDA) – or develop your own. PDAs are also a great place to store a list of patients for hospital rounds, medication contraindications and formularies, procedure scheduling and so forth. Look for a coding and charge capture product that allows for a direct, wireless interface with your practice management system.

Communication

Use e-mail and instant messaging to communicate internally about staff meetings, policy changes, or general announcements. Instant messaging can also be handy to alert staff to immediate issues, such as when a patient with bad debt presents to the front desk. The receptionist can instant message the billing office to come to the front office to handle it. Instead of causing a scene, or violating the patient's confidentiality, the communication to the billing office can be handled with ease. That said, recognize that these channels may not be secure; add encryption or set policies to avoid transmitting a patient's personal health information.

Payer Interface

If you're sending your claims through a clearinghouse, look into direct transmission of claims. A number of payers offer direct transmission at little or no cost; some even accept claims through their Web site or Web portal. It saves you costs, and most payers will train you, as it saves them money as well.

Information Technology Support

No matter what technology you deploy, you need solid technological support for your practice management software so you can minimize system downtime. The technology is sophisticated enough that your IT specialist should be versed in medical practice software. For small medical practices, an outsourcing arrangement may work best. Larger medical practices often realize the benefits of having their own on-site support.

Information Technology Priority and Action List

To ensure that the billing office receives appropriate levels of priority by your IT department, maintain a running priority list of projects, the responsible party and deadlines. Practice leaders should regularly review this list, noting priority discrepancies, with the appropriate individual held accountable for performance results. In some practices, the billing office is not afforded the same priority in terms of technology needs as is, for example, an EMR or in the case of a practice affiliated with a hospital, hospital IT needs. You may need to bring the IT issues associated with your practice management system and billing office to an individual who can give priority to professional fee billing needs.

The efficiency and performance of your billing operation can be greatly enhanced by technology. Although it's a tremendous asset to have an EMR, the billing office can benefit from a myriad of technology applications – from simple to sophisticated.

CHAPTER 12

The Debate: Centralize, Decentralize or Outsource?

Medical practices, particularly large ones or those with more than one site, must make a decision regarding centralization or decentralization of the billing office. Many practices also ponder whether to outsource billing. Although there are no hard and fast rules, we define centralized billing offices as those with all functions and responsibility for the billing process residing in a staff unit that is separate (often geographically) from the rest of the practice staff. A decentralized billing office means that all functions stay at the practice site; for a multisite practice, each site has its own insurance follow-up staff working the accounts for that particular practice.

There are advantages and disadvantages to each approach: We do not intend to indicate a bias toward any method based on the order we discuss them. Each medical practice needs to assess its own particular circumstances in order to resolve the centralization, decentralization and outsourcing question.

In this chapter, we discuss:

- Advantages of decentralization
- Advantages of centralization
- Outsourcing

Advantages of Decentralization

The key advantage of decentralization is that the billing staff is closer, emotionally and physically, to the medical practice. This facilitates communication and information exchange between physicians and billing staff and contributes to the development of a team approach between the front-office and billing office. Billing costs typically are lower in a decentralized model.

Loyalty to the Organization

Particularly in large organizations, the billing staff's loyalty to the organization tends to decrease when billing is centralized because employees are farther removed from the physicians, and, just as importantly, from the patients. The centralized business office (CBO) manager can create the same loyalty, but it is difficult, particularly given that many billing employees formerly worked directly with or for physicians. It is much more difficult to be loyal to a central billing operation than it is to be loyal to a physician, provider or manager at the practice site.

Relationship with the Physician

A key component of the billing process is charge capture and coding. Speed and accuracy are critical, and they depend heavily on the relationship with the physician. Employees in a decentralized setting can easily ask the physician questions: "Did you mean to put this modifier with this procedure code?" or "Do you have some time to review the linkages of the multiple procedure codes and diagnosis codes for this patient?" In a CBO structure, interaction with the physicians may require filling out a form, faxing it to the provider and waiting a few days – or even weeks – for it to be returned. The staff time, as well as the time the charge is held, can really add up.

Patient Collections

If you centralize billing and remove it from the practice, staff can quickly take the "it's not my job" attitude. Many front-office staff assume that since their billing colleagues have been shipped down the road, so too has the work. Freed of billing duties, they make no qualms about telling patients to call the CBO if they have questions. At times we have witnessed front-office staff refuse to accept payment of prior account balances: They told the patient to "send it to the CBO." At the same time, the CBO is desperate to get these same patients on the telephone. Thus follow-up work may expand at the CBO, even though the front-office staff could easily collect payments at the time of service.

The Unit of Work Does Not Change

The unit of work in physician billing, which is a claim, remains largely unchanged whether it is centralized or decentralized. Staff still have to key the charge, edit and transmit the claim, process the denial, post the payment and call the payer. Although it's easier to stay current with payer requirements in a CBO because of its expanded and focused resources, the time to perform the work is the same whether it is performed centrally or not.

A CBO Adds More Activities – and Costs

Because a practice may have functioned without a CBO for years, a CBO almost always adds several new resources. These include coding, compliance, reporting, contract analysis, training and application support. Clearly, practices need these activities in today's health care environment, but for many practices, they represent new costs. These new resources are not without a price – though some do contribute directly to increased revenue.

Communication

It is easier to communicate in a decentralized billing office. Paper, telephone calls and e-mails fly back and forth between the practice and the CBO. When places of business are disjointed, communication is difficult to maintain. So, what happens is ... *meetings*. The CBO management team spends a significant amount of time in meetings, making sure everyone is current with data, information and reporting. This heightened communication can have its advantages in terms of staying current with coding and reimbursement issues, but it also has a cost in staff time and resources.

Advantages of Centralization

A centralized billing office can be more focused on aspects of billing such as performance monitoring, compliance and coding. In addition, a larger billing office often justifies the purchase and use of time-saving information systems. Centralized billing offices are often disconnected from the physicians, however, and typically result in higher billing costs for a practice.

Communication

Because the billing employees are under one roof, communication about billing issues can be swift and effective. If a payer bulletin publishes information about billing for a new service, staff or managers can communicate it very quickly throughout the CBO.

Compliance

In a large organization without centralization, it is difficult to keep compliance in check. There are a number of ways that the billing process can become noncompliant. It is critical to recognize that the medical practice is responsible for everything that happens in its billing process. By centralizing the refund process, monitoring coding, managing internal controls, and standardizing policies and procedures via centralization, the organization may reduce its business risk.

Performance Monitoring

By forming a CBO, a practice takes tasks that multiple staff members once performed and locates them into single functions so that one employee performs only these tasks. The CBO can therefore track and monitor performance, including accuracy rates for payment posters and productivity measures, such as number of transactions posted per day.

Expert Management

An organization with a CBO can employ a manager who is focused and professionally trained to manage billing and collection operations rather than a manager who has this responsibility as one of many. Sophisticated management can improve performance.

Training

A practice can perform targeted orientation and training that can bring results. As the medical practice environment gets increasingly sophisticated, it is hard to train on the job. A CBO can offer training and expertise to new employees, as well as competency assessments for all employees. Although this is possible in a decentralized environment, it is much easier in a centralized one.

Information Systems

Typically, capital for information systems and technology is more readily available in large, centralized practices. To pay off, however, those "bigger and better" systems really have to save money by automating processes or improving revenue by catching mistakes. Medical practices are often sold by the fact that technology can perform such tasks, but the implementation or processes often do not capture these positive effects because the training, implementation or even the users are inadequate.

Shared Accounts

If the medical practice is billing for multiple physicians who cross specialty lines, a CBO can work accounts that are shared by different specialties. For example, patients who undergo surgery are also likely to have anesthesia, pathology and radiology services. A practice can organize billing and collection teams to include surgical specialties with these ancillary services, with this integrated team fully working the account.

There is no right answer as to how to structure your billing office, yet the practices with the best performance in accounts receivable have found effective results from a hybrid model that combines the best features of both decentralization and centralization.

To Outsource or Not to Outsource?

For those of you contemplating outsourcing, we recommend that you conduct a formal analysis of your practice to see if outsourcing is for you. An outsourcing arrangement must ensure that the dollars invested generate a positive return. That is, you should outsource only if you are going to boost revenue or save money.

Next, you need to consider the outsourcing service or product. There are four basic factors to consider: control, performance, communication and cost. To illustrate, we will review the four factors in terms of outsourcing your billing operation:

Control

Physicians must have the ability to control the quality of the outsourced product or service. This is especially important with billing, a process for which physicians are responsible whether it is managed in-house or at an outside billing service.

Performance

To achieve a positive outcome, the performance of the outsourcing service must be equal to or greater than that of the in-house service. Gauge the performance of the billing service by measuring its three critical indicators – percentage of A/R over 120 days, days in A/R and net collection rate – against industry standards. This indicates the current level of performance and the opportunities for improvement.

Communication

No matter what product or service is being considered, effective communication is essential. By its nature, outsourcing hampers the communication channel, but hiring a good internal or external manager can bridge the gap. Also, ask for and call the references of the billing vendor to inquire about the effectiveness of its communication methods.

Cost

The cost of the product or service must be equal to or less than the cost of managing the product or service in house. Otherwise, why bother? The cost of the billing operation should be considered as a percent of collections or revenue. Typical billing costs for back-end billing range from 4 percent for surgery practices to 12 percent for emergency medicine practices, with primary care and most medical specialists somewhere in the middle around 8 percent (See Chapter 13 and Figure 13.7 for a detailed discussion of billing costs). Comparing your costs against these industry averages should indicate whether there are opportunities for improvement.

After analyzing these four factors, ask yourself the following questions:

- How much control must I have over the management of this service? Can I afford to give up some control?

- What is the current performance of the service? Do I believe that someone else can do it better? How much better?

- What level of communication do I need to manage the service? Can I afford to reduce that level?

- What is the current cost of managing the service? Do I believe that I can operate the service at a lower cost? How much lower?

- Which is most challenging for my practice – front-end billing or back-end billing?

Look for a compelling answer to all of these questions (and others that might arise). In other words, be sure that the overall performance of the outsourced billing service will be improved and the cost will be lower. If one of these two factors is achievable, and another is neutral, that may be acceptable as well. However, the control and communication levels must be equally maintained, so make sure that outsourcing does not drop below acceptable levels.

If your medical practice has outsourced your billing and collection process to an external billing vendor, document the scope of services to be performed and the performance expectations of the billing vendor and review these expectations at least annually.

The following billing and collection services are typically included in the scope of services for billing vendors:

Pricing and coding: Analysis of codes used, suggestions to improve accurate coding of services performed; fee schedule analysis and recommendations

Registration and charge entry: Demographic updates, new registration, charge entry

Account management and follow-up: Accounts receivable evaluation, follow-up on insurance and patient pay balances, telephone follow-up with patients, claims appeals, customer service support with office hours from 8 a.m. to 5 p.m., automated services for off-hour and weekend messages

Payment posting: Ensuring consistency with expected levels of reimbursement, billing secondary payers, line-item posting, validation of bank totals and reconciliation of month-end and daily batch runs to deposits, management of credit balances

Cash management/financial: Development of payment plans, appropriate separation of duties, cash management controls, time-of-service payment programs, banking and/or lockbox services, financial reconciliation, budget variance analysis

Production: Patient billing statements, paper claims, e-claims

Information systems support: Support for peripheral devices, daily backup/month-end process, computer maintenance, version updates, module updates

Compliance and legislative updates: Established compliance program, legislative updates communicated to practices and physicians as appropriate

Management reporting: Standardized reports delivered at specific days following month-end, ad hoc reports as required

Physician education: Coding, changes in billing guidelines, chart documentation, dictation

Staff education: Front-office staff related to insurance pre-authorization, pre-existing condition exceptions, insurance validation, payment policies, charge entry, time-of-service collections, patient account history

Meetings with physicians: Monthly meetings to review charges, collections, capitation, accounts receivables, collection requests, coding issues

Meetings with administration: Quarterly meetings to review management reports, problems and issues; additional meetings to discuss and plan for changes to billing and collection practices pursuant to federal or state requirements, plan changes, etc.

Optional services: The following services are typically considered optional, often with additional associated fees:

- Enrollment and credentialing: Completion of credentialing packets, follow-up on credentialing status;

- Charge capture, charge controls: Procedures to ensure inpatient and outpatient charge capture, for example, comparison with patient schedules, admission, discharge and transfer reports;

- Contract analysis and negotiation: Evaluation of managed care contracts from an economic and business basis on specialty, assistance in negotiating managed care and capitation agreements;

- Physician coding/audit compliance: Chart audits to determine coding and audit compliance;

- Managed care analysis: In-depth review of capitation performance, including utilization management statistics and analysis; and

- Collection agency: Pursuit of patient payments owed to the practice, skip tracing, legal collections.

The cost of outsourcing varies significantly based on the services that the vendor offers. In addition to the services, however, it is critical to evaluate the vendor's performance. Like many products and services, it may be worth it to pay more if you are realizing better quality and performance.

Many practices make a decision to outsource only a portion of the billing process. In fact, the majority of practices send their past-due accounts to a collection agency, which is a form of outsourcing, and many outsource patient statement mailing. There is no formula to guarantee the best results for the least investment. You must make a careful review of your internal strengths and weaknesses, as well as the sources available to you, before you can select the processes to outsource. With proper planning and research, you can choose the best organizational structure for your practice and determine if all or a part of the billing process should be managed by an external party.

CHAPTER 13

Managing and Analyzing the Revenue Cycle

When a practice experiences low collections, physician and administrative leaders often focus attention on accounts receivable follow-up to determine what went wrong. This narrow view does not permit a medical practice to examine *leading* indicators in the practice that may have contributed to the low collection levels. In this chapter we explore the reasons for low collections and present reimbursement management techniques that a practice can employ to ensure that it is receiving expected revenue levels. We also benchmark the performance of the revenue cycle and present methods to evaluate the cost of your billing and collections operation.

In this chapter, we cover:

▓ Benchmarking billing and collection performance

▓ Reasons for low collections – leading financial indicators

▓ Calculating the cost of your billing and collection operation

▓ Reimbursement management techniques

▓ Keys to management reporting

▓ Billing policies and procedures

Benchmarking Billing and Collection Performance

How do you know if your billing operation is performing well? This is a critical question because the financial viability of a medical practice depends on the performance outcomes of its physician billing process. In this section, we will provide benchmarks for key performance measures so that you can determine whether your revenue cycle is performing at optimal levels.

Net Collection Rate

The net collection rate lets you know how much money you collected of the money you could have collected. It is a ratio of cash to the net charges (net charges are gross charges minus contractual adjustments agreed to as part of the practice's contracts). For example, if the procedure code is priced at $125, but the contractual allowance (the money that you have agreed to write off as a function of your contract) is $50, then the billing office should be held accountable for collecting $75 rather than the full price of the code.

Many benchmarking sources use a definition of the net collection rate that permits deductions for non-contractual adjustments, bad debt, charity care and other similar adjustments. By adding deductions beyond contractual adjustments, the medical practice is essentially "accepting" its current level of bad debt and non-contractual adjustments, rather than minimizing these types of adjustments. When you're comparing your medical practice's net collection rate with benchmark sources, read the data definitions carefully and adjust your calculation accordingly to ensure you are benchmarking accurately.

Calculation: This is (collections less refunds) divided by (gross charges less contractual adjustments). *Note*: Gross charges minus contractual adjustments is also referred to as net charges.

Expected outcome: We recommend an overall net collection rate of 95 percent or greater. When you examine a collections analysis report that links gross charges with collections by dates of service, you should see an increase in the net collection rate over time. The difference between the net collection rate and 100 percent includes bad debt, A/R in transition and administrative errors. If your practice experiences a higher than normal amount of charity care, it will be difficult to achieve a net collection rate in the high 90s.

We are not recommending that you benchmark your *gross collection rate* to other practices. The gross collection rate is calculated as: collections divided by gross charges. This rate is highly subject to interpractice fee variation as well as interpractice payer mix fluctuations. The net collection rate represents a more advanced performance indicator and lets you benchmark billing outcomes against other medical practices, even those with dissimilar payer mix and fee schedules.

Days in Accounts Receivable

Days in accounts receivable translates the dollar value of the current accounts receivable into the number of days of gross fee-for-service charges. It tells you how long it takes, on average, to collect a day's worth of charges. You calculate it by taking the total accounts receivable and dividing it by the average daily gross charges (based on 365 days). It is of note that although the industry standard is the average daily charge over a year, this method can lead to misleading fluctuations in days in A/R for practices with seasonal variability in production (for example, an allergy practice). To control for the fluctuation, management can use the average daily charge based on the last one to three months.

Calculation: This is total accounts receivable/(12 months of gross charges/365).

Expected outcome: This varies by specialty and payer mix. However, approximately 50 to 60 days in accounts receivable is a typical goal for many practices.

Percent of A/R Greater Than 120 Days

The aging of the receivables is also an important aspect of receivables management, as a dollar today is more valuable than a dollar in the future. In addition, the longer the accounts age, the more difficult it is to collect the balance due. The higher the percent of A/R over 120 days, the higher risk that accounts will be written off to bad debt. The aging of the accounts receivables is calculated by viewing an aged trial balance (ATB). You can observe the ATB for both insurance and patient receivables and review them in the following aging categories: 0–30 days, 31–60 days, 61–90 days, 91–120 days and more than 120 days. Just because your practice management system reviews aging beyond 120 days does not mean that you should tolerate aging at these levels. Reviewing the percentage of total accounts receivable that is over 120 days old and comparing this level against benchmark norms lets you assess the medical practice's aging of accounts compared with its practice counterparts.

Calculation: Percentage of accounts receivable is defined by amounts owed to the practice by patients, third-party payers, etc., that are more than 120 days old.

Expected outcome: Having 15 to 18 percent of accounts receivable greater than 120 days is an acceptable performance indicator.

Additional measures of revenue cycle performance can be benchmarked as well. These can also help you determine opportunities for improvement in revenue performance. These performance measures are outlined below:

Bad debt per physician: These data vary based on payer mix of a medical practice. However, bad debt write-offs are one of the most controllable expenses for a medical practice. To calculate this, divide the amount of accounts receivable written off to bad debt (including collection agency write-offs) by total charges for the same time period (for example, 6 or 12 months). Then divide this figure by the number of full-time equivalent (FTE) physicians in your practice. *Note:* Measuring bad debt over time is credible only if you have an established policy and procedure for writing off accounts to bad debt. If you are not consistently applying the policy and are writing off invoices quarterly, instead of monthly, the trend could be misleading.

Total A/R per physician: This measure, which varies depending on the specialty and productivity of your medical practice, is calculated by dividing 12 months of A/R by the number of FTE physicians in your practice. Because accounts receivable is a reflection of production (that is, the more charges a physician puts on the books, the more money is owed to him/her), the accounts receivable per physician is higher for those practices that have higher productivity than their benchmark counterparts – but it should not be older. Another useful measure is the ratio of accounts receivable to charges. This essentially "controls" for the higher production levels of a particular practice.

Net collection rate by payer: Evaluate each major payer with respect to the net collection rate. Over a 12-month period you should expect 95 percent or greater for each contracted payer. Comparing rates among payers may identify issues that you may not have noticed in other performance measures.

Payer mix analysis in comparison with benchmarks: As you compare your practice with external benchmarks, evaluate whether your payer mix is similar to the benchmark data source. This analysis ensures that the medical practice is comparable regarding performance indices of the benchmark data. For example, a medical practice with a higher level of Medicaid patients may require more billing resources than a practice with a high level of Medicare that is using e-claims submission and electronic remittance processes.

Benchmarking the billing and collection performance of a practice requires identification of the source of relevant benchmarks. We have provided a list of benchmarking sources in the additional resources list at the end of this book. It is important to recognize that benchmarking is only a tool to determine performance at one moment in time. Managers and leaders must interpret this data, take action, assign responsibility and deadlines and initiate change in the medical practice to improve performance over time.

We offer the following case study as an educational tool to help you identify action items associated with benchmark findings.

Benchmarking Case Study

Practice Anywhere, a multispecialty practice, has performed a benchmarking analysis of its key billing and collection indices. The outcome of this analysis is presented in the following table.

Performance measure	Practice Anywhere	National median[1]	High-performing practice bench-mark median[2]
Percent of A/R > 120 days	20.5%	21.32%	10 – 12%
Days in A/R	51.15	52.32	35 – 40
Net fee-for-service collection rate*	93.67%	97.13%	98 – 99%

Benchmark sources:
1. *National Benchmark: MGMA Cost Survey: 2003 Report Based on 2002 Data*, Multispecialty Practices-All, Median
2. *High Performing Practice Benchmark*: Walker, Larch, Woodcock, 2004.

*For purposes of this table, the MGMA definition in the MGMA *Cost Survey Report* for the net fee-for-service collection rate is used. This definition is: (net fee-for-service revenue X 100)/adjusted fee-for-service charges. "Net fee-for-service revenue" is defined as revenue collected from patients and third-party payers for services provided to fee-for-service, discounted fee-for-service and non-capitated Medicare/Medicaid patients. It includes portions of withholds returned to the practice as part of a risk-sharing arrangement, bonuses and incentive payments paid to a practice for good performance, and other related revenue. "Adjusted fee-for-service charges" is defined as the difference between gross fee-for-service charges and the amount expected to be paid by patients or third-party payers. This includes Medicare and Medicaid charge restrictions (the difference between the practice's full, undiscounted charge and the Medicare limiting charge); third-party payer contractual adjustments; and charitable, professional courtesy and employee adjustments.

Case Analysis

- The percent of A/R greater than 120 days and the days in A/R are better than median benchmark norms, but they fall short of the levels reported by better performing practices.
- The net collection rate is lower than both benchmark sources.

Action Plan

If you were the practice executive for this medical practice, what action would you take? Below are some of the action steps we recommend to improve revenue performance for Practice Anywhere:

Review account follow-up activity: Find out if your staff have been able to fully work the A/R report each month. Review account notes for high dollar balances in the more-than-120-day category to determine if staff have been systematically conducting account follow-up.

Review aged trial balance by payer: Determine if one payer is skewing the results by making problematic or late reimbursements.

Review net collection rates by payer: Determine if the problematic performance is endemic or if it resides with only one or a few payers. Determine if staff are appropriately recording contractual and non-contractual adjustments by sampling the payment posting activity and comparing it to the explanation of benefits (EOB).

Review credit balances: If you have a high level of credit balances, your A/R may be understated. In this case example, your performance may be worse than the case findings would indicate.

Review collection agency activity: Because accounts are typically written off when they are sent to collections, review the success of the agency in collecting outstanding accounts and the method by which your practice records this money in the practice management system.

Review aging by date of service: Try to match your gross charges and collection activity by date of service (a number of practice management systems provide this analysis for you). This helps you focus on areas that may need follow-up attention.

Review contract management activity: Make sure your payers are reimbursing at contractually agreed-to levels.

Verify front-end accuracy: Determine the extent to which front-end billing processes are contributing to problematic back-end billing functions by reviewing claim denials. A clean front-end billing process minimizes rework and account follow-up work.

Review payment posting and adjustments: Determine the timeliness of payment posting and ensure that payment posters are flagging $0 accounts and accounts to be appealed. Make sure payment posters are using the appropriate adjustment codes – contractual or non-contractual – to the level of specificity needed to analyze performance.

Verify that claims submission is timely: Verify lag times from date of service to date of claims submission. Review claim edit reports to determine if a lack of clean claims is contributing to delayed claims submission.

As this case demonstrates, once you know your practice's performance in comparison with the benchmarks, you can evaluate potential problem areas to improve revenue performance. You should undertake benchmarking on a systematic basis (we recommend at least quarterly) to ensure that you are identifying key indicators that impact revenue performance.

Once you have benchmarked your practice's performance, you are also in a position to perform a gap analysis.

Performing a Gap Analysis

Once you have benchmarked your performance, a gap analysis lets you identify your revenue opportunity. You can conduct a gap analysis on a number of billing and collection indices to determine the opportunity you have to enhance revenue for your practice. This type of analysis is also useful when you are trying to determine the need for additional resources for billing and collection operations. An example of a gap analysis for Medical Practice Anywhere follows:

Case facts:	
Adjusted fee-for-service charges:	$720,000
Net fee-for-service collections:	$600,000
Net collection rate:	83.33%
Gap analysis:	
Expected net collection rate:	97%
Expected revenue if net collection rate were 97%:	$698,400
Revenue gap:	$98,400

To close the revenue gap, the practice needs to take steps to improve its net collection rate. By performing a gap analysis, the practice is also in a better position to determine the level of resources to devote to this effort.

You can perform a gap analysis on a number of billing and collection measures. For example, if your practice could change its payer mix, you could determine the revenue impact and gap between current and potential revenue. Once you perform a gap analysis for payer mix, you are in a better position to allocate resources for contracting and marketing efforts and to determine whether you want to be more aggressive in managing your payer mix.

Reasons for Low Collections – Leading Financial Indicators

While benchmarking is important to permit you to compare your practice's revenue cycle with others and to identify areas of opportunity for your practice, you'll want to do more than benchmark performance. Once you have measured and reported the above indicators of performance for your billing and collection process, it is a little late to effect change in revenue for your practice. We know of many medical practices that diligently benchmark their billing and collection performance yet are surprised when their revenue takes a turn for the worse. That is because the benchmark measures represent *lagging* indicators rather than *leading* indicators for a medical practice. In this section we review the reasons for low collections. These serve as early warning signs or leading indicators to identify fluctuating revenue performance. By investigating the reasons for low collections, you can actively manage the performance of your billing and collection operation.

The figure below outlines a blueprint of possible reasons a practice may experience low collections.

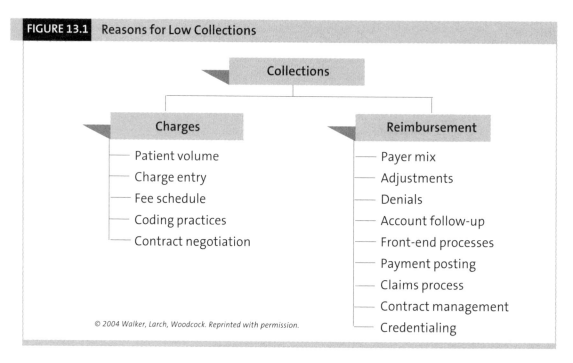

FIGURE 13.1   Reasons for Low Collections

Collections

Charges
— Patient volume
— Charge entry
— Fee schedule
— Coding practices
— Contract negotiation

Reimbursement
— Payer mix
— Adjustments
— Denials
— Account follow-up
— Front-end processes
— Payment posting
— Claims process
— Contract management
— Credentialing

© 2004 Walker, Larch, Woodcock. Reprinted with permission.

When medical practices examine each of these reasons, they often find that there are a number of factors that contribute to the practice's fluctuating and/or low collection levels. You should regularly monitor leading indicators so you can anticipate low revenue and take action *before* revenue declines. For example, if you recognize an increase in payer denials early on, improving the percentage of clean claims submitted or providing coding education to physicians can minimize or prevent negative impacts to revenue performance. As another example, by tracking referrals by referring physician, payer mix and type of case, you can intervene early on if you recognize a change in referral patterns – or at the very least, you can anticipate a drop in revenue rather than be surprised. We explore the reasons for low collections in two main categories: (1) fluctuating charges and (2) fluctuating reimbursement, and suggest issues to investigate in your own medical practice.

Fluctuating Charges

Your medical practice may experience low collections because of fluctuating charge activity. Fluctuating charges may be due to changes in patient volume, problems with charge entry, your fee schedule or coding practices, or the problem may rest with the payer contracts that you have negotiated or that have been negotiated on your behalf. We will explore each of these areas as it relates to fluctuating revenue levels for your medical practice.

Patient volume: A change in patient volume impacts revenue performance. Review new-to-return patient ratios, procedure volumes and type of patients who are presenting to the practice. Also review changes to practice style (such as the addition or deletion of services), patient volume per session, physician leave policies and coding patterns and referral patterns of the practice's key referring physicians. Perform these reviews on an ongoing basis. This allows you to anticipate fluctuations in revenue so that there are no surprises. It also lets you mitigate the impact on revenue performance through such actions as marketing strategies or changes to provider scheduling. Issues to investigate include:

- How many billable services do you provide?
- What is the mix of procedure codes that you bill?
- What percent of total patient visits are new patient visits?
- Are referring physicians continuing to send the volume and type of referrals as in the past?
- What is the visit-to-procedure ratio this year compared with last year – by physician? Has a physician changed or altered his/her practice style so that it impacts procedure or visit volumes or type of services performed?
- Has there been a recent change in vacation or leave policies for physicians and/or nonphysician providers that is impacting patient volume?
- Has a physician changed his/her coding patterns?
- Are you capturing charges for all services performed?
- What audits are you conducting to ensure that services performed at each hospital are captured, that all visits and procedures in the office are billed?
- How many surgeries were performed? How many operating room minutes were used?

Charge entry: You may find that the charge entry function is backlogged. If physicians are holding encounter forms until the end of the week or end of the month, this will impact revenue and provide wide fluctuations in staffing workload and realized revenue. If staff are behind in posting charges and there is a lag time from date of service to date of entry, this could also mean reductions in revenue for a particular month or quarter. Issues to investigate include:

- When are office, outpatient and inpatient charges entered with respect to date of service? Track by physician and location.
- Do you have the appropriate number of staff to enter the charges?
- Do you have staff with the appropriate skill mix and tools for charge entry?
- How many encounter forms are stacked on staff desks? How much revenue is backlogged if you have one or two inches of forms waiting to be entered? When charges are backlogged, pull a cross-trained staff member who normally handles another function, authorize overtime or add a part-time staff member.

Fee schedule: We often find that medical practices are charging fees that are below reimbursement levels for some payers. You can easily quantify it with data available to the practice. Issues to investigate include:

- When did you last review your fee schedule?
- Examine the EOBs for your top 25 codes from all of your payers. Do the allowances match your fees, or are your fees too low?

Coding practices: Coding education is available for physicians and nonphysician providers from a number of organizations. These include educational workshops as well as both on-site and off-site prospective audits performed by certified coders. See Additional Billing and Collection Resources at the end of this book for some coding resources. Improved coding will ensure that accurate levels of services are billed and appropriate reimbursement received. Issues to investigate include:

- Have the codes and/or levels of codes used shifted?
- How do your coding practices compare with national data, such as those published by the Centers for Medicare and Medicaid (CMS)?
- Are your physicians actually documenting everything they do? Spend a half day observing each one to ensure that they are documenting and coding appropriately for the services they render.

Contract negotiation: The initial contract negotiation could have a detrimental effect on revenue performance. If the contract terms initially established do not cover the expense of practice, for example, revenue will not be optimized. Issues to investigate include:

- When was the last time the contract was negotiated? When is it up for renewal?
- Are you getting the patients and mix of services you expected when you negotiated the contract?
- Do you track problems with the payer so that you can work to resolve them at meetings or at contract negotiation?
- Are you being paid the agreed-upon fee schedule stated in the contract and are the annual increases to your fees effective on the date specified? Ask that a copy of the actual fee schedule for the codes relevant to your specialty be attached to the contract; that way, you'll avoid misunderstandings about the meaning of "110 percent of Medicare." What year of Medicare? 1993 or current?

Fluctuating Reimbursement Levels

In addition to changes to your charges, there may be critical indicators of fluctuating revenue because of reimbursement issues and/or lack of due diligence in managing this portion of the revenue cycle. We have outlined below leading indicators for fluctuating reimbursement levels, along with issues the practice should investigate regularly.

Payer mix: If the payer mix has changed in the practice so that a lower-reimbursing payer represents more of the business, this will decrease revenue. Many practices actively manage their payer volumes so that they do not become unduly dependent on one payer for the majority of their revenue stream. Issues to investigate include:

- What is your payer mix (based on charges) for your top six payers during the past 12 months and the prior 12-month period?
- What is the average gross collection rate for each payer? Use a weighted average to calculate your practice's expected gross collection rate and compare variance with actual revenue.
- Has your payer mix shifted toward payers with lower payment schedules? Or are the more complicated cases being directed toward your physicians without higher reimbursement? Are there services for which your payers have discontinued payment and/or now consider noncovered services?
- Do more of your payers require the patient to pay a copayment or co-insurance portion? If so, are you successfully collecting these?

Adjustments: As we discussed in Chapter 6, if the payment posters are adjusting accounts inappropriately, this obviously has an impact on revenue. Payment posters should code adjustments accurately; we recommend instituting a second level of review for adjustments at a particular dollar threshold. Issues to investigate include:

- How do you define a contractual allowance in your practice? We consider a contractual adjustment to be uncontrollable, as contractual adjustments were agreed to at the contract negotiation. A missed filing deadline should not be considered a contractual write-off because you are able to meet this deadline. Determine separate categories for those controllable losses and train staff to identify these.

- What is the amount of contractual adjustments your practice made during the past 12 months by payer? How does this compare with the previous period?

- What is the amount of non-contractual adjustments your practice made during the past 12 months by type of adjustment? By payer? By location?

- Can your billing system verify that payments from payers received on every claim are appropriate and if not, have ad hoc reports been instituted to verify payment levels?

- Do your payment posters know how to read an EOB and how to select the appropriate adjustment code? Are you performing payment audits to evaluate performance?

- What is the adjusted or net collection rate for each payer?

Denials: Your medical practice could be experiencing higher denials from a particular payer. Unless your staff systematically work the denials and conduct an appropriate appeal process, revenue may drop precipitously. Issues to investigate include:

- What is the percent of claims that are denied by the payer on first submission?

- What are the major denials by category, for example, coding, incorrect/incomplete registration, patient not eligible on date of service, no referral/pre-authorization, medical necessity and so forth?

- Are the denials due to payer error, practice error or a combination?

- What action can you take to reduce these denials?

Account follow-up: Once you have investigated patient volume, payer mix, your fee schedule and other factors that could contribute to low collections, it's time to look into account follow-up. As we discussed previously, we recommend that staff follow accounts every 30 to 45 days. This ensures that you identify inadequate coding, potential denials and e-claims submission failure before it becomes a larger problem for the practice. Issues to investigate include:

- What is your policy regarding insurance follow-up after the claim is submitted but before it has been paid, for example, if there is no response from the payer?
- What is your policy regarding appeals?
- What is your policy regarding patient follow-up to include statements, telephone calls, letters, payment plans and collection agency accounts?

Front-end processes: The saying "garbage in, garbage out" applies to physician billing. If the demographic and insurance data are not accurate, a denial is assured. The ability of a practice to "bill it right the first time" ensures a revenue stream that minimizes wide fluctuations. Issues to investigate include:

- What percentage of denials was due to mistakes made during the registration process (demographics or insurance)?
- Are you reviewing your procedure, modifiers and diagnosis codes to ensure accuracy based on payer guidelines and documentation?
- Are you verifying insurance and benefits eligibility?
- Are you collecting the patient's portion of the bill – copayment, co-insurance and patient account balance – at the time of service?
- Are you accepting credit and debit cards?

Payment posting: When a medical practice delays the payment posting process, it does not record revenue during the appropriate period. The practice also may not be taking advantage of interest earnings on bank deposits. If the practice makes inaccurate payment postings, there will be problems in revenue, and daily reconciliation will fall short, requiring rework. Practices need to move to e-remittances when possible to reduce staff expense and minimize manual errors. Issues to investigate include:

- What is the lag time from receipt of the payment to posting of the payment?
- When are payments deposited at the bank?
- Are payment posters flagging $0 or low payments for appeal – by line item?
- Do you have the appropriate number and level of staff to enter the payments?
- Are the payment posters categorizing adjustments correctly?
- Have you maximized the use of electronic remittance and funds transfer?
- Do you compare actual payments versus contracted or expected payments regularly to identify incorrect payment amounts?

Claims process: The claims process may be encumbered. If a practice is sending out less than 75 percent of its claims electronically, the claims process has not been optimized. (This assumes that 75 percent of your payers accept claims electronically.) Practices that have moved to e-claims for the majority of their claims submissions have realized substantial savings and faster turnaround time for remittance. If staff are not working the edit reports – the reports received back to the practice on claims that have not passed through the clearinghouse because of a problem – this will also impact revenue performance. Issues to investigate include:

- What percent of your claims do you submit electronically?
- How quickly do you mail out paper claims?
- Do you daily work edit reports (paper and electronic) and examine them to eliminate the cause of problem edits?
- If you are using a claims clearinghouse, what process are you using to monitor claims reaching the payer?

Contract management: After you sign contracts, you need to manage them. It is possible that the payer is not paying at the contract level. It is also possible that there is a delay related to payment or that the payer is requiring pre-authorization when the contract states otherwise. Issues to investigate include:

- Are you getting the volume and type of patients you expected?
- Are you competitive in scope, delivery and quality of services provided?
- Did you comply with contract provisions such as access, timely filing, pre-authorization?
- Is the payer in compliance with contract provisions such as pre-authorization and timeliness of payment?
- Is the payer responsive to claim/payment inquiries? Do its staff answer the telephone or respond to e-mails?
- How much of your resources do you spend on collecting? That is, does the payer deny every claim, hold payment in a pending status or otherwise encumber the follow-up process?
- Are you positioning yourselves for contract renegotiation and renewal?

When you review your contracts and payer performance, you may want to use a liquidation table. This type of analysis compares payer mix with account receivables. For example, if a payer represents 45 percent of your payer mix, but only 30 percent of your receivables, that tells you that this payer pays you faster (liquidates cash at a faster rate) than other payers.

This is only one measure of payer performance and should not be used alone. Use Figure 13.2 to format your own liquidation table.

| FIGURE 13.2 | Liquidation Table | | |

Payer	Percent of payer mix	Percent of A/R	Liquidation rate
Blue Cross	14%	10%	Faster
Commercial	12%	6%	Faster
HMO	11%	13%	Slower
Medicaid	6%	9%	Slower
Medicare	40%	15%	Faster
Worker's compensation	5%	15%	Slower
Self-pay	10%	30%	Slower
Other	2%	2%	Even
	100%	100%	

© 2004 Walker, Larch, Woodcock. Reprinted with permission.

Credentialing: Another reason for low collection levels could be a delay in credentialing new providers in the practice. Many markets are experiencing a six- to nine-month process to credential new providers. Each practice needs to identify someone who is accountable for getting new providers credentialed with the payers, your local hospitals and other accrediting bodies. Initiate this activity as far in advance of the provider's arrival as possible to ensure s/he is paid for services. Otherwise, you can expect cash flow disruptions related to referrals, authorizations and, of course, payments. Although you submit the information to the payer, it can be another 30 to 90 days before the payer enters that new provider's information into its information system.

If the physician is seeing patients but not fully credentialed, you'll need to determine if these services need to be written off, submitted as non-participating claims or held until credentialing is completed and paid as participating. It is important to review each insurance contract regarding how to bill for non-credentialed providers. It may be that the payer allows you to bill if another physician in your group supervises the services that are performed, or the payer may offer retroactive coverage or allow another mechanism so the practice is assured of payment. You should not routinely write off these charges without checking to determine the contract provisions with the particular payer related to credentialing. If your contracts do not include language regarding the treatment of non-credentialed physicians, consider adding it. Issues to investigate include:

■ Are you actively managing the credentialing process to maintain data related to timeliness?

■ Do you know how each payer handles claims for non-credentialed providers?

■ What process is in place to ensure that new physicians have accurately completed their credentialing paperwork prior to arrival? Each payer has different rules related to credentialing. Some offer checklists to help you ensure the forms are completed correctly. Figure 13.3 is a sample of Medicare's enrollment checklist, identifying the more frequent errors or omissions.

FIGURE 13.3   Sample Medicare Enrollment Checklist

☐ Signatures and dates are missing.

☐ Wrong person signs the forms. A billing agency cannot sign.

☐ Section 4 – the date the applicant started working at a location is missing.

☐ Attachments are missing.

☐ Section 2A5 – nonphysician practitioners fail to complete information about their training.

☐ Legal business name does not match the name on the tax documentation.

☐ Section 2 – correspondence address cannot be the billing agency's address.

☐ Section 3 (adverse legal actions and overpayments) – this question is not answered.

☐ Income reporting method is not completed or is incorrect.

☐ Section 6 (physician's signature) is missing.

For more specifics go to www.cms.hhs.gov/providers/enrollment/forms/checklist.pdf.

In the detailed discussion above, we intended to assist medical practices in recognizing fluctuations to revenue performance *before* they affect the practice's bottom line. Figure 13.4 summarizes the issues to investigate on a regular basis by a medical practice related to its revenue and collections activities.

FIGURE 13.4   Key Revenue Indices: Issues to Investigate

What causes low collections?

LOW CHARGES

Low volumes
- How many billable services do you provide?
- What is the mix of billable services?

Charge entry
- When are outpatient and inpatient charges entered with respect to date of service ("lag time")?
- Do you have the appropriate staff to enter the charges?

Low fees
- When did you last review your fee schedule?
- Identify your top 25 codes and extract an EOB for each code from a sample of payers. Do the allowances match your fees? If so, they are too low.

Coding practices
- Have the codes and/or levels of codes that you bill for shifted toward codes with lower or no reimbursement?

Credentialing
- Have the providers for whom you are billing been credentialed by all carriers? If not, what is the status of their applications?

LOW REIMBURSEMENT

Payer mix
- What is your payer mix (based on charges) for your top five payers during the past 12 months and the prior 12 months?
- Calculate the average gross collection for each payer, and use a weighted average based on your payer mix to determine estimated gross collection rate.
- Has your payer mix shifted toward payers with lower allowance schedules?
- Are there services for which your payers have discontinued payment and/or are considered noncovered services?

Adjustments
- What is the amount of contractual adjustments your practice made during the past 12 months?
- What is the amount of non-contractual adjustments your practice made during the past 12 months?
- Can your billing system verify that payments from insurance companies received on every claim are appropriate?

Denials
- What is the percent of claims that are denied during the first submission?
- Identify your five major denials by category (coding, incorrect/incomplete registration, patient not eligible on date of service, no referral/pre-authorization)

Account follow-up
- What is your policy regarding insurance follow-up after the claim is received (the appeal process)?
- What is your policy regarding insurance follow-up after the claim is submitted but has not been paid (no response from the payer)?
- What is your policy regarding patient follow-up, to include statements, telephone calls and payment plans?

Front-end processes
- With regard to the denials above, what percent were due to mistakes made during the registration process (demographics or insurance)?
- Are you editing your procedure and diagnosis codes and modifiers to ensure accuracy (based on payer guidelines)? (assuming you document appropriately)
- Are you verifying insurance and benefits eligibility, if applicable?
- Are you collecting the patient's portion of the bill at the time of service (copayment, co-insurance, balance)? Can you accept a credit card or debit card?
- Are you collecting on past-due balances at the time of service?

Payment posting
- When are payments entered with respect to their receipt by the office? When are they deposited at the bank?
- Do you have the appropriate staff to enter payments? Are they categorizing adjustments correctly?

You can also develop a snapshot of leading financial indicators to regularly review and monitor. These represent performance expectations for each step in the revenue cycle. Your medical practice's performance in comparison with your expectations lets you intervene at an early stage so you can take action to enhance revenue performance. Conduct a comparison of your medical practice's performance with expectations at least quarterly so you know ahead of time if a key element of your revenue cycle is broken or performing at suboptimal levels. We have provided a sample snapshot of leading financial indicators for the revenue cycle in Figure 13.5. These indicators serve as early warning signs for your practice. If they are systematically monitored you should have no surprises related to fluctuating revenue for your medical practice.

FIGURE 13.5 Sample Snapshot of Leading Financial Indicators

Billing Function	Service Expectation	Actual Performance	Target
Registration	Obtain demographic and insurance information		98% accuracy
Prior authorization	Determine prior authorization for services		98% accuracy
Time-of-service collections	Collect copayments, patient accounts balances, deductibles, co-insurance		Copay: 98% Others: document attempt
Coding	Physician coding Certified coders for surgical procedures		Chart audits for coding accuracy Rejections for incorrect coding 0 to 1% of visits All certified by (date)
Claims/statements	Supporting documentation for claims Edits completed Claim denial/rejection rate		100% same day 100% same day <5%
Charge entry	Days lag (date of service to date of entry)		24 hours outpatient 48 hours inpatient
Account follow-up	Every 30 to 45 days Percent A/R >120 days Net collection rate		100% accuracy 15 to 18% 95% or greater
Payment posting	Cash posted and balanced Credit balance report		100% same day Fully researched and resolved within 60 days
Collections	Patient account to collections		110 days
Denials	Percent denials due to referrals Percent denials due to past filing limits		2% 0%
Management reporting	Reports available within 10 days after month end		100%

© 2004 Walker, Larch, Woodcock. Reprinted with permission.

Now that we have benchmarked performance and investigated leading indicators to ensure an optimal revenue cycle, let's calculate the cost of your billing operation.

Calculating the Cost of Your Physician Billing Operation

There are five measures to evaluate when you're analyzing the cost of your physician billing operation. These include:

1. Cost of front-end billing as a percent of net collections;
2. Cost of back-end billing as a percent of net collections;
3. Cost of back-end billing per claim;
4. Cost of back-end billing per full-time equivalent (FTE) physician; and
5. Percent of key cost categories.

When you're analyzing billing office costs – particularly when comparing costs with other practices – it is important to recognize the billing and collection functions included in the cost analysis. For example, one practice may include the front-end billing functions in its reporting of billing costs, while another may only report back-end billing functions. Front-end billing functions (registration, coding, charge capture and charge entry) typically are at a cost equal to 2 to 3 percent of net collections (see Figure 13.6). Many practices, however, have elected to spend more on the front-end billing functions, resulting in less cost on the back-end because claims are essentially clean prior to submission. Therefore, the current trend is to see this percent of investment into front-end functions increasing, while the investment into back-end functions is declining.

Cost of Front-end Billing

Medical practices typically overlook the cost for the front-end billing functions. This is due to the fact that the staff involved in front-end billing typically reside in the clinical area and their costs are not considered to be part of the "billing office" for financial reporting purposes. You should assess the cost of the staff involved in front-end billing. Estimate the time they spend in the performance of registration, chart abstraction/coding and charge entry – three of the key functions of a front-end billing operation. Compare your charges with the average costs for front-end billing operations reported in Figure 13.6 on the next page.

FIGURE 13.6	Front-end Billing Costs

Billing Function	Cost as a Percent of Net Collections*
Registration	1%
Chart abstraction/coding	1%
Charge entry	.50%

Note: Costs will be higher than these levels if your staff are highly multitasked, or if work processes are encumbered.

© 2004 Walker, Larch, Woodcock. Reprinted with permission.

Cost of Back-end Billing

The cost of back-end billing can be computed as a percent of net collections, on a cost per claim basis, or on a cost per FTE physician basis. The average billing cost as a percent of net collections is 8 percent (see Figure 13.7), the typical cost per claim ranges from $5 to $7 (see Figure 13.8), and the cost on a per FTE physician basis will vary depending on your specialty; however, it averages $30,000 to $60,000 per FTE physician. Specialty-specific benchmarking resources are available to compare cost on a per FTE physician basis and are listed in the additional resources list at the end of this book.

Cost as a Percent of Net Collections

Typically, the cost of back-end billing as a percent of net collections varies based on (1) the specialty and (2) the services performed. When you're comparing your cost of billing with other practices, it is important to understand the services included in the cost calculation supplied by other practices. The ranges for back-end billing costs as a percent of net collections that we typically find are reported in Figure 13.7. Note, however, that the actual cost for your back-end billing operation depends on a number of factors including your range of services in the pricing mechanism, payer mix, resources devoted to front-end billing to ensure a clean claim and other practice-specific factors.

FIGURE 13.7	Back-end Billing: Cost as a Percent of Net Collections

Specialty	Cost as a Percent of Net Collections*
Surgery and anesthesiology	4 – 6%
Medical specialties	6 – 8%
Primary care	7 – 9%
Radiology and pathology	8 – 10%
Emergency medicine	11 – 13%

Note: This cost is for back-end billing functions only (once a charge becomes a claim and all the steps that follow). Actual cost depends on the level of service and communication, range of activities provided, specialty, market and payer mix (for example, a high percentage of self-pay patients will increase costs, perhaps even above these ranges). If you have extraordinary reimbursement management, analysis and/or reporting, these activities may also result in a higher cost.

© 2004 Walker, Larch, Woodcock. Reprinted with permission.

Cost per Claim

Isolate the cost of the billing office from the general operating expense of the practice to determine whether your practice has allocated sufficient resources to the billing office function. You can then calculate the cost per claim, so you can identify whether you have allocated appropriate resources to your billing operation.

We have provided an example of determining the cost of a billing office in Figure 13.8 on the next page. In this example, the cost per claim is $5.93. Because the cost per claim medical practices typically face is from $5 to $7, the overall cost in this particular example falls within this threshold and is acceptable.

FIGURE 13.8 Back-end Billing: Cost per Claim

Cost per Claim

1. Determine billing office costs
2. Compute cost per claim* (billing office costs divided by claims)

Example:

Billing Office Costs	Practice
Hardware/software	$75,000
Claims/statement processing	$72,000
Staff compensation	$220,000
Staff benefits	$50,000
Office supplies	$15,000
Space	$30,000
Telephone/communications	$9,500
Miscellaneous	$2,500
Total	$474,000

Assuming 80,000 claims:

Cost per claim = $5.93   Benchmark = $5 to $7 per claim

© 2004 Walker, Larch, Woodcock. Reprinted with permission.

Percent of Key Cost Categories

In addition to the cost calculations for front-end billing and back-end billing outlined above, you can calculate your mix of costs in the billing operation to determine whether you have appropriately resourced your revenue cycle. Regardless of specialty, the costs allocated to the billing operation are, on average, reported in Figure 13.9 on the next page. These include the percent to total billing expenditures for three key expenditure categories: (1) personnel, (2) technology/practice management system and (3) operating and all other expenditure categories. By calculating the cost of these expenditure categories as a percent of total billing expenditures you can determine if you can redistribute your resources within your billing operation.

FIGURE 13.9 Percent of Key Cost Categories

Regardless of specialty, the average costs associated with the billing operation as as follows:

Expenditure Category	Percent of Total Billing Expenditures
Personnel	58 – 62%
Technology/practice management system	18 – 22%
Operating and all other expenses	18 – 22%

Actual levels will vary based on practice-specific factors such as leveraging technology, resources devoted to front-end billing and others.

© 2004 Walker, Larch, Woodcock. Reprinted with permission.

The Efficient Frontier – Balancing Performance and Cost

When you're analyzing your cost of billing, don't forget to include your performance expectations. If the cost of your billing operation is at 8 percent and you'd like it to drop to 6 percent, how much performance are you also willing to decrease? Are you able to cut the right costs out so that performance (net collection rate, for example) will not be hampered? Perhaps one of the questions you need to answer is, "*How much* billing office cost are you willing to fund to obtain *what level* of revenue performance?"

There is no absolute answer, but the key is to be close to the optimal balance of costs and performance. This balance is reaching the point at which you cannot spend any more money to give you a positive return. In other words, each additional dollar invested in your billng operation would return less than $1 in net collections. The "efficient frontier" describes the ideal ratio of performance to cost – along the spectrum of costs. Reaching the "top" of the efficient frontier is achieved when you are maximizing your performance at the minimum cost. This concept is depicted in Figure 13.10 on the next page.

Maintaining this balance requires constant vigilance. Only those practices that monitor their revenue cycle process, the individual performance of each resource in that process and the impact of technology will achieve the balance on a long-term basis.

FIGURE 13.10 The Efficient Frontier

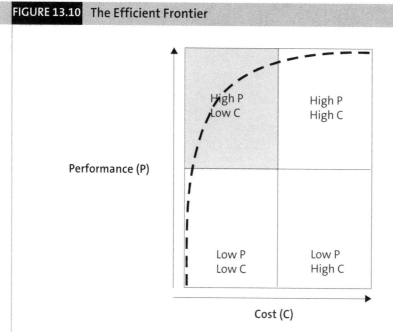

P = measure by key performance indicator, such as days in A/R
C = measure by key cost indicator, such as cost of billing as a percent of collections
— — = efficient frontier

High P/Low C: The "efficient frontier": Ideal scenario. Practice maintains high performance at a low cost. It is likely that front-end revenue cycle processes and payer strategies have been maximized, thus putting a lower cost burden on the billing staff. Cash flow, A/R and costs are optimized.

High P/High C: Next-to-ideal scenario, *unless* costs are significantly more than benchmarks. Note that every practice could get to this quadrant with enough spending. Thus, performance may be "high" but at a significant cost.

Low P/Low C: If performance is low *and* costs are low, there may be an opportunity to improve performance *by investing* in the revenue cycle.

Low P/High C: ALERT. There is a problem. The practice is spending above the benchmarks, and the performance is lower than industry averages. A full review of the revenue cycle is recommended.

We will now turn to techniques for reimbursement management, then discuss key management reports, policies and procedures.

Techniques for Reimbursement Management

We recommend the following techniques to ensure optimal reimbursement. These techniques do not take the place of the work needed to capture a charge, generate a claim and follow up on that claim. Rather, they represent additional steps that you can take to ensure that your medical practice receives appropriate compensation for the services it performs.

Keep Current on Newsletters and E-mails from Payers

If your practice's physicians participate in third-party contracts, you must stay current on changes dictated by the payers. Payers communicate key information regarding reimbursement matters such as which services are covered and changes in requirements for claims submission. Payers communicate in many ways – via newsletters, faxes, e-mails – and increasingly via their own Web sites. Someone on your staff must regularly read this information and promptly implement practice changes consistent with payer instructions. The practice manager or billing manager is often responsible for reading payer communications and transferring the relevant information to the physicians and staff. The billing manager can delegate this responsibility to billing staff, but it's important to ensure that someone is responsible for this duty. Rotating this assignment is an excellent way to educate and provide a development opportunity for staff. Some practices have the assigned individual read the payer news, highlight what is important for the practice and post it in the staff lunchroom. Others have the staff member present the information at the weekly staff meeting. Rotating the assignment to other staff members over time will keep a fresh perspective on the material.

Institute Formal Reimbursement Management Practices

We recommend the following reimbursement management practices in the billing office:

- Review the top 25 procedure codes (by frequency and by dollar) for your practice and actual-versus-expected payer reimbursement for your top six payers;

- Develop tools for payment posters to ensure flagging of low or incorrect reimbursement;

- Audit your payment posters. At least quarterly, pull 10 payments and review the accuracy and timeliness of payment posting, use of contractual and non-contractual adjustments and appeal processes;

- Ensure that the maximum number of payer reimbursement schedulers are loaded into your practice management software to permit automatic adjustment and comparison with expected reimbursement levels;

- Analyze non-contractual adjustments by reason and correct the cause of the problem;

- Develop an appeal process for $0 payments. There are different filing deadlines for appeals — usually they involve shorter deadlines than claims submission;
- Develop payer-specific plans to manage billing for non-credentialed physicians;
- Monitor the percent of payments collected at time of service — for example, track how much money was collected that could have been collected at the time of service;
- Calculate the net collection rate by payer. The net collection rate is (collections — refunds) divided by (gross charges — contractual adjustments);
- Ensure follow-up of payment plan accounts;
- Ensure follow-up of "do not bill" or hold accounts;
- Prioritize the management of inbound mail. Staff should manage the patient correspondence when it is received as patients may be providing new information to ensure payment;
- Develop a patient collections policy to ensure equitable treatment for those with financial hardship; and
- Track collections and appeals for timeliness, appropriateness and trends.

Track Revenue That Is Still Outstanding

It is also important to manage and monitor the level of revenue that is still outstanding. This extends beyond simply knowing the level of the practice's outstanding accounts receivable. You must understand the detailed reason for and dollar amount of the revenue owed to the practice.

Below are a number of categories to investigate:

- Payments in process;
- Contractual adjustments not yet adjusted;
- Bad debt not yet adjusted;
- Claim edit lists not worked;
- A/R follow-up accounts;
- Encounter forms not entered;
- Claims not mailed; and
- Denied claims pending and past filing deadlines.

Keys to Management Reporting

We strongly encourage using data to determine opportunities to enhance billing and collection performance, rightsize the billing office and provide the appropriate education, tools and resources for individuals involved in the physician billing process.

Share unblinded data: Share unblinded data when possible by including physicians' names or practice locations on reports. The use of data to influence behavior and change cannot be underestimated, as physicians and practice executives will become actively engaged in identifying areas of opportunity and improvement. Remember, peer pressure is a powerful influencer of change.

Produce timely reports: Issue monthly billing and collection data by the 10th working day of the month; otherwise they lose their relevancy and prolong the opportunity to implement changes. If you are unable to produce reports this quickly, consider eliminating nonessential reports or reducing the number of pages in reports. You can produce these later and use them as historical documents.

Include benchmarks on reports: Include internal and external benchmarks on the graphs and reports so physicians, staff and managers have a measurement tool to determine the appropriateness of current performance outcomes.

Conduct full benchmarking at least quarterly: Full benchmarking should include a financial and performance review of the billing office.

Ensure all reports reconcile to a system report: Do not have financial reports generated in the accounting office that do not reconcile with billing reports from your practice management system. Or if there are variances between reports, explain these variances.

Use exception reporting: Use exception reporting to analyze reimbursement, timeliness, cost and other parameters as appropriate. On a quarterly basis, select new measures to examine.

Exercise caution when using rolling averages: Rolling averages are an excellent way to identify trends, smooth over monthly variations and perform revenue projections for budgetary purposes, but they can mask recent variations in billing and collection performance, preventing you from noticing problems.

Match reports to your audience: Identify the practice's decision makers and clarify what they require in their management reports. If they are detail oriented, provide them with detailed reports. If they are not, present a brief oral summary. Do not provide more reports than necessary. The data provided to the audience should be exactly what they want to see and how they want to see it so you can initiate active discussion of the current state and plan for future action.

Tell your story: Use your reports to tell your story. Do not simply provide a graph or a report without reflecting your analysis or conclusions. For example, if February is your lowest collection month every year, note that in a footnote in the report. Physicians and others who read the report may not remember this annual trend, but the footnote will avert unnecessary stress about revenue that month.

Picture yourself in the monthly physician board meeting while you are presenting an analysis of last month's revenue performance. Ask yourself if your physicians really understand what you are presenting and whether you are doing a good or bad job managing the billing and collections functions. What if days in A/R are up, yet percent of A/R over 120 days is down and bad debt write-offs are up – how are you doing? Some practices translate the traditional performance measures into a scorecard or report card with a letter grade, such as A, B, C, D or F. This can help your physicians interpret performance more easily.

You should regularly analyze a number of month-end reports, as well as ad hoc reports specific to a particular billing function. We have provided a list of recommended routine and ad hoc reports below. If you are unable to obtain these reports from your practice management system, contact your vendor. The vendor may have had some new updates or releases that are critical to robust reporting or there may be new options.

Month-end, routine reports include:

- Collection analysis;
- Aged trial balance summary;
- Aged A/R ratio analysis;
- Income analysis report;
- Service analysis report;
- Outstanding credit balance report;
- Month-to-date transaction summary report;
- Monthly batch proofs report;
- Monthly adjustment code summary report;
- Payment analysis report; and
- Credit balance report.

Ad hoc reports include:

- Summary of cash collected by location;
- Copayment billing by site;
- Insurance plan changes;
- Lag time, payment receipt to date posted;
- Lag time, date of service to date of entry;

- Claim edit report and categories, determined by percentage of claims;
- Non-contractual adjustments, by category;
- Top 25 procedure codes (by frequency and by dollar) linked to reimbursement by top six payers; and
- Percent of claims fully paid by 120 days.

Tools 28 through 34: Sample Management Reports (see pages 213-217)
With these tools, we have provided examples of management reports to demonstrate the relevancy of including trend data in your reports. In this fashion, the practice manager and/ or billing manager is able to provide a relevant comparison of the current state over time and tell the story regarding conclusions drawn from the data. You can also add benchmark sources to determine if your medical practice is competitive with its peers.

TOOL
28 SAMPLE A/R AGING REPORT
This format makes it easy to see which aging buckets are increasing and decreasing.

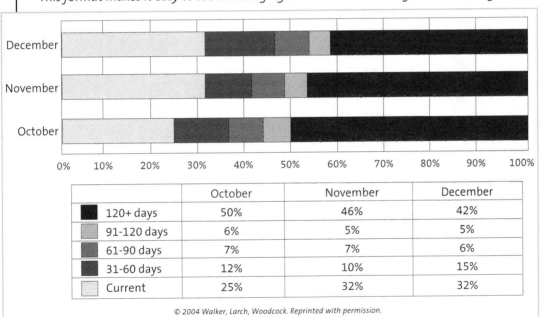

		October	November	December
■	120+ days	50%	46%	42%
□	91-120 days	6%	5%	5%
▨	61-90 days	7%	7%	6%
■	31-60 days	12%	10%	15%
□	Current	25%	32%	32%

TOOL
29 SAMPLE BILLING FINANCIAL REPORT
One-page reports force you to focus on only the most important indicators for your practice.

Financial Activity
For the period ending month, year

$\boxed{\text{\textit{Data is provided as sample only}}}$

(in millions)	Month, year			Fiscal YTD		
	Actual	Budget	Variance	Actual	Budget	Variance
Gross charges	$ 26.00	$ 25.00	$ 1.00	$ 161.00	$ 153.00	$ 8.00
Contractual adjustments	$ 11.70	$ 11.25	$ 0.45	$ 72.45	$ 68.85	$ 3.60
Net charges	$ 14.30	$ 13.75	$ 0.55	$ 88.55	$ 84.15	$ 4.40
Gross collections	13.70	12.50	1.20	81.00	78.00	3.00
Refunds	(0.50)	n/a	n/a	(2.00)	n/a	n/a
Net collections	$ 13.20	$ 12.50	$ 0.20	$ 79.00	$ 78.00	$ 2.00
Net collection rate	92.3%	90.9%	1.4%	89.2%	92.7%	-3.5%
Days in A/R	68	73	5			
Days in A/R >90 days	23.9%	30.0%	6.1%			

Payer Mix

	Percent A/R total	A/R >90 days
Blue Shield	21.3%	22.5%
Commercial	12.8%	28.0%
HMO	17.4%	16.1%
Medical assistance	9.1%	37.6%
Medicare	18.9%	11.1%
Miscellaneous	5.8%	36.9%
Patient responsibility	14.7%	25.0%

Notes
• Gross charges are above budget by 7% month-to-date and year-to-date.
• Net collections are favorable to budget month-to-date and year-to-date.
• Days in A/R are favorable to budget by five days.
• Blue Shield is the payer with the largest portion of total A/R (21.3%).
• 38% of medical assistance receivables are greater than 90 days.

TOOL
30 **SAMPLE CHARGE LAG REPORT**
This report shows several types of charge lag measures.

		Mar xx	June xx	Sep xx
Average charge entry lag days	Inpatient	27	22	19
Definition: Number of days between	Outpatient/office	12	9	5
date of service and date charge was entered				
Average claim lag days		6	6	5
Definition: Number of days between date charge entered and date claim produced				
Average payment lag days		47	38	31
Definition: Number of days between the date the claim was produced and date of first payment				

TOOL
31 **SAMPLE COLLECTION TARGET GRAPH**
Most practices also monitor collections on a monthly basis.

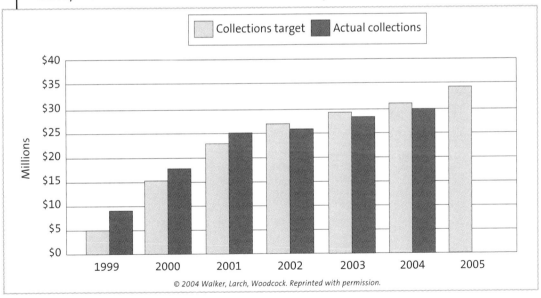

TOOL 32 SAMPLE DENIAL GRAPH

Another one-page report that shows denial detail and trends over several time periods.

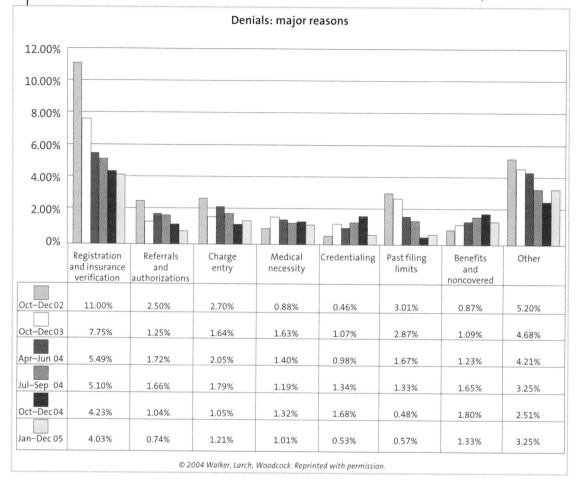

Denials: major reasons

	Registration and insurance verification	Referrals and authorizations	Charge entry	Medical necessity	Credentialing	Past filing limits	Benefits and noncovered	Other
Oct–Dec 02	11.00%	2.50%	2.70%	0.88%	0.46%	3.01%	0.87%	5.20%
Oct–Dec 03	7.75%	1.25%	1.64%	1.63%	1.07%	2.87%	1.09%	4.68%
Apr–Jun 04	5.49%	1.72%	2.05%	1.40%	0.98%	1.67%	1.23%	4.21%
Jul–Sep 04	5.10%	1.66%	1.79%	1.19%	1.34%	1.33%	1.65%	3.25%
Oct–Dec 04	4.23%	1.04%	1.05%	1.32%	1.68%	0.48%	1.80%	2.51%
Jan–Dec 05	4.03%	0.74%	1.21%	1.01%	0.53%	0.57%	1.33%	3.25%

TOOL
33

SAMPLE DASHBOARD INDICATORS

Create this report with your practice's top 3-5 measures to track every month.

	Dec-20xx	Dec-20xx	Dec-20xx	Dec-20xx
A/R days	155	96	76	70
% A/R >90 days	49%	36%	30%	28%
Net collection rate	64%	81%	89%	86%
E-claims	41%	45%	81%	89%
Claims on edit list	$500,000	$300,000	$200,000	$100,000

TOOL
34

SAMPLE CHARGES AND A/R TRENDS

Tracking two variables on a report permits a more advanced examination of trends and relationships between variables.

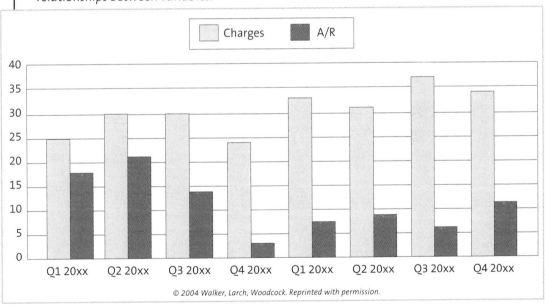

Policies and Procedures for Billing and Collection

Well-documented policies and procedures are considered primary tools to ensure an appropriate compliance environment and to measure, evaluate and systematically improve business processes. As part of the overall compliance environment, we strongly recommend that you create formal policies and procedures relating to all aspects of the billing, collection and claims processing functions. Key components of such billing policies and procedures should be consistent throughout the *entire* practice. Even if you have several entities sharing a practice location, it is important to have just one set of policies and procedures. Staff and patients perceive the practice as one entity and can become frustrated by changing rules and processes. Variable policies and procedures can also increase business risk to the practice.

We have provided samples of policies and procedures for key billing functions throughout this book. A complete list of policies and procedures that you should address in a formal policy and procedure manual for a medical practice include the following:

- Coding;
- Charge entry;
- Data entry;
- Charge and appointment reconciliation;
- Charge correction;
- Billing third-party payers;
- Billing capitated plans;
- Billing secondary insurance;
- Claim edits;
- Payment posting;
- Payment posting – bank deposit/lockbox;
- Payment posting – interest payments;
- Credit balances and refunds;
- Claim denials;
- Insurance follow-up;
- Capitation follow-up;
- Contractual write-offs and adjustments;
- Small-balance adjustments;
- Collection payment transition;
- Budget plans;

- Collection agency policy;
- Collection agency payment posting;
- Documentation of collection accounts;
- Settlements;
- Bankruptcy;
- Charity care;
- Deceased patient;
- Workers' compensation;
- Estates;
- Bad address;
- Non-sufficient funds;
- Collection letters/statement notes;
- Collection follow-up;
- Collection disputes; and
- Telephone collection.

Conduct regular audits of compliance with policies and procedures using a systematic audit plan. You can routinely consider updates to policies and procedures by reviewing one policy and procedure at each monthly staff meeting and discussing current processes and any policy updates that may be required.

As we discuss in this chapter, by actively managing and analyzing your billing and collection operation you can avoid surprises associated with fluctuations in revenue performance. By carefully benchmarking your billing operation, investigating reasons for low collections, monitoring leading indicators, examining the cost of your billing operation and creating accurate and timely management reports, policies and procedures you can be proactive in managing reimbursement for your practice.

CHAPTER 14

The Compliance Benefit

Developing, implementing and operating an effective corporate compliance program is simply good business. An effective compliance program ensures that services are documented, coded and billed appropriately – steps that effectively contribute to optimal revenue performance. While many practices have adopted compliance plans intending to establish a safeguard from government action, a compliance plan really represents good business practices for a medical practice on its journey to getting paid.

Federal and state agencies' tolerance levels have narrowed, and there is heightened scrutiny regarding billing and other areas related to the delivery of health care services. High-profile enforcement actions have demonstrated the harsh reality that an effective, well-coordinated compliance program must be a critical, high-priority component of any health care delivery network.

Developing a compliance plan may mitigate some of the damages associated with a problem audit, though this is not assured. What is assured, however, is that a medical practice should not develop a compliance plan simply to say that it has one. If it is not actively following the plan, establishing a compliance plan may do more harm than good as the practice may be going from an unintentional violation to an intentional violation by not adhering to its formalized plan.

In this chapter, we discuss:

- Resourcing your compliance efforts
- HIPAA privacy
- HIPAA transactions and code sets

Resourcing Your Compliance Efforts

Key components of a compliance plan include the following:

- Compliance officer;
- Committee roles and responsibilities;
- Code of conduct;
- Billing policies and procedures;
- Educating and training;
- Developing open lines of communication and reporting;
- Developing and enforcing disciplinary requirements related to non-compliance; and
- Implementing and monitoring an effective auditing component.

In today's enforcement environment, an effective corporate compliance program should consider at least the following potential risk areas as part of its overall compliance initiative:

- Billing for items or services not sufficiently documented;
- Data system integrity;
- Creation of employment and contractual or other relationships with excluded individuals and/or organizations;
- Anti-kickback laws, Stark law, HIPAA and other regulatory compliance;
- Compliance with applicable requirements associated with tax status, including those related to fair market value and intermediate sanctions legislation;
- Risk associated with billing vendors as it relates to coding compliance and liability, supervision and other areas;
- Proper collection and submission of copayment and other amounts received at the time of service;
- Compliance with patient, medical record and other health data confidentiality provisions and information practices; and
- Appropriate security hierarchy related to user account management in your practice management system.

Coding and billing compliance training should focus on the following topics based on Office of the Inspector General (OIG) guidance. Physicians and staff should understand and be able to apply the concepts of:

- Not billing for undocumented items or services;
- Bundling of services/procedure codes;
- Not engaging in upcoding;
- Ensuring that inappropriate balance billing does not occur;
- Proper resolution of overpayments;
- Maintaining confidentiality of patient information;
- Appropriately using provider identification numbers;
- Using proper modifiers;
- Not engaging in "assumption" coding, instead coding from complete documentation; and
- Not billing for services provided by unqualified or unlicensed clinical personnel (state laws vary).

Most practices have already determined their staffing needs to ensure a dynamic compliance program. If you haven't reviewed your compliance resources lately, it may be appropriate to evaluate this area of your practice. The size and complexity of your practice impact your need for a dedicated compliance officer and the number of staff assigned to these functions. Answering the questions listed in Figure 14.1 on the next page will assist in your evaluation.

You should attend to all of the above activities whether or not the medical practice has adopted a formal compliance plan. They will let you enhance revenue performance in the medical practice by doing things right the first time and attending to critical business functions.

FIGURE 14.1 Evaluating Your Compliance Needs

The questions below will help you evaluate your practice. The larger and more complex your practice is, the more dedicated resources you will need to lower your compliance risk.

☐ Do you have a separate office/department for billing?
- • Do you have more than five full-time staff in billing?
- • Is your billing process automated?
- • Is your registration process automated?

☐ Do you have more than three medical specialties?
☐ Do coders use coding software?

What are the:
☐ Average monthly claims?
☐ Number of providers?
☐ Number of payers?
- • Percent claims Medicare
- • Percent claims Medicaid

☐ Number of computers interfacing with billing system?

© 2004 Walker, Larch, Woodcock. Reprinted with permission.

Health Insurance Portability and Accountability Act (HIPAA)

Medical practice leaders must also stay current on other laws and regulations. The Health Insurance Portability and Accountability Act (HIPAA) of 1996 is being implemented over several years. HIPAA's many areas of focus have caused practices to make operational and policy changes.

What was HIPAA intended to do? Its many goals include:

- Allowing people to keep their health insurance coverage when they change or lose their jobs;

- Reducing health care fraud and abuse;

- Establishing administrative standards to promote electronic health care transactions;

- Streamlining medical claims processing; and

- Protecting patient information.

When medical practice leaders first heard about HIPAA, they were encouraged to see the administrative simplification goals. Standardizing electronic transactions should, over time, reduce the cost of billing and communicating with payers, though the greater emphasis on patient privacy and security standards has caused increased costs for many practices.

HIPAA Privacy

In April, 2003, the HIPAA privacy regulations went into effect. The regulations have three major points:

- Define who may see or use health information and what they can do with it;

- Place limits on the uses and disclosures of health information to the "minimum necessary" amount needed for the task; and

- Establish new patient rights concerning their health information. The new patient rights include the following:
  - receive the Notice of Privacy Practices;
  - access and copy medical and billing records;
  - request an amendment of a medical or billing record;
  - accounting of some disclosures;
  - request restrictions on uses and disclosures of protected health information (PHI);
  - request alternative channels of communication of PHI; and
  - complain to the practice/covered entity, or to the federal Department of Health and Human Services.

FIGURE 14.2   HIPAA Privacy

You do not need a patient authorization in order to share Protected Health Information (PHI) for the following reasons:

Treatment
May use and disclose a patient's health information to provide health treatment or services. This information may be disclosed to all doctors, nurses, technicians, pharmacists, students or other people who are involved in the care of that patient.

Payment
May use and disclose patient health information to an insurance company or third party so services and treatment received may be billed to that patient and payment may be collected.

Health care operations
May use and disclose a patient's health information for administrative and operational purposes. Some types of operations include:
- Case management, care coordination and medical reviews, clinical guidelines and protocols;
- Teaching activities, accreditation, certification, licensing;
- Business management/administrative activities; and
- Internal grievances, legal services, audits and compliance programs.

© 2004 Walker, Larch, Woodcock. Reprinted with permission.

As we learned the HIPAA privacy regulations, we realized with relief that there are no barriers to exchanging information with others in the health care community when it is for treatment authorization or for billing purposes.

HIPAA Transactions and Code Sets

The HIPAA Transactions and Code Sets regulation is being implemented over time. If implemented as written, medical practices should benefit from this regulation. Practices should expect to experience reduced transaction costs, reduced business office and registration staff, improved claims management, decreased payment lag times and increased patient satisfaction. As we are writing this book, however, most practices are still wary about whether this regulation will be implemented as planned. This has caused some medical practices to delay (1) modifying their current billing workflow and data collection processes, (2) implementing changes to current practice management systems and/or (3) purchasing "HIPAA-ready" e-commerce services until they are sure that payers are moving in this direction in a timely fashion.

As we noted at the beginning of this chapter, we believe that attention to compliance-related activities is simply good business. It focuses both physician and staff attention to critical elements of the billing and collection process that help ensure a clean claim. It also ensures that your practice will pay attention to critical front-end billing functions, such as charge capture, coding and charge entry and back-end functions such as account follow-up and collections. A focus on data is in everyone's best interest and can lead to enhanced revenue performance.

Conclusion and
Future Implications

In this book, we have shared our recommendations to improve the revenue cycle of your medical practice. Many of these strategies have been adopted by better performing medical practices to enhance revenue performance. Successful billing and collection performance is dependent on avoiding the potholes in the road to getting paid and establishing specific performance outcomes expected at each step in the process. We deem the following elements critical to successful revenue generation in the medical practice:

- Articulated accountability and responsibility for the entire revenue cycle;
- Effective staffing organization, infrastructure and expertise;
- Appropriate leverage of information technology and management reporting;
- Monitoring of *leading* indicators to assess billing and collection performance;
- Streamlined and systematic billing and collection processes (avoiding the potholes): previsit, patient check-in, charge capture and charge entry, claims process, patient posting, account follow-up, denial management and patient collections;
- Compliance-driven policies, procedures and practices; and
- Leaders at all levels of the organization involved in leading change.

Clients often ask us to assist them in prioritizing the actions they should take to enhance the billing and collection process in their medical practices. Each practice needs to determine those priorities based upon comparison of the current process with benchmarks, expected levels of performance and other indicators. It is important that medical practices avoid simply adding more staff to perform work the way they've always done it. As we have described in this book, the work itself – the processes, tools and methods by which your staff perform the work – may need to change before your practice can optimize its revenue cycle.

We offer the following top three priorities to assist medical practices that have embarked on the journey to enhance their revenue cycle.

Priority 1: Decrease Rework

Rework is costly for a medical practice. Not only are additional costs associated with rework, but rework also typically translates to more billing staff required for the back-end billing process.

Immediate tasks to decrease rework:

- Increase collections at time of service including copayments, co-insurance, deductibles and patient responsibility balances;
- Decrease denial rates;
- Increase quality of data captured at previsit and at check-in; and
- Evaluate staffing levels devoted to front-end billing.

Priority 2: Increase Automation

Technology can greatly assist in enhancing billing office efficiency and effectiveness.

Immediate tasks to increase automation:

- Increase e-claims and payment remittance;
- Increase online eligibility and claims status; and
- Investigate document scanning technology.

Priority 3: Increase Productivity

The key to ensuring optimal process outcomes is to hold staff accountable for specific billing and collection functions.

Immediate tasks to increase productivity of billing office staff:

- Define staff performance expectations;
- Measure and report performance outcomes and results and share data with physicians and staff;
- Help staff prioritize their activities to optimize performance; and
- Avoid batching work.

We certainly expect that in the near future we will have a smart card that permits instantaneous transmission of services performed and electronic transfer of payment for these services. In the meantime, however, we hope that this book has given you a broader understanding of the detail required to achieve successful billing and collection process performance and to optimize revenue for your medical practice. Most importantly, we hope that it will serve as a useful tool in helping you, the leaders of your medical practices, avoid the potholes in the road to getting paid so that you can continue to do the important work you have chosen – meeting the health care needs of your community.

As we conclude, let's remember the recurring themes we mentioned early in the book:

- Putting patients first by developing a patient-oriented billing and collection process;
- Doing the work right the first time, minimizing rework and lost revenue opportunities;
- Performing work in real time, rather than batching work to be performed at a later date, thus enhancing efficiency;
- Measuring performance outcomes – both quantity and quality – to recognize early warning signs through leading performance indicators;
- Taking action to lead change in the medical practice involving billing and collection so advanced billing practices can be adopted and implemented; and
- Using data to communicate the need for change and to measure and analyze change efforts.

Let's collect what we are due on behalf of the physicians and other providers who provide medical care across the country. Reduce your errors, increase your automation and increase your productivity – don't leave any money that is due your practice uncollected!

Additional Billing and Collection Resources

This list of resources has been compiled for your reference, and does not represent our commercial endorsement of any particular product. You may want to investigate these and other resources as you continue to refine your journey on the road to getting paid.

Quick Start Library

- Current-year procedure and diagnosis code books (for some specialties, additional coding manuals are appropriate);
- Medical dictionary;
- Book on human anatomy;
- Medicare and/or Medicaid carrier updates and specialty billing guides (many practices keep these in a three-ring binder);
- Current payer guides;
- Three-ring binder with all third-party payer contracts;
- Physician credentialing data;
- Health Insurance Portability and Accountability Act (HIPAA) summary; and
- *Federal Register* subscription (or www.thomas.loc.gov for online access).

Books

American Medical Association, *Assessing and Improving Billing and Collections*, 2000, order #OP318600, 800.621.8335 (ISBN: 1-57947-078-5)

American Medical Association, *Handbook of Physician Office Letters*, 2000, order #OP318700, 800.621.8335 (ISBN 1-57947-081-5)

American Medical Association, *Mastering the Reimbursement Process*, 3rd edition, 2001, order #0P080000BEV. 800.621.8335 (ISBN 1-57947-142-0)

Aspen Publishers, *Medical Group Practice Legal and Administrative Guide*, 1998 with annual supplements. Available from MGMA, 877.275.6462

Atlantic Information Services Health, *A Guide to Auditing Health Care Billing Practices*, looseleaf service, www.aishealth.com

Department of Commerce, *Practical Guide to Medical Billing* (report #PB98-114374), 1997, 703.605.6000

Noelle Floreen, *Medical Practice Reimbursement Manual*, Healthcare Financial Management Association, 1998. Available from MGMA, 877.275.6262 (ISBN 0-07-022015-8)

HCPro, Inc. *Maximize Your Reimbursement Success,* 2004, www.hcmarketplace.com

Thomas G. Hajny, *Looking for the Cashcow: Action Steps to Improve Cash Flow in Medical Group Practices*, MGMA Center for Research, 2000, 877.275.6462. (ISBN 1-56829-022-5)

Medical Group Management Association, *Coding Profile Sourcebooks*, three book series: (1) medical specialties, (2) primary care and (3) surgical specialties, pathology and radiology, 2002, 877.275.6462

Medical Group Management Association, *MGMA Cost Survey Report* and *MGMA Performance and Practices of Successful Medical Groups*. Benchmark data for billing performance, published annually. 877.275.6462

Courtney Price, PhD, and Alys Novak, MBA, *Governing Policies Manual for Medical Practices*, MGMA, 1996, 877.275.6462 (ISBN 1-56829-079-9)

Robert J. Saner, Marla Spindel, Amy Nordeng, *Understanding Compliance*, MGMA, 2004, 877.275.6482 (ISBN 1-56829-144-2)

St. Anthony Publishing, *Billing Compliance Q&A for Physicians*, 1st edition, 1998, 800.632.0123

Reed Tinsley, CPA, and Joe D. Havens, *Performing an Operational and Strategic Assessment of a Medical Practice*, John Wiley & Sons, 1999, (ISBN 0-471-29964-2)

Deborah L. Walker, MBE, FACMPE, and David N. Gans, MSHA, FACMPE, *Rightsizing: Appropriate Staffing for Your Medical Practice*, MGMA, 2003, (ISBN 1-56829-149-3)

Bette A. Warn, CMPE, and Elizabeth W. Woodcock, MBE, FACMPE, CPC, *Operating Policies and Procedures Manual for Medical Practices*, MGMA, 2001, 877.275.6462 (ISBN 1-56829-145-0)

Associations Related to Billing and Reimbursement

- Medical Group Management Association, www.mgma.com
  The Medical Group Management Association (MGMA), founded in 1926, is the nation's principal voice for medical group practice. MGMA's 19,000 members manage and lead 11,000 organizations in which approximately 220,000 physicians practice. MGMA leads the profession and assists members through information, education, networking and advocacy.

- Professional Association of Health Care Office Management, www.pahcom.com
  PAHCOM is a communications network and support system dedicated to enhancing productivity and efficiency. Through increased knowledge of basic health care management principles, continuing education and networking opportunities designed to solve medical management problems, PAHCOM members gain the edge.

- Healthcare Financial Management Association, www.hfma.org
  HFMA is the nation's leading personal membership organization for health care financial management professionals. HFMA brings perspective and clarity to the industry's complex issues, preparing its members to succeed. HFMA is comprised of about 32,000 members employed by hospitals, integrated delivery systems, long-term and ambulatory care facilities, managed care organizations, medical group practices, public accounting and consulting firms, payers, government agencies and other health care organizations.

- Healthcare Billing and Management Association, www.hbma.com
  Healthcare Billing and Management Association (HBMA) is the only trade association representing third-party medical billers. HBMA members process physician and other provider claims integral to the health care delivery system. They not only bill for medical services, but frequently perform all of the physician's administrative functions.

- American Association of Medical Billers, www.billers.com
The organization offers certification as Certified Medical Biller (CMB) or the Certified Medical Billing Specialist (CMBS). Its Web site is a source for locating billers.

- Medical Association of Billers, www.physicianswebsites.com
Medical billing association for billing, coding, electronic insurance claims and compliance education and training. Offers education, training, salary survey and products.

- America's Health Insurance Plans, www.aahp.org
America's Health Insurance Plans (AHIP) is the national trade association representing nearly 1,300 member companies providing health insurance coverage to more than 200 million Americans. One of its goals is to provide a unified voice for the health care financing industry.

Discussion papers and sample forms are available on the AHIP Web site:
"Improving Claims Processing and Payment: A Self-assessment Tool for Providers"
This checklist helps providers take the steps necessary to improve claims processing and payment.

"Coordination of Benefits: Tips for Reducing Payment Delays and Improving Accounts Receivable"
To address top reasons for coordination of benefit (COB) delays, this one-page tip sheet was developed to convey information about steps that can be taken to reduce COB-related claim delays.

"Claim Correction Form"
Designed to assist providers to resubmit claims that they have corrected or amended with additional information or documentation related to a specific claim, this document can be filled out on line and submitted as an e-mail attachment or printed and sent by mail or fax.

Articles

"Benchmarking the Billing Office," Elizabeth W. Woodcock, MBA, FACMPE, CPC; Scott Williams, CMPE; *Healthcare Financial Management*, 56(9):42–46, September 2002.

"Billing Basics: A Review Course," William C. Fiala, *MGM Journal*, 47(16):16–25, November/ December 2000.

"Capturing Lost Revenues," The Advisory Board, Health Care Advisory Board Cost and Operations Center Presentation, 2002.

"Making Accounts Receivable Analysis Understandable," S. Thomas Dunlap, *MGM Journal*, 40(3):70–76, May/June 1993.

"A Medical Group Practice Imperative: The Practical Use of RVUs for Managing and Contracting," by W. Robert Wright, Jr, FACMPE; A. Scott Williams, MBA; and Elizabeth W. Woodcock, MBA, FACMPE, CPC, *MGM Journal*, September/October 1994.

"We Didn't Get the Claim and Other Payer Excuses," Judy Williams, *MGM Journal* 47(6):58-62, November/December 2000.

"The Whys and Ways for Analyzing your Claims Processing and Denials," Lisa Stavrakas, *MGMA Directions*, 5(3): 1–3, Summer 2003.

Audio Conferences and CD-ROMs

Organizing for HIPAA Compliance
A comprehensive, three-part CD-ROM series covering electronic transactions and code sets, privacy of patient information and security in the group practice setting. Content is presented in a case study format by experienced MGMA practice administrators and industry experts.
   CD-ROM 1 – Electronic Transactions and Code Sets (item #5941)
   CD-ROM 2 – Privacy of Patient Information (item #5942)
   CD-ROM 3 – Security in the Group Practice Setting (item #5943)
Available from MGMA, 877.275.6462

Benchmarking the Billing Office for Improved Efficiency
With Elizabeth Woodcock, MBA, FACMPE. Audio conference recorded Aug. 23, 2001. Available from MGMA, 877.275.6462, www.mgma.com

Billing & Compliance Audits/Education: A Systematic Approach
With Betsy A. Nicoletti, consultant. Audio conference recorded Aug. 7, 2003. Available from MGMA, 877.275.6462, www.mgma.com

Denial Management for Medical Groups: Turn Your Denials into New Cash
With Sara M. Larch, MSHA, FACMPE. Audio conference recorded April 5, 2001. Available from MGMA, 877.275.6462, www.mgma.com

Improving Business Office Performance: Setting the Benchmark
By Laura Jacobs, MPH, and Katherine Sorenson. Audio conference recorded March 27, 2003. Available from MGMA, 877.275.6462, www.mgma.com

Newsletters

The Receivables Report, Aspen Publishers
Most articles are focused on hospital patient accounts, but content is usually relevant to physician billing.

Managed Care Contracting & Reimbursement Advisor, www.brownstone.com

Web Sites

Billing and collection tools
www.physicianspractice.com/pearls/tool.htm
Sample appeal letters collections letters and other key billing and collection tools; free e-mail newsletter: *Physicians Practice Pearls*

Billing competency exams
www.physicianswebsites.com/medical_association_of_billers_books.htm

Centers for Medicare & Medicaid Services (CMS)
www.cms.hhs.gov/providers/pair
New CMS site tailored to the needs of the practice administrator: *Practice Administrative Information Resource for Medicare*. Start here when you are looking for CMS information. The site includes payment/billing, coding, enrollment, policies and regulations, education, compliance, HIPAA and contacts/links.

Coding resources
www.ingenix.com – Ingenix
www.ama-assn.org – American Medical Association
www.aapc.com – American Academy of Professional Coders
www.coderyte.com – CodeRyte, Inc.
www.cms.gov/mcd – Medicare's "Medical Coverage Database"

Custom reports
www.monarch.datawatch.com or www.proclarity.com
Software to create custom reports from the data in your practice management system

Denied or disputed medical claims
www.appealsolutions.com and www.eappealsolutions.com
Services and products focusing on the resolution of denied or disputed medical claims

The Fair Debt Collection Practices Act
www.ftc.gov/os/statutes/fdcpa/fdcpact.htm

Imaging for patient accounts
www.medcard.com
Software to attach an electronic image to the patient's account, so you can, for example, scan insurance cards and attach them to the patient's account in your practice management system.

Listserv: Patient Accounts Management List (PAMLIST)
www.dekaye.com
Free subscription includes procedure code utilization by specialty and participation/ enrollment, policies and regulations, integrity and medical review, contacts, payment and billing, Medicare secondary payers, Medicare education.

Medicare
www.medicare.gov
Key information source for Medicare beneficiaries — you will find it very helpful if your practice has the same information as that of your Medicare patients.

OIG's (Office of the Inspector General) Compliance Program Guidance for Third-Party Medical Billing Companies
www.hhs.gov/progorg/oig/modcomp/thirdparty.htm

Patient online environments
www.yalehealthonline.yale.edu
dukehealth.org/patientchannel/entry.html
www.alexian.org/billing
www.afwomensmed.com
Examples of medical groups creating "patient online" environments for appointment scheduling and paying bills, etc.

Prompt payment laws by state
http://info.insure.com/health/lawtool.cfm

Personal digital assistant (PDA)-assisted tools

A number of PDA-assisted tools for coding and pharmaceutical prescription processing have been developed. We did not intend the list below to be exhaustive of the many vendors that have entered this market but as a useful starting point for the reader's own research:

www.mdeverywhere.com
www.mdanywhere.com
www.iscribe.com
www.pocketmed.org
www.emd2.com
www.allscripts.com
www.mdpad.com

Index